Brave Girls

Brave Girls

*Raising Young Women with Passion
and Purpose to Become
Powerful Leaders*

STACEY RADIN, PSYD

with Leslie Goldman

ATRIA BOOKS

New York • London • Toronto • Sydney • New Delhi

ATRIA BOOKS

A Division of Simon & Schuster, Inc.
1230 Avenue of the Americas
New York, NY 10020

First Atria Books hardcover edition January 2015

ATRIA BOOKS and colophon are trademarks of Simon & Schuster, Inc.

For information about special discounts for bulk purchases, please contact Simon & Schuster Special Sales at 1-866-506-1949 or business@simonandschuster.com.

The Simon & Schuster Speakers Bureau can bring authors to your live event. For more information or to book an event contact the Simon & Schuster Speakers Bureau at 1-866-248-3049 or visit our website at www.simonspeakers.com.

Jacket design by Janet Perr
Jacket photograph by Getty Images/Purestock

Manufactured in the United States of America

1   3   5   7   9   10   8   6   4   2

Library of Congress Control Number: 2014003404

ISBN 978-1-4516-9930-2
ISBN 978-1-4516-9932-6 (ebook)

This book is dedicated to my father, Laurence Bernstein, whose unconditional love inspired me to reach for my dreams and imagine what life could be if I believed they could come true! His words of wisdom are ingrained in my soul even though he is no longer physically here to speak them. I hope he can hear me now when I say, "You were the greatest influence in my life, unleashing my power to change the world. Everything I have accomplished has been because of you!"

To my children, Justin and Jordyn, both of you always remain my number one priority. The greatest gift I have ever received was motherhood. Thank you for being patient and understanding throughout this amazing but frenzied journey! I owe you both a few family trips and undivided attention. As a great man once said to me and now I say to you, "You are meant to do great things in the world. It's up to you to figure out what that means."

Before Unleashed started, I was scared about what to say. Now I can say what I feel.

—Lillian, fifth grade

Usually we're told that we're too young, but here you can help out firsthand.

—Julia, seventh grade

Unleashed is a program where a girl can walk into the room and learn to use her power for a good reason instead of having power and not knowing what to do with it. You can use it to change society and help dogs and change the world and make it a better place.

—Kristina, seventh grade

I think of it as more than a dog rescue program. It's not just about dogs; it's about working as a team and supporting each other to make change.

—Traciann, eighth grade

We are still as strong as boys; they may be physically stronger but not strong in words.

—Adanla, sixth grade

[During a discussion about dog fighting] It's like putting a Band-Aid over the issue of aggression.

    —Anna, eighth grade

I went into Unleashed hoping I could make a change in animal welfare, and now that I've come out, I know I can make a change in not just that part, but other aspects of society.

    —Charlotte, eighth grade

Just because we are dainty and cute doesn't mean we aren't powerful.

    —Ivana, sixth grade

Being an Unleashed girl is an opportunity for girls to have a voice.

    —Samantha, eighth grade

I am only one person, but I can make a difference.

    —Marie, eighth grade

Contents

Brave Girls

Introduction

O ur society as a whole is lacking in opportunities designed to help preadolescent girls feel confident, secure, and emotionally safe. Middle school isn't all sleepovers and smiles: It is the purgatory of childhood, wedged between the nurturing elementary years and the maturity attributed to a high school teen. The majority of middle school girls are riding the proverbial emotional roller coaster without a safety net or a seat belt. Defying the values of and severing ties with family, asserting autonomy and independence and defiance, are all normal aspects of this second stage of separation-individuation (the first having taken place during toddlerhood). However, it essentially causes a state of crisis, leaving a young girl feeling alienated, anxious, and powerless. Just mention "middle school," and each and every woman I have encountered seems visibly shaken, running off a litany of bad memories and social mishaps. It is a time when self-esteem plummets, bullying is pervasive, and the decibel level of a girl's voice dramatically lowers to the point of being practically inaudible.

Compounding matters, the structures that were once in place to support middle school girls are now nonexistent: Cultural institutions (i.e., family, school, and community) are weakening, empathy at a societal level is declining, pressure to achieve and weighty expectations permeate every aspect of a young girl's life. The DNA of girls makes them much more sensitive to pressure than boys, and girls succumb to the indirect and direct messages of their environment. They morph behaviors and beliefs based on cues from media, peer, and family influences, much like a chameleon's color adjusts to varying temperatures and backgrounds. Grown women reflect on this time in their childhood and report feeling frustrated and disappointed in how simply being a girl filled them with a sense of restriction, and that adults—sometimes total strangers—often treated them in a way that reinforced the "nice little girl" gender norm.[1]

At school, one building houses popular girls and academics, jocks and outcasts, queen bees and wannabes. More likely than not, the groups stick to themselves (at best) or tear each other down (at worst). Rampant use of Facebook, IMing, and texting has made it possible for girls to be bullied from the usual safety of their own bedrooms—all during a time when young women need the comfort and support of sisterhood more than ever.

For all of these reasons and more, adolescence is the ideal time for girls to develop the critical tools needed to be a brave, powerful female. Not only are they at the crux of identity development, challenging the status quo, redefining the norms for themselves and others, but they are flooded with biological, physiological, cognitive, social, and emotional change. Planting the seeds during this formative stage, as they experiment and define who they are and whom they want to be, establishing templates for leadership, civic engagement, communication, self-awareness, and positive interpersonal relationships, will ultimately affect their futures.

In 2010, I founded Unleashed, a middle-school-based social-justice program empowering girls to take a stand against an injustice they are passionate about by offering them the opportunity to become experts in animal rights and welfare. They design educational awareness campaigns, spread their message by speaking to the community, host events that engage others in their mission, lead school assemblies, and tap into social media, gaining hands-on experience as social activists. Integrated into the program is the opportunity for girls to engage in community service with our rescue organization, selecting puppies from lists provided by overcrowded shelters across the country, conducting behavioral assessments on animals being transported to New York, and recruiting temporary and permanent homes for them.

Over twelve weeks, they are provided with critical tools they can use to solve complex social issues throughout their lives. They develop a deep understanding of animal rights and welfare; the nationwide inhumane treatment of dogs and other pets; the synergy that exists between the animal and the human rights movements; and how the issues faced by animals are reflective of society's larger problems. Girls learn to diagnose a social problem, digging deep beneath the surface to address the root cause of the issues they have identified, to create change, and to engage others in their cause. As a result, they graduate from Unleashed feeling unbelievably powerful, realizing that because of their newly developed tools, they have the ability to positively impact their community and *can* make a difference in the world. Nola, eleven, who participated in sixth grade, explains, "Unleashed taught me how to speak my mind and express my opinion about certain things. I didn't always used to do that before. I learned that I had a lot more to say than I thought."

Unleashed was developed based on the overarching need to revolutionize gender in today's society. Despite progress stemming from women's suffrage, the second wave of the feminist movement in the 1970s, legislative amendments, and increased opportunities, American society continues to force women to struggle to find their voices and seek out opportunities. At first glance, it may appear that women and girls no longer have to fight for equal rights—opportunities to gain an education, play sports, earn a living in nontraditional careers, and enjoy freedom of choice all exist. Yet, look slightly beneath the surface and the picture morphs dramatically: there is pay disparity and a scarcity of C-level positions in corporate America; few women inhabit political leadership roles; and both men and women adhere to unspoken gender stereotypes, consciously or not. Our society is still wedded to beliefs reflecting a male-dominated culture.

Serious consequences exist if our culture retains embedded archaic beliefs predicated on unchallenged gender norms. If so, neither women *nor* men will ever be able to fully achieve freedom of choice and exercise their inalienable human rights. It is 2015, and we are still debating whether women have the right to make decisions about their own bodies, cutting budgets and limiting access to proper health care and benefits, failing to incorporate women's history into educational curriculums and textbooks, judging other mothers' child-care decisions, not deterring violent crimes against women, and violating women's basic human rights around the globe.

Legislation and external changes have advanced the gender revolution only so far. Much of Betty Friedan's *Feminine Mystique* still applies in 2015. Throughout my decade-long career in developing powerful women in business, and the past three years of Unleashed, I have witnessed women and girls, regardless of ethnicity, socioeconomic status, or race, become frustrated and disappointed about being judged based on outdated norms, struggling with society's proverbial shoulds and shouldn'ts. We need to unhinge the stereotypes that predate the US Constitution and create dialogues between men and women, examining what lies at the heart of the issues, if we want to move the needle further along. Recognizing that gender is a social problem for all of humanity, not solely a women's issue, is a path leading to true change.

Unleashed is my version of a modern feminist movement, connecting generations of women with a common platform to collaborate and redefine the relationship between women and power. Feminism, sadly, remains vastly misunderstood. Without a visible, well-defined mission, women of all ages shun the notion of being a feminist. They see some women shattering the glass ceiling and hold on to a false sense of security that things are getting better, denying the reality of statistics set before them. When I speak publicly about Unleashed, numerous young female audience members approach me and tentatively ask, "Are you a feminist?" When I proudly claim that I am, my response is met with "I am so glad! Finally, a woman who is not afraid to say the word." The truth is, a movement working toward equality is still needed. Silent oppression prevails and repeatedly rears its ugly head whether women choose to believe it or not.

The Unleashed mission, then, is simply to unleash the power of girls, investing in the next generation of female change-makers.

The truth is, an impressionable twelve-year-old girl and a self-doubting thirty-six-year-old woman are two sides of the same coin; how we empower our younger generation dictates whether that coin will gleam or grow dull. For better or for worse, most leadership programs focus on either girls *or* women, neglecting to see the continuum between the two. Unleashed was created in an effort to leverage that link. When I launched my consulting firm, Corporate EQ, in 2003, I began helping behemoths such as Pfizer, Bear Stearns, and the NBA achieve their leadership goals. After a decade of working with hundreds of powerful women, I had reached a point where I could predict what female executives in top-level positions would say en route to strengthening their leadership abilities and increasing their power. Common sentiments included "I feel like a fraud—I am just waiting for everyone to figure out that I shouldn't be VP" or "I'm afraid of being called a bitch for speaking my mind." Remember, these are women with MBAs and corner offices . . . yet they were struggling mightily with identifying with the notion of being a powerful leader.

An unmistakable connection between gender, power, and the leadership equation was blatant. What I wanted desperately to figure out was the rationale underlying this phenomenon. Why were so many women afraid to speak their minds, defy the status quo, or effectively utilize their power, even when they were being paid to do so? What if I identified a diverse group of influential women across the country who were impacting their respective industries—VIPs such as ABC News anchor Deborah Roberts, Burberry Americas president Eugenia Ulasewicz, and *New York* magazine COO Kit Taylor—and interviewed them to explore: "What does a powerful woman look like?" "Where did she fail and how did she respond to setbacks?" "What are her challenges and how does she manage them?" "What influences have played a role in her career?" Every woman, no matter how senior her position or how tight her schedule, was *dying* to have this conversation. Hundreds of interviews were conducted over the next two years, filled with frustration, tears, laughter, and insights, giving candid recounts of how women navigated a system designed and operated by men. Each woman shared a deep yearning for change. Two highly significant findings were that childhood experiences and relationships shape a woman's perception of her power and how she leverages it; and women are more likely to utilize their power when passionate about a cause and given an opportunity to create impact. When women are emotionally connected and attached to a purpose, they will take necessary risks and refuse to conform to outdated norms when seeking desired outcomes. Passion motivates women to push limits and defy the status quo.

One day, during a morning run, I found myself thinking, "If this is true for women, could these same hypotheses be applicable to girls?" Maybe if passion was tapped into at a younger age and seeds of leadership were planted and cultivated during preadolescence—a critical time of identity development—then girls would evolve into women who could embrace their power as they matured. What if I created a proactive approach, providing young women with critical tools to influence their lives so that by the time they reached their thirties, forties, fifties, and sixties they would be fully aware of who they are and unafraid of disclosing their authentic identities? This is how Unleashed was born. It is a culmination of my years as a clinician working with females across a broad age spectrum; my dissertation examining adolescent feminine identity; consulting with executive women and designing leadership initiatives; and the original research I conducted studying powerful women. It is a model created to change our society's beliefs about gender and advance progress by focusing on the next generation of powerful women—our girls.

Over three months, Unleashed girls move through a definitive process not unlike therapy, but disguised as a combination of social justice, leadership development, community service, and fun. They learn about the societal issues surrounding animal welfare and rescue; become familiar with ways to reframe these problems to better understand precedents and consequences; align with one another to form a strong community; become adept at articulating strong messages; and take on the responsibility and ownership of project management, similar to how an adult would. The building blocks of strong, ethical leadership are formed as girls execute their plans to take action against injustices. Feeling capable and confident in this, many of these girls experience a sense of power for the first time in their lives. Our society needs more effective leaders who follow their moral compass, using power appropriately; Unleashed is laying the groundwork for the future.

During the program, a heated group discussion might be sparked when girls are asked, "Who are some powerful women you look up to?" Names such as Michelle Obama, Rosa Parks, Amelia Earhart, and Harriet Beecher Stowe fly out of their mouths; when these are listed on a flip-board, the group realizes how much they admire women who speak their minds, are true to themselves, and are not or were not afraid to overcome adversity. Each session slowly pushes them toward developing a true sense of who they are as young women—their identities and values begin to crystallize. They learn how to cultivate the Michelle Obama and the Amelia Earhart who live within them.

In her book *Lean In*, Facebook COO Sheryl Sandberg posits that women must take risks and learn to advocate and negotiate, adding that self-generated internal barriers that interfere with a woman's success (professional and personal) deserve much more attention than they currently receive.[2] Unleashed was designed to create a movement not unlike Sandberg's. In the pages that follow, you will witness the evolution of numerous girls as they complete Unleashed, gaining insight into how to ignite power and purpose in the lives of the young girls in your own life. Through the lens of Unleashed, you will deepen your understanding of the middle school girl, her inner social and emotional life, which is often hidden beneath a multilayered facade. For the past four years, not unlike an anthropologist studying another culture, I have been privy to their thoughts, their unique spoken and unspoken language, how they experience the world, and the misperceptions they encounter along the way. My hope is that by imparting my own discoveries and newfound knowledge to other adults, the myths of the middle school girl will be dispelled; our culture will provide the scaffolding and support needed at this critical age of development; and open and honest dialogues will ensue, influencing our relationships with the next generation of young women. Cracking their code has been life altering for me as a woman, inspiring me to reevaluate my own sense of power and purpose. As you read each chapter, embark on this journey through the eyes of a young girl, envisioning yourself as she does every day. No doubt, your perceptions of yourself and the girls and the women in your life will never again be the same.

In the 2012 computer-animated Pixar film *Brave*, a young Scottish princess named Merida dares to challenge an age-old custom of being married off by her king and queen parents. For the first time in the animation studio's seventeen-year history, a female was taking the lead—a strong, confident young girl who had better things to do than maintain the royal status quo. Merida knew her strengths—she was skilled at archery and horseback riding—and she was unafraid to show them. She spoke her mind, even when her opinion was unpopular. At a young age, she grasped the concept of a young woman's power and refused to let anyone put a cap on her potential. She was, as the title states, brave.

Today's middle school girls are capable of becoming a generation of Meridas: powerful, determined, comfortable in their own skins, willing to take risks (and, yes, to be wrong sometimes), undeterred by archaic societal norms, and resolved to get women and men standing on equal ground. *Brave Girls* will provide a lens to look at various aspects of a girl's experience, her constitution from both physiological and social-emotional perspectives, the challenges she faces, the contexts she functions within, and how she navigates the world to break through barriers, leveraging her strengths and self-insight. This can be used as a foundation from which to dig deeper, reexamine our educational, political, business, and family systems, and begin unhinging stereotypes where we have impact. Parents, teachers and administrators, business and organizational leaders, researchers—we all have the capacity to make a difference in the lives of women and girls.

This book looks at the continuum of female development from girl to woman and vice versa. Not surprisingly, many parallels exist between the various stages of a female's development. Chapter after chapter will explore various aspects of power and will relate real-girl and real-woman vignettes that highlight the concepts presented. The experiences and insights of the Unleashed girls can be applied to women and girls of all ages, serving as an inspiration to all. Any woman eager to unleash her power will read this book and be inspired to experiment, leverage her strengths, and find her passion. And any adult, female or male, who is concerned about the state of women today, who wants to empower them to become change-makers, will know that it is possible to foster a brave new generation of strong girls who will continue to influence and shape our world for decades to come.

Chapter 1

"Who Am I?": The Girl Problem

*M*adison was your typical girlie girl, long, blond hair, giggles, and flirtation. Eleven years old when she started Unleashed, I noticed she talked—a lot—about looks, weight, and boys. She had more curves than many of her classmates, and she knew it, flaunting them in belly shirts and tight tank tops. Most girls adopt a persona at this age, whether it is "the athlete" or "the mean girl" or "the class clown," because they are unaware of who they are. Madison was trying on the role of "sexy girl."

As the weeks progressed, I noticed a marked decrease in her comments about makeup, eating disorders, and cute football players. She attended an animal rescue and worked with potential adoptive parents; I even named a puppy after her to honor the stellar job she did writing and organizing a skit on dog euthanasia for a schoolwide presentation. Madison began to realize the impact she could have on the world—and that that impact had nothing to do with her looks. One day she told me, "I love Elle Woods—she's so powerful." Elle Woods is a pink-obsessed sorority girl played by Reese Witherspoon in **Legally**

Blonde, *who strategically enrolls at Harvard Law School to win back her ex-boyfriend. To an outsider, Madison's comment might seem worrisome, but I was thrilled. I told her, "I agree! Elle is a fabulous role model for girls because she's so much more than her veneer. She was passionate about a cause and enlisted her fellow sorority girls to get things done." Unleashed helped Madison find a way to blend her girlishness with a sense of power and, like Elle, became a modern-day feminist.*

Adolescence is the stage of life most marked by identity development. The overriding quest is to answer the daunting question "Who am I?" At no other time in a woman's life will she face as many physiological, psychological, cognitive, and social-emotional changes as during her adolescent years. Newly acquired reasoning skills, hormonal fluctuations, and differences in her social milieu thrust a young girl full speed ahead into self-discovery and experimentation. But this exciting new phase of development is complicated by other factors that make it surprisingly difficult for a girl to answer the question "Who am I?" Our society is largely male dominated, deeming men's experiences and developments the prototypes for cultural norms. In 2015, girls and women still struggle to establish a strong sense of self in an environment flooded with pressure to conform to expectations that disregard the uniqueness of a female's experience. The developmental theories studied in school by the next generation of psychologists remain largely based on the clinical observations and research of men such as Kohlberg, Freud, Erikson, and Piaget, who either minimize gender differences or go as far as viewing females as deviants from the norm. Erikson states, when discussing the adolescent girl, "Female identity is held in abeyance while attracting men."[1] Freud believed the superego (an individual's executive functioning) was compromised in women, labeling them incapable of having a sense of justice as compared to men. And

Piaget, who exerted tremendous influence on our educational system, discussed how girls lack respect for rules because they are willing to make exceptions if necessary (adding that respect for rules is highly correlated to morality). What meaning does this have for girls and women? As girls embark on their journey to discover their passions, values, and strengths, they confront the harsh reality that they may need to morph their identities to assimilate and succeed.

We live in a world that places great emphasis on autonomy, independence and self-sufficiency. But a relational, interconnected approach is the cornerstone of a female's psychological health and growth. Researchers such as Carol Gilligan and Peggy Orenstein continuously report women's and girls' identities are defined in accordance with relationships, intimacy, and communities, motivated by a sense of connection to their world; empathy and mutuality are instrumental to their functioning. These vast differences in psychological models of health result in the distortion of a woman's experience as pathological or insufficient. Societal perceptions dampen our females' ability to develop authentic identities; instead of asking themselves "Who am I?" the question becomes "Who am I supposed to be?"

Worsening matters, middle school girls are not used to having leadership programs designed specifically for them. Most after-school programs focus on elementary-school children or high school and college women, rendering middle school a developmental purgatory. (According to the Afterschool Alliance, nearly 4 million sixth through eighth graders find themselves unsupervised after school.)[2]

There is a popular misconception about this group: People categorize middle school girls as oppositional, difficult to work with, and hard to engage. The media depicts them as self-involved, superficial, materialistic mean girls. Even psychologists and teachers confess to reluctantly working with sixth-, seventh-, and eighth-grade girls, easily overwhelmed by sassy retorts, vacillation from one emotional state to another, or being stonewalled with silence.

But what others tag as oppositional, I view as feisty, passionate, and eager to experiment. In my eyes, these girls are diamonds in the rough: unique, possessing great potential, and capable of shining brilliantly when succeeding. What they need is a trusted adviser to actively listen to their ideas and thoughts, empathize with their experiences, and guide and navigate them as they weather the storm. Our girls need adults who will provide them with opportunities to take risks and embrace ownership of projects for which they care deeply. Given the right tools, middle school girls will fly.

Unleashed fills a void created by society, providing girls with a forum to develop a strong sense of self. The organization is largely based upon my model of power, developed from the research I conducted studying powerful women (which will be discussed at greater length in chapter 4). The model integrates personal power, relational power, and assertive power to form a triumvirate, each component as critical as the others. Developing a strong identity and an authentic sense of self is largely contingent upon strengthening a girl's personal power. Its basic tenets include identifying and leveraging values, strengths, passions, and needs; tapping into empathy and emotional intelligence; strengthening self-esteem and confidence; and increasing self-awareness and insight.

"What do you think Unleashed is about?" I ask the group in our first meeting.

"Puppies!" shouts back Tess, a ten-year-old redhead wearing a tank top and blue Converse high-tops. "Doggy rescue!" calls out Maia, a twelve-year-old with wire-rimmed glasses and wavy brunette hair. It is my job to fill in the blanks: "Yes, it's all of that . . . and more. It's about being a powerful girl and having a voice. It's about fighting for something you believe in. It's about a concept called social justice and why animal welfare and rights are much more important than you might think. And it's about learning how to work well with other girls while you learn so much about yourself." Within minutes of the first session, they are already learning, absorbing information, but this is unlike any education received in school.

On that first day of Unleashed, the classroom hums with energy and excitement. The air is filled with both promise and hesitation: The girls know they will be working with dogs, but they have no idea about the personal transformation they are about to undergo. For most of them, this will be their first experience where their opinions will be heard, their points of view valued, and their leadership skills utilized.

"I'm Stacey," I say, introducing myself. "I'm the founder of Unleashed, and the reason I'm here is because I believe girls deserve to have a voice." My words are often met with skeptical looks, and I can practically see the words scrolling across their foreheads like a news ticker on the bottom of a television screen: "Who *is* this woman? And how do I know I can trust her?" It is depressing to say, but by the age of nine or ten, girls have already been forced to put up with being patronized, condescended to, or treated as "less than" by teachers, parents, and society at large. With few exceptions, they have had at least one experience where an adult, consciously or not, behaved differently toward them than they would a boy. It could be as overt as being denied the opportunity to try out for a sport because they are not male, or more subtle, such as when they report feeling passed over by teachers to serve as leaders of group projects. So now, to have a stranger telling them she believes in them, that they have the power to make a change in the world? They simply do not trust that it is possible.

Unleashed is an all-female program for a reason: Not only does society hinder girls' quest for an authentic identity, it fails to provide girls and women with opportunities to be different; it also reinforces the building of fences between various groups and the establishment of cliques. During the first few sessions of Unleashed, many of the girls, ranging in age from fifth to eighth grade, are strangers, despite sitting next to each other in algebra or passing by one another in the hallway daily.

From the popular cheerleader or soccer star to the computer whiz, an Unleashed team encompasses many different types of girls with one common passion: animal rights. Yet they feel intimidated by one another. The Unleashed philosophy is to align with the developmental trajectory of women, their need for community and relationships, fostering a sense of sisterhood.

Middle school girls are greatly in need of this intimacy with and connections to others. Girls thrive in supportive social settings, experiencing autonomy in a different way from boys; they are able to better assert their independence when they feel connected; and attachment to others is a vital component of their identity. Without these strong connections, girls and women feel isolated and dissatisfied. While some might view dependency and interrelatedness as weaknesses, I strongly adhere to the notion that women and girls assume a position of strength when they are able to create a shared experience among them. Ultimately, when females defy the need to conform to gender biases and stereotypes, ignoring the shoulds and shouldn'ts placed before them, a strong sense of self will ensue.

Keeping in line with girls' need for shared experiences, every Unleashed session launches with a Check In. Not only does the Check In serve as a transition from school to social-justice mode, it also functions in several other capacities. First, it offers me a snapshot of the girls' personalities. On the first day, I can get a sense of who is willing to take a risk and speak up first, versus those who are reluctant to even whisper their name and grade aloud. For every girl who craves the spotlight and takes the floor with ease—"I'm Gemma! I'm eleven years old and I have a Goldendoodle named Cookie at home and a little brother named Asher and last week my mom let me see Justin Bieber in concert and OMG we had fourteenth-row seats!"—there is one who rarely participates in school because she fears raising her hand and using her voice. These initial impressions help me establish individualized goals to enhance each girl's personal power. As sessions progress, Check In allows me to pose a provocative question to inspire the girls to dig deeper, think critically about issues that impact them, and discuss what it feels like to be female—the challenges faced and how to manage them effectively. Check In conveys the message that Unleashed was designed as a space to develop and hone their sense of power, to figure out who they are, how they relate to others, and to build their dreams for the future. Middle school girls need an outlet to openly express their confusion about identity (who they are and whom they are supposed to be); articulating their ideas and challenges aloud each week helps them clarify their self-perceptions in the context of their peers' experiences.

Unfortunately, opportunities for girls to speak about their unique experiences of being a female in today's world are limited. Check In often lasts for a half hour because girls crave a forum to explore issues that are not addressed in school. As they become aware that their feelings are not abnormal, it sets a tone to deeply explore who they are based on strengths, how they describe themselves, and their visions for the future. By the end of the program, Check In responses reflect an identity that is much more crystallized than in the beginning sessions.

Identifying Values in the Search for Self

Identifying, leveraging, and aligning behavior with values is critical for our current and future generations of powerful women. A girl's identity is largely predicated on her core values. As she experiments, faces new situations, and is exposed to new ideas and information, she constantly reevaluates her decisions. Observing this, one might perceive a middle school girl as fickle or noncommittal; she seems to be constantly changing her mind about friends, clothing style, music, and interests. But this process is a prerequisite for crystallizing a strong sense of self; in its absence she resigns herself to accepting the personality characteristics she first tests out, never knowing what could have been if she continued her search.

Up until now, girls have mirrored their parents' values, accepting them as truth. During adolescence, they begin questioning those values and rethinking if those values make sense to them. Defiance is a healthy part of identity development as they establish themselves as separate individuals who are capable of having their own thoughts and opinions. As they mature, it will be essential to keep their sense of self intact by refusing to veer from what is most important.

Many times I have heard women recount situations where they compromised their values because of pressure to conform. Our goal in Unleashed is to lay the groundwork for the girls to develop mental templates so they are equipped to manage adversity throughout their lives. During one session, I hand out a sheet of paper that lists fifty values—family, beauty, education, honesty, self-confidence—and ask the girls to circle those that appeal to them, gradually narrowing it down to their top five. What values resonate most with them and how do they manifest those in various aspects of their lives? I explain that powerful and ethical leaders know their values, align their behavior to correspond to those values, and recognize when they are straying. Most girls tell me they have never even thought about what is most important to them, let alone prioritized their principles. When we debrief their insights, they openly discuss how much they have learned about themselves, and they now see how their values can be similar yet different from those of other girls without destroying their relationships. Over the twelve weeks, we strive for increased self-awareness, which has a direct, positive effect on identity and sense of self.

Without the ability to engage in "aha" moments and identify and articulate their values, girls will continuously rethink what is important to them. An integral piece of personal power, values shape a girl's identity; they serve as a launching pad, enabling them to venture out into the world and guiding them in their decision-making. Without a strong sense of self, girls will struggle to define who they are, repeatedly becoming stuck in conflict and self-doubt. They tend to conform and assimilate to cultural norms versus defying the status quo, and they are more inclined to tolerate unhappiness rather than to make a change. Lastly, they continue to experience an unhealthy relationship with power and control.

How the Pressure to Achieve Diminishes the Search for Self

The middle school years can be incredibly daunting. The world has never been an easy place for young girls, but today's environment is likely the toughest it has ever been due to advances in and access to technology, earlier onset of puberty, dramatic shifts in the family system, and a culture where children are encouraged to act mature before their time. Our younger generation faces issues such as bullying and popularity, pressure to conform, academic stress, distorted body image, and perfectionism and is at risk of drinking and premature sexual activity.

As we now know, all of this is happening during a pivotal time of identity development, as girls struggle to develop an authentic sense of self. Compounding the fragile state of middle school girls today, these youth are, as I said before, the "forgotten population," with most after-school programming targeted at elementary and high school students. And despite all of these factors conspiring against them, young girls are often raised with the belief that one day they can and should "have it all"—a happy family, high-powered career, bustling personal life. A recent survey by *Junior Achievement USA* found that half of teen girls say they feel either "a lot" or overwhelming pressure to succeed in academics, no matter the cost.[3] They experience anxiety over achievement (73 percent of sixth through eighth graders), appearance (74 percent), fitting in (64 percent), and getting along with their parents (32 percent).[4]

These types of early influences during childhood and adolescence lay the foundation for future perceptions of power and how they will influence experiences and behavior. Some girls grow up believing overachievement is the only solution, compensating for low self-esteem and feeling powerless. Others are similar to a highly prestigious lawyer I interviewed, transferring their self-criticism to other women, forming a generalized opinion that men are more capable of being in powerful positions. Not until women begin to feel confident and competent in their own abilities can they acknowledge the value proposition (inherent worth) in other females, debunking the male-supremacy theory. This is a critical milestone in establishing a strong, authentic identity.

Many experts believe early adolescence—particularly from ten to twelve years old—is the ideal time to formally introduce a girl to the concept of leadership. The middle school brain is developing at exponential speed, rendering her interpersonal relationships, academic pursuits, and involvement in art, music, and sports more likely to stay with her, or at least resurface, later in life.[5] The more she practices these skills in early adolescence, whether it is arguing on the debate team, advocating for someone more vulnerable, empathizing with the plight of a friend, or expressing her emotions, the better equipped she will be to reenact them during adulthood. Analogous to learning how to ride a bicycle, learning how to lead will be impossible for her to forget.

Girls could then use their strong sense of self as a launching pad, enabling them to venture out into the world, develop intimate connections, feel secure about themselves, and continuously make a difference for others and themselves.

Creating a Safe Space to Foster a Brave Sense of Self

Our culture repeatedly minimizes the degree to which it directly and indirectly shortchanges our middle school girls. Girls this age need access to supportive environments that will continuously permit them to be authentic, experiment with new skills, and gain unconditional acceptance while forming close intimate relationships. These settings generate a sense of security, act as a container for girls to share emotions, fail without repercussions, process thoughts and ideas, and engage in age-appropriate questioning, frustration, and setbacks. Adolescence is a transitional phase, bridging girls from childhood to young adulthood. Underestimating the significance of this rite of passage is detrimental—girls feel that they are devalued, not taken seriously, and their needs are insignificant.

Girls this age also covet a safe space where they can discuss real-life issues—a place where they can share what is bothering them with others and feel listened to and not judged.[6] Unleashed was designed to serve as a container, an emotionally and physically secure base that encourages girls to be honest and authentic. Middle school girls often need emotional refueling, a place that is positive and optimistic where they can gain recognition and acceptance, subsequently bolstering self-esteem. So real is the need that the Population Council has labeled it "urgent," stating that "by developing new interventions that seek to give girls 'a safe space of their own' . . . we will begin to positively influence the life trajectory of adolescent girls."[7]

Girls internalize this sense of security, symbolically carrying it with them and drawing upon it when feeling uncertain. During sessions, girls report how they have transferred the self-awareness they have developed in Unleashed to other contexts of their lives. Some even report that when facing a dilemma, they think about what a teammate or coach might say if she was there. Our girls recognize that they can act independently, take greater risks in their world, and showcase their true selves because they have an accepting community readily available to them.

But just as important as it is to encourage the expression of emotions and ideas, it is equally crucial to set limits and establish boundaries if an environment is to feel safe. In Unleashed, girls share their innermost thoughts, allowing themselves to be vulnerable; they need to trust that they will not be criticized or judged. By the end of the three months, they truly believe their team will accept them regardless of who they are, regardless of their differences or blind spots ("Nobody is perfect" is another Unleashed philosophy).

Development is not linear; there are stops and starts, setbacks and movements forward. A middle school girl who appears to be making leaps and bounds in identity development might suddenly seem to regress, wanting to crawl into her parent's lap or play with her favorite childhood toys, longing to be younger again. It can be confusing to adults: one minute, these preteens want to be perceived as older and capable of more responsibility; the very next, they are clamoring to climb into bed with their mom. During one session, a bubbly twelve-year-old named Chrissy who often enjoyed the limelight volunteered to participate in an exercise as the other members observed:

Chrissy was asked to reveal a secret that she keeps hidden. We were ten sessions in and nearing graduation, and she was feeling safe and comfortable enough to reveal "I still play with Barbie dolls." Some outsiders might think this sounds childish, but it's perfectly normal for a sixth grader to be playing with dolls; during the emotionally and physically tumultuous middle school years, it's not uncommon to want to revert back to childhood a bit and feel taken care of and protected. Chrissy cringed as she stated this, fearful of being judged by the group. But she waited, and what transpired was indeed magical: One seventh grader spoke about her own American Girl doll collection, which she still loved and refused to put away. Other sixth graders revealed how they wished they could still play with their dolls but their parents had given them away. Nobody in the room responded negatively or thought Chrissy's Barbies were strange. In fact, the consensus was that they wanted to feel as they did in earlier childhood. Chrissy would never have shared intimate information as she did unless she truly felt safe. She would have kept her Barbie dolls a secret, harboring a perception

that her regression was shameful and not the norm for a girl her age.
This not only impacts identity but also perpetuates a pattern that con-
tinues throughout life: shame, doubt, and the need to keep "dirty little
secrets" hidden. The silencing of needs or thwarting of aspects of self
will manifest when there is no place to be authentic.

Finding Their Passion

I always say, "Passion and purpose . . . that's what girls and women
are made of," as a way of reframing the age-old "sugar and spice and
everything nice" mantra. What I have observed time and time again
in my research and consulting work is that passion is a requirement
for the majority of women. Central to both their identity and sense
of self is the ability to articulate and change those issues that inspire
them; if they don't feel engaged with a cause, they will opt out. (Men,
on the other hand, are socialized to pursue a linear career that is as
lucrative as possible, regardless of whether they are passionate about
the cause. This stems from their preconceived image of the male as
the major breadwinner.) Unsurprisingly, my research examining
power showed that when women are attached to a cause, they are
willing to take risks, defy the status quo, be the lone voice in the
room, and use their power effectively.

Unleashed is predicated upon the girls' passion for animal welfare
and rights; without it they would not choose to embark on a transformative personal journey. Girls are much more willing to examine
who they are, explore aspects of themselves they have never considered, stretch outside their comfort zone, and receive feedback when
it is presented as the necessary leadership skills that will strengthen
their capacity to advocate for the dogs. There is a method to my mad-
ness: Unleashed leverages the girls' passion for puppies, inspiring

them to channel their newly found sense of injustice into making a difference, and, at the same time, feeling powerful. Girls embrace a sense of purpose at a time when things might be confusing to them; the world as they once knew it is dramatically changing. Not only does it give them a sense that they are needed and valued, it also allows them to focus on something external rather than the changes taking place in their bodies and minds.

Most important, their passion becomes a catalyst for the development of personal power and a strong sense of self. As their self-awareness deepens, a shift occurs. Girls will say, "This program isn't about the puppies, it's about us." Fast-forward to graduation when the girls, now considered experts, sit on a panel, discussing Unleashed in front of parents, school faculty, donors, and Unleashed board members. When asked, "What has been the best part of the program?" girls' responses include "The sisterhood"; "I learned I can make a difference"; and "I feel powerful"—without any mention of the puppies.

Society has failed girls and women by making it difficult, if not nearly impossible, to develop an authentic, untainted sense of self. Our culture remains largely focused on the male experience, erroneously characterizing autonomy and self-sufficiency as the norm. That's not surprising considering that, even tracing back to the Bible, men have historically assumed the majority of leadership positions, taking ownership of business, politics, religion, and more.

But what if the reverse were true? What if traits such as empathy, intimacy, and mutuality were considered signs of overall psychological health and well-being? What if women felt emboldened to defy stereotypes and not succumb to the male point of view? What if our girls learned to craft a strong sense of self from an early age, recognizing their values and aligning with them versus veering away out of

fear of being seen as dependent, overly emotional, passive, or irrational? Maybe we wouldn't have so many women who, despite outward
appearances, are afraid to truly succeed; who grapple with insecurity
and self-doubt; who suffer from a scarcity of authentic leadership positions in law, medicine, finance, academia, government, and corporate America. Maybe women wouldn't still be purchasing 6 million
self-help books a year (74 percent of all self-help books sold),[8] and
making sixty-nine cents for every dollar a male CEO makes.[9]

By offering safe spaces to grow and experiment, easing the wide-
spread pressure to overachieve, and helping them to name and contemplate their values and passions, we can enable middle school girls
to give an answer—too-often highly elusive—to the basic question
"Who am I?"

The feminist movement is far from over, glass ceilings still exist,
and women are still afraid to truly seize their power. Now is the time
to give girls and women permission to be themselves, to have big
aspirations, and to own their potential. If we keep adjusting our values and beliefs to fit in with male-focused societal norms, it will be
our demise. Cultural change is daunting, but we owe it to ourselves,
our daughters and students, our feminist leaders of the past, and our
change-makers of the future to make the effort.

1. One of my favorite questions to pose during Check In is "If you were sixty-five years old and sitting on a park bench and a stranger sat down next to you and asked you about your life, what would you tell them?" In response, I have heard everything from "I discovered a cure for cancer" or "I'm a vet with a humongous house and six rescued dogs" to the simpler "I graduated college" or "I lived a happy and peaceful life." Aspirations and dreams are significant aspects of developing a sense of self. On the girls' path to defining who they are, the chance to venture down a variety of roads will only broaden their horizons. Try posing this question in a casual setting (during mealtime or while running errands if you are a parent, as a writing assignment or during an advisory session if you are a teacher), and be sure to follow up by asking the girl what she thinks her answers reveal about the type of person she hopes to become. Share your own responses, serving as a role model and acknowledging the differences in and equal value of individuals' aspirations, hopes, and dreams.

2. Girls need and deserve female-centric safe spaces to develop, mature, and cultivate intimate relationships with other girls and women. Think about an average day of the middle school girl in your life: Are there opportunities for her to develop a sense of sisterhood? Is she spending time in any all-female environments where she can interact with different types of females and tap into her passions?

Examples include athletic teams, Girl Scouts, same-sex camps or activities, or even community-service opportunities to help younger girls.

3. Designate one technology-free (no cell phones, computers, iPads, or TV) night a week to enjoy dinner as a family. Use this as an opportunity to prompt reflection about passions, values, and strengths. Pose a question similar to one in an Unleashed Check In: "What was the best part of your day and the most challenging?" or "What was something that happened today that you are proud of?" Be sure to respond to your own questions as part of this activity. As you begin to spark these conversations regularly, look for patterns and themes in the dialogue: You may find your girl mentions collaboration or socialization consistently as a high point of her day, or that may be her largest challenge. She may be proud of helping a partner study for a test or standing up for someone else despite being afraid to do so. Acknowledge the information you are observing and provide reinforcement and support when needed; for example, "Wow, that was amazing how you got to work together with someone you didn't know before. It might have been awkward in the beginning, but what did you learn from that?" or "You really love being creative. I noticed that last week when you told me about your art class and now this week in writing. I can't wait to see what else you do with your imagination . . . not everyone is so creative!"

Chapter 2

Strengths and Resilience

hy do strengths matter? Strength is a capacity for thinking, feeling, and behaving in a way that allows optimal functioning to pursue a valued outcome.[1] Strengths serve many purposes: They function as a woman's "core," motivating her to broaden her repertoire of skills; they equip her to manage adversity; and they create a foundation for the development of additional strengths. Understanding and owning her strengths enables her to make sense of her world; it builds confidence to expand her horizons. The ability to articulate one's strengths is highly correlated with self-confidence, mastery, and self-worth. While the possibilities to build on weaknesses are limited, there are ample opportunities to maximize strengths.

However, far too many females are fearful of embracing or even acknowledging their strengths. I regularly consult with highly accomplished women who are unable to see their own value proposition, or who do see it but hold back showcasing their assets for fear of being perceived as arrogant or aggressive. One client, Mindy, is a prime example of those who hire me soon after securing a powerful position. In her early forties, Mindy had recently been promoted to senior vice president of the Finance and Technology Division of a major global investment banking company and, while preparing for maternity leave, had requested a performance review from her boss. On a coaching call a few weeks before the evaluation, I asked her to describe how she would articulate her success to her manager, resulting in minutes of silence. "I have no idea," she replied. "I've been in this position for such a short period of time." What was shocking, but common among talented, competitive, driven women, was her inability and reticence to showcase and own her inherent strengths and value.

This same dynamic is at play among girls as young as nine, ten, and eleven years old. Like Mindy, they fight to conceal their worth, the characteristics that may set them apart from others or make them unique. They struggle with touting their strengths for fear that this might be misconstrued as selfish, narcissistic, and unduly self-promotional. Complicating matters, they hold back from owning an accomplishment for fear that others might feel it's unworthy of praise and that they might not live up to the expectation set forth by their description. I have witnessed girls become the judge and jury of their own court; they vacillate, trying to justify why they could label themselves a good swimmer or call themselves an athlete. They fear someone may say, "How many medals did you win? Where is the evidence for a statement such as that?" Unless a girl has her testimony fully prepared, she hesitates to proclaim her value. Consequently, perfectionism and stringently high self-expectations follow suit.

Unfortunately these girls' apprehension is warranted. They live in a society that perpetuates and reinforces high performance and overachievement. Are girls allowed to identify themselves as good swimmers without an adult asking, "Which swim team are you on?"

"What are you ranked?" Setting such high and often impossible expectations without support, reinforcement, and acknowledgment of success is dangerous. The modern female is immersed in a black hole searching for her perfect image, repeatedly coming up empty and dissatisfied. Her looking glass is distorted, and no wonder. There is an absence of realistic reflections illuminating her true self. We say to every Unleashed girl throughout the program, "Nobody is perfect . . . we all have our strengths and weaknesses . . . we all make mistakes . . . when you let go of the pressure to be ideal, you will discover wonderful pieces of yourself."

Acclaimed psychologist Martin E. P. Seligman, PhD, is the founder of the field of positive psychology—the scientific study of the strengths and virtues that enable individuals and communities to thrive.[2] Positive psychology challenges the traditional, pathology-based view of mental health and medicine, proposing that a strength-based approach, with an emphasis on competencies and resources, would prove far more effective in promoting psychological health and welfare.

The positive-psychology model pinpoints strengths and positive emotions as the starting point, reframing adversity in such a way that it is seen as a challenge rather than a setback. This asset-based approach has been successfully used in health care,[3] child welfare,[4] community development,[5] and more. In the field of education, it has been repeatedly shown that positive psychology impacts academic and social learning; scholastic achievement, student engagement, and overall student happiness are enhanced when classroom philosophies integrate optimism, empowering children to create solutions based on their strengths and utilizing their individual successes to increase motivation and satisfaction.[6] As Aristotle argued, "Educating the mind without educating the heart is not education at all."

Strength-based approaches provide the framework for doing just that: educating the heart; recognizing and appreciating individual and collective strengths and potential; leveraging these competencies across many contexts; and adjusting one's lens to view situations from various vantage points rather than immediately jumping to negative conclusions.

As a strength-based organization, Unleashed is heavily influenced by the principles of positive psychology. My inherent philosophy is that transformation occurs when girls understand their assets, gain a deep understanding of their value proposition, and use their skills to maximize success. I purposely integrated multiple Seligman-like theories into Unleashed's culture from the onset: the belief that girls have the potential to thrive; the emphasis on capacity building and increasing overall life satisfaction; the notion that solutions are not only possible but within reach. Few opportunities exist for girls to identify and embrace their strengths without being chastised; our society continually maintains a pessimistic perspective, with much more attention directed at deficits versus assets. Our younger generation, socialized to avoid adversity and failure rather than utilizing them to develop healthy coping mechanisms, is at a major disadvantage.

When people are asked to identify their successes, their view of their situation becomes colored by it in a positive way.[7] The identification of strengths is a large component of Unleashed, based on the premise that understanding and leveraging one's value proposition is an aspect of one's personal power (one of the three components in what I consider a woman's triumvirate of power, which will be further explored in chapter 4). Early on in the program, girls are encouraged to list their strengths. We do this anonymously at first, respecting their discomfort and inability to state their value. But the practice enables me to stretch girls to think about the importance of articulating their worth, then helps them to process the feelings that emerge as a result and to understand the consequences of allowing their talents to remain unrecognized or minimized. Later in the program, I hang posters across the classroom, each with a heading: DREAMS, STRENGTHS, ADJECTIVES, and THINGS I WANT TO IMPROVE ABOUT MYSELF. This is designed to motivate them to revisit the concept of self-worth; the rationale being that the more frequently a girl assesses her capabilities, the higher likelihood that she will not only make them visible but leverage them.

Gradually, girls are stretched to embrace recognition for their accomplishments and talents, reinforcing the notion that it is not only acceptable but critical for girls to showcase their expertise. This might be discussed explicitly during Check In, when I ask, "What are you most proud of about yourself?" and field a variety of responses ranging from "I care about people" to "I am an excellent soccer player" to "I don't know." For a girl who is reluctant to respond or struggles to articulate what she admires in herself, it is an opportunity to explore the barriers. "What is getting in the way of acknowledging yourself?" I ask, encouraging her to ask her teammates for support.

Donald O. Clifton, a well-respected advocate of strength-based psychology and coauthor of *Now, Discover Your Strengths,* has said, "Each person's greatest room for growth is in the areas of his or her greatest strength . . . to avoid your strengths and to focus on your weaknesses isn't a sign of diligent humility. It is almost irresponsible . . . the most honorable thing to do is face up to the strength potential inherent in your talents and then find ways to realize it."[8]

Implicitly, Unleashed validates and reinforces girls for being transparent about their strengths. Coaches acknowledge girls in the moment for taking risks, revealing an intimate insight or fact about their lives, achieving a goal, having an innovative idea, or acting as a role model or leader. I might tell them, "I love how you were honest about your feelings" or "You did a great job leading the discussion today." Initially, they are reluctant to accept the compliment, but they quickly become desensitized, reveling in the praise. Witnessing a smile beam across the face of a young girl when admired, watching a teen jokingly stand and take a bow in response to applause or even just nod her head in acceptance, underscores how vital a strength-based environment is for youth empowerment and their overall health and well-being. I often half-kiddingly remark, "Who in this room can complain of receiving too many compliments? Let's see a show of hands for those who do." Never has a hand been raised in response.

When it comes to strengths and gender, women and girls remain in a double bind. Qualities such as communication and empathy are labeled "feminine" and tend to be undervalued and perceived as inconsequential, while those characteristics attributed to "masculinity" (confidence, assertiveness) are coveted and admired. Girls' and women's strengths are viewed as trivial and expendable, so to tout them may not hold any weight. But when a woman minimizes feminine qualities or adopts more masculine characteristics, she risks being labeled "aggressive" or "dominant." It also compartmentalizes her; women resort to siloing their strengths, exhibiting certain characteristics in some contexts but not others. This style of behavior has tremendous consequences: it perpetuates feelings of inauthenticity and fraudulence; it hinders a woman's ability to leverage her strengths that could actually differentiate her from others; and it is highly disengaging and de-energizing.

Society socializes women to focus on deficits, limitations, and weaknesses; hardwired to pay more attention to failures and shortcomings, a woman has little room to reflect on the positives and develop her value proposition. "People think you're full of yourself when you talk about what you're good at," Shaylee explains. "Boys roll their eyes, like we think we are so perfect," Giselle reveals. Starting young, girls receive an undeniable message that making their talents visible has serious consequences. Gender research shows that success and likability are positively correlated for men but negatively linked for women—successful men are admired; successful women are rebuffed.[9] Girls and women are sensitive to the messages their environment is conveying and struggle to figure out which strengths are socially acceptable. To illustrate this to the girls and my clients, I often joke that a man files a piece of paper in a cabinet and makes sure that everyone in the office knows about it as if he just knocked down the Berlin Wall, but a woman would not even stop to reflect, continuing on to the next task. Remember Mindy, who was hesitant to "admit" she had successfully reorganized a division of hundreds of employees within a colossal global company? The concealing starts young: one study found that 65 percent of gifted adolescent girls hide their ability in school, while only 15 percent of gifted adolescent boys do the same.[10] In another study of female graduates who attended a school for gifted students, researchers discovered that three out of four women did not believe they had superior intelligence.[11]

Growing Stronger through a Search for Meaning

More than ever, overall life satisfaction is a desperately needed commodity. People search for meaning, purpose, and engagement to make sense of their existence: Fifty-eight percent of Americans report thinking about the meaning and purpose of life.[12] Overall life satisfaction is one of the constructs measured in all Unleashed participants, using a research tool designed to assess the differences both pre- and postprogram. One of my primary goals was to ensure that the framework of change created for the girls was being transferred to other aspects of their lives, not exclusively being enacted in the twelve-week sessions. Unleashed serves as a microcosm of life, providing a window of opportunity to hone specific strengths and develop additional ones, reinforcing permeation of this new-found knowledge across contexts—school, community, family, to name a few. Psychological research clarifies the benefits of happiness, satisfaction, and optimism on health, well-being, learning, productivity, and achievement, but educational systems and institutions repeatedly fail to take these claims into account when developing culture or curriculum. In one of the first few team meetings of Unleashed, I highlight that fun is a virtue, valued in our work together. The time commitment and dedication put forth warrant enjoyment—essentially, there must be a win-win. Privy to the information I gained from my interviews with hundreds of successful women, which told me that women crave the feeling of contributing to a system larger than themselves, I want to implant this concept of mutual benefit early on.

Dominating our world today are the values of overachievement, aptitude, and success. The expectation is that people should be matching the speed and accuracy of technology—which is entirely unrealistic. Ironically, we have what economist Daniel Pink calls the "paradox of prosperity," referring to how our society has more abundant material goods than ever before, yet satisfaction has not improved.[13] As Columbia University professor Andrew Delbanco states, "The most striking feature of contemporary culture is the un-slaked craving for transcendence."[14]

The digital revolution has provided a multitude of benefits: flexibility, continual access to resources and information, nontraditional work arrangements, and the ability to connect and communicate regardless of location or time zone. Yet, these advances simultaneously present numerous dilemmas. Our world no longer shuts down, operating on a 24-7 schedule, creating pressure to be constantly available and causing stimulus overload. The emerging and ever-changing world of technology has largely shaped lives; the majority of people are struggling to manage and adapt to these shifts because humans are much more resistant and slower to change than computer science.

These beliefs, expectations, and phenomena are trickling down to our younger generations. Our educational system is preoccupied with standardized testing and grades; parents are consumed with their children's performance in hobbies such as music and sports and anxious about popularity and socialization. Children are flooded with activities and pressure to perform, enjoying little time for reflection or fun.

Parallel to the need to highlight overall life satisfaction is the need for girls to be encouraged to dream, to create a vision for their futures even if it morphs over time. Girls and women both are more hesitant to venture into the realm of possibility, remaining cautious about revealing goals that might seem impossible. Dreams not only motivate but also provide inspiration for the future. Unfortunately, women are more likely to downscale their dreams as they move through college.[15] I want girls to imagine what could be and create a vision for themselves without worrying that someone else might find it ridiculous or stupid. Previously, I described how I write DREAMS on a poster, inviting girls to jot down their hopes and visions for the future. This is their first step toward beginning to decipher not only what is important to them, but also toward uncovering their true aspirations. (Later, the same lesson gets embedded in discussions about projects and hopes to change the world.) Simply stating "I want" and filling in the blanks sets the stage for them to be able to put a stake in the ground and to carve their own path, refusing to accept what is expected and defying the conventional plan. At first I may hear softly, "I want to be president," resulting in other members of the team asking, "Of what . . . a club? The school?" I caution the girls not to interfere with their teammate's vision and to allow her to complete her sentence without feeling pressured. This same girl will continue to bring up the dream in other contexts and at graduation, where I may hear her proclaim her goal to an audience of thirty people. By that point, there is no hesitation in her voice . . . and no one in the room questions her choice.

Resilience and Strength

Being able to step back and reflect on a challenge, resulting in growth and development, is the hallmark of resiliency. Renowned psychologist Abraham Maslow, creator of the "hierarchy of needs" model, outlined a principle, the "continental divide," to describe how stress can make or break a person depending on the person's level of psychological health—what psychologists identify as resiliency or invulnerability.[16]

Although no universal definition of resiliency exists, most agree it is an adaptive response of individuals facing various levels of adversity. In recovering from suboptimal circumstances, people experience a wide range of negative emotions, become overwhelmed, but then recover from the setback and move forward. Often new strengths and opportunities emerge along with a host of other vulnerabilities and challenges; an absence of stress and adversity leaves little room for growth or for discovering meaning, purpose, or opportunity. Harnessing the power of difficult moments and the wisdom gained from them is what separates resilient women from those who are more vulnerable.

This valuable trait is shared by successful, powerful women. They might have faced alienation on the way to the top; been labeled "bad" mothers because they worked; were thought to be crazy because of their ideas or decisions; received diagnoses of serious illnesses; and even faced being fired from organizations they created when outside investors were brought in. Regardless of the obstacles, these strong women persisted, breaking through barriers that were continuously erected, relying heavily upon their strengths and their passion to persevere. How did they overcome such adversity? It was not a matter of coincidence or circumstance . . . these women reframed the negative experiences into challenges. The language they used was more positive, perceiving problems as tests of endurance, increasing their drive to surmount hurdles. Reflection was another common coping strategy, as they believed insight and purpose could be derived from understanding the root cause of their situations. The question "Why?" motivated them to move forward, energizing their effort to reach new goals.

Resiliency's value spans all contexts of life. When Accenture surveyed more than five hundred senior executives in twenty countries, more than two-thirds of world global corporate leaders rated resilience as extremely important when deciding which employees to retain.[17] It is no surprise that those communities hit hardest by September 11 and Hurricane Sandy bonded, volunteered side by side, and comforted and supported one another. Tragedy forces people to reevaluate their lives, search for meaning and purpose, access all resources (internal and external), and connect to others who have experienced similar circumstances. The road to recovery depends largely on the constitution of each individual: her perception of the events, her view of herself, her ability to cope, her support system, and the strengths she employs to rectify what has happened.

Gabriela was an avid animal lover and would do anything in her power to rescue animals—dogs, cats, you name it. In sixth grade, she recruited a group of girls who successfully raised a few hundred dollars and collected donated bedding, blankets, food, and toys for a New Jersey animal sanctuary. Bursting with pride, Gabriela brought her friends to hand-deliver the goods . . . only to discover the facility was crammed with dirty cages and neglected-looking animals. The sanctuary, it turned out, was under investigation by PETA.

Gabriela was so upset, she became racked with anxiety and lost her appetite; she was embarrassed and ashamed that she hadn't properly researched the facility beforehand. Her father told me I was the only one she felt comfortable speaking to about this mess outside of him and her mother. Together, we explored the entire scenario—what her true role had been, what aspects were and were not under her control, and where the blame truly lay. I helped her turn her focus toward the strengths she'd demonstrated throughout the entire process: passion, drive, collaboration, and leadership. I also shared stories of times I felt that I had failed, such as when a tiny, two-pound pup died in transport, or when a foster parent defamed my name on Craigslist. I promised Gabriela that part of growing up includes giving yourself permission to make mistakes.

We formulated a plan of attack to restore in her a feeling of justice. She decided to report the sanctuary to authorities, ask for her donations back, and request permission from her school principal to share the story with her friends so she wasn't being dishonest. With that, Ga-

briela headed into the Unleashed team room relieved and reenergized. She realized she could believe in the rescue world—and herself— once again.

When it comes to resiliency and how girls are socialized to manage adversity, profound gender differences pervade our culture. From an early age, little girls are perceived to be more fragile and less capable of risk taking. In one enlightening study, mothers were shown videos of children engaging in potentially risky playground activities and asked to intervene by stopping the tape and explaining how they would react in the situation depicted. Researchers found that mothers of daughters stopped the action more quickly and frequently than those with sons. Little girls heard many more warnings such as "Be careful—you could get hurt!"—whereas boys were actually encouraged to take risks on the monkey bars and slide.[18] Girls frequently report to me that they have more stringent curfews and rules than their brothers; the adults in their lives act as though girls need more protection. During discussions about the challenges facing girls, responses include "Boys think we are weaker"; "We are treated like we can't manage anything"; "We aren't dolls"; "I am not glass and I don't break."

The consequences of safeguarding girls from adversity, of thwarting their ability to take risks—even if it means failing—and adopting an overprotective stance are enormously detrimental. If girls continue to receive messages that they are vulnerable and at risk of being harmed (whether it be on the playground or in life), they will never develop the ability to bounce back from less than ideal situations and navigate the labyrinth essential for a woman to succeed. Avoiding failure or risk is not the solution; in fact it actually increases the likelihood that girls will develop a sense of learned helplessness, viewing negative incidents as beyond their control and reinforcing dependency. "Learned helplessness is a barrier to empowerment," Seligman states in his research about building immunity to setbacks.[19] It undermines a person's ability to function, setting the person up for increased frustration and failure. Whether parents innocently do their daughter's homework to keep her from getting a bad grade or finish her science project because she is overwhelmed and they want to ease her stress, it sets up a vicious cycle. Not only does it send the message "You must be perfect," it keeps her from building up a capacity for the future challenges she will undoubtedly face and reinforces the notion that she is incapable of managing anything too complex.

Carol Dweck, a leading psychologist in emotional development, found that girls respond differently to criticism from boys. When receiving feedback, they attribute failures to a permanent flaw in their personality versus circumstances that can be altered.[20] For example, when failing a math test, a girl might respond, "I am bad at math; I can't do this" versus "I didn't study much; I can do much better next time." Engaging in the self-blame game, women are more likely to ascribe their own lack of ability to a negative situation (even if it has nothing to do with them). Men, on the other hand, attribute failure to motivation—"I didn't try hard enough"—but do not perceive it to have occurred because of a lack of aptitude.

From my early work as a child psychologist, my framework has always been to leverage strengths as a means to build resiliency. My philosophy is to accentuate capabilities, reframe the negative into a positive light, and use failures and mistakes as learning opportunities. Unleashed is predicated on this philosophy because of the dire need for girls to not only articulate and leverage their strengths and create a value proposition differentiating themselves from others, but to gain a deep recognition that failure is a vital aspect of life.

Our girls need to become aware that it is acceptable to confidently proclaim they do not have the answer; that doing so does not diminish their self-worth. During team meetings, girls will plead with me to tell them how to spell a certain word; despite my assuring them, "Spelling doesn't matter in Unleashed, it's more important to generate ideas," they struggle to write down a specific word, paralyzed by fear over making a mistake. Similarly, in the initial stages of project planning, they will ask, "What do you think we should do?" My response is always "Your ideas are so much better than mine. What do *you* want to do? What are *your* thoughts?" These replies are always met with smiles as girls admit, "This is the first time I really feel an adult is being honest when they say I can do anything."

During the 2012 presidential election, Jaye was discussing what she considered to be stereotypes about female candidates. I couldn't help but grin as she spoke, causing her to stop. I encouraged her, "Go on . . . I am interested to hear what you are about to say." She looked at me and said, "I would rather hear what you think." And my response was "Your ideas are so much more important to me than mine." Jaye then discussed how disappointing it was to hear candidates talk about women's rights or lack of them. At the end of her critique, she announced, "I would love to have a candidate from the Libertarian Party win an election." Everyone shifted to hear more, and she proudly continued. In retrospect, this was a huge risk for her. Her out-of-the-box political views could have caused alienation, questioning, or criticism. Yet this budding political activist was willing to put her ideas forth . . . and that's incredibly important.

Empowering girls to take huge risks extends beyond team meetings. I never prepare the girls before they speak in front of large audiences; it goes against the grain of the Unleashed philosophy. Speaking from their hearts is more important than being perfectly scripted. Initially, girls hesitate to respond without any research or rehearsal. Yet what always intrigues me is that, midway through the program, when asked to speak on expert panels or host a booth at a community event, girls never even bother to ask what they will be speaking about; an overriding sense of trust in their ability to be spontaneous supersedes their fear of making a mistake.

Resilient girls are optimistic, possessing a sense of self-efficacy (the belief that one can master one's life). They refuse to define themselves by failure, nor do they give up in less than ideal circumstances. These girls are more apt to be energetic and passionate, determined and persistent. A powerful connection exists between resiliency and mental and physical health, happiness and overall life satisfaction, not to mention productivity and success.

I had asked a team to identify an animal-welfare issue close to their hearts and plan a three-week project around it. After heavily researching dogfighting, they learned that pit bulls are the breed most at risk of being enlisted for this cruel and brutal form of "entertainment," primarily because their high tolerance for pain and complete devotion to their caretaker allow them to last longer in the ring. The more the team researched, the more they realized how this breed-specific form of animal cruelty has led to negative, dangerous stereotypes of pit bulls (not the other way around), resulting in plummeting adoptions and increased euthanasia.

The team planned a talent show as a way to combine fun and education, but quickly realized they could not execute an entire production in less than three weeks. Their next idea: a weekend "dog-a-thon" meetup in the park, complete with a walk and educational booths. To raise money, they presented their plans to their classmates in homerooms, selling $3 NUT (No Uniform Today) cards in order for students to have a choice not to wear a school uniform for one day during the school year.

The next week, they dejectedly reported back that they had raised only $50. So I posed a difficult question: "Are we realistically going to be able to get this done in two weeks?" A sea of faces dropped; it was like letting air out of all their balloons. Disappointed, they began grappling for ways to amend their plans. To focus them, I asked, "We have fifty dollars. How can we help pit bulls with fifty dollars?" Morgan, twelve, said her local shelter posted pictures in their window of dogs needing sponsorship. "Maybe we can sponsor a part of a dog?" she suggested. That ignited the girls' interest, and they quickly became energized, searching online for the shelter's website and reading aloud a list of dogs and their stories. Eventually they selected Melissa, a fifty-pound American Staffordshire pit bull who loved humans but tended to be aggressive toward other dogs. They redesigned their NUT cards, featuring Melissa's picture and a one-sentence description of Unleashed, and agreed that even if they raised only $50 total, it would be worth it. That was Wednesday afternoon. On Friday, I learned that, during an indoor recess due to rain, ten of the girls had (with permission) jumped onstage and loudly announced why they needed students to buy NUT cards and save Melissa. Naomi (one of the stronger girls) went first, but was having trouble commanding the attention of three hundred rambunctious students. Then all of a sudden, Shelby—the quietest girl in the group—yelled, "Be quiet and listen to what Naomi has to say!" The auditorium went silent . . . and the girls raised $300 in a low-income school. They were so proud of themselves for refusing to give up. We talked about how they took action even when the original plan did not work out, and how it is normal to feel upset and disappointed— but what matters is how to rebound and recover from those situations. Later that week, they arranged to visit the shelter as a group and personally present the check to Melissa.

Consciously or not, resilient individuals see obstacles as opportunities, subscribing to the motto "When one door closes, another door opens." Not only do young girls benefit from an opportunity to fail, they are privy to Unleashed coaches who serve as role models, transparent about their own setbacks and mistakes. Our world values superficial elements, highlighting success in the form of celebrities, high-performing athletes, socioeconomic status, and material wealth. Business and political leaders alike refuse to take accountability for decisions that go awry, and many adults dismiss or minimize any mistakes made on their pathway to success. This is problematic as girls look at women in positions of power and influence, unaware of the challenges they faced or the struggles they are in the midst of.

I always tell the girls about one of my own biggest failures: I spent hundreds of hours in 2008 and 2009 researching and writing a book proposal focused on my philosophies about women, leadership, development, and power. Rewriting and editing the proposal three times while managing a leadership consulting firm, collaborating with Wharton's Total Leadership Program, and raising two kids was no easy feat. But after all that, the book never got a publisher.

In fact, I received dozens of rejections. I had poured my heart and soul into this project, only to have editor after editor send letters deeming it "not the right fit." This devastating experience could easily have caused me to give up. Instead, it catalyzed me to reanalyze my priorities and think about how else the research could be utilized other than in a book. "Unleashed would not exist if I didn't fall flat on my face and fail miserably," I tell the group. "If I had received a book deal, I would have written a book and still be working full-time as a leadership consultant." Immediately, hands shoot up, with girls screaming, "I wanna make a mistake! I wanna make a mistake!"

[S]he who has a Why to live for can bear almost any How.

—Nietzsche (with a slight gender modification by me)

The will to find meaning and purpose is the window into the human soul.[21] Everyone is born with that drive, but not all rise to the occasion. Conviction is a risk; it may end in disappointment if the desired outcome isn't reached. Some stave off connecting with this feeling for fear that engaging in a search for something unknown may lead to defeat or simply wind up feeling anticlimactic.

Yet, not embarking on this quest has an even higher cost. Meaning and purpose is a fundamental drive, a motivational engine that powers human existence. For some, such as survivors of the Holocaust, it is a matter of life and death, sustenance for survival, literally and figuratively. But whether the situation is as catastrophic as the aftermath of a tsunami or recurring abuse, or more of an everyday (yet still devastating) loss, such as sudden unemployment or divorce, it is human nature to dig deep, tapping into one's inner strength to withstand adversity of any magnitude.

My Personal Quest to Help Girls Embrace Their Strengths

From a very early age, I was determined to find meaning in my life, attempting to understand my purpose and the reasons why I faced tremendous struggles. I was born in the Bronx, and my childhood and early adulthood were filled with adversity, as I was raised in a working-class family struggling to make ends meet. As a young adolescent, I didn't have any other option but to care for my three younger siblings since my parents worked long hours. Camp and after-school activities were luxuries; I had to babysit and later take on a part-time job during high school to afford clothing and to save for college. At the age of seventeen, I left home to attend college, but the onus was on me to support myself and fund my tuition. Upon graduation, I was accepted into Columbia University and faced a dilemma: put graduate school aside and get a job to support myself, or struggle financially and put myself through school. Deep in my soul, I realized that an education was the key to power and success and chose graduate school. For five years, I worked full-time while enrolled in a competitive doctoral program (I later transferred to a medical school because I wanted a more intensive education). Living on $5 a day, at times sleeping on friends' couches when I couldn't afford rent, I never once imagined leaving graduate school. I perceived it as a test of strength, a challenge that pushed me beyond my limits, but one I was determined to win. Fueling me: I felt that I was on a quest, a journey to discover meaning and purpose in my life. I believed deeply in possibility and knew something was waiting for me—I just didn't know what. My father, the most influential person in my life, provided emotional support, reiterating again and again, "You were meant to do great things—remember that!"

While working multiple jobs, interning in schools and clinics, and earning my doctorate in clinical psychology, I began to notice the number of girls and women who came into my life who lacked the sense of purpose and determination that I had. They devalued their worth, refused to believe in possibility, and accepted less than optimal situations because they thought they didn't deserve anything more. Harnessing and leveraging power was not part of their repertoire. Deep inside, I yearned to change this mentality, wishing I could empower these females to embrace their uniqueness, take a stand to advocate for themselves, and go after their dreams. Gradually I began to recognize that this was my calling: I was meant to strengthen the power of women and girls. I would be an activist fighting for the rights of females (I even attended a few NOW meetings), and it became clear that I was a feminist, despite its dirty-word connotation.

Without those struggles propelling me to search for meaning and purpose, I am not sure I would have landed where I did. Adversity taught me many lessons that I have used in my life, in my career, and when raising my children. A deep understanding and confidence that I have the capacity to create impact and change enabled me to take many more risks in my life. Fully aware of the skills I developed along the way, relying on my strengths, and fueled with passion, I learned from my informal education that I was resilient enough to manage just about anything life had to offer . . . and that felt powerful!

In 2003, I founded Corporate EQ, a leadership consulting firm. My passion was partnering with companies that were committed to investment in female leaders across all industries and at every level—from administrative assistants all the way up to senior VPs. Five years of development and advancement of women of all ages and career paths left me intrigued by the concept of leadership—how few female leaders struggled to embrace their power and their ability to bounce back from—and triumph over—negative situations. Based on my philosophy that to gain a deep understanding of any phenomenon one must study those who have been successful at it, I felt the only way to learn more about women and power was to examine highly influential female leaders.

So I conducted hundreds of interviews, exploring the challenges, necessary risks taken, and unique career trajectories of women who had figured out how to effectively leverage their power—inspirations such as Facebook's Global Marketing Solutions VP Carolyn Everson;

Oxygen cofounder Lisa Gersh; former NBC news correspondent and Young Women's Leadership Network creator Ann Tisch; American diplomat Prudence Bushnell; and Marlene Sanders, the first woman to anchor a prime-time network newscast (for ABC) and the first female TV journalist to report from Vietnam. Each of these women could clearly articulate her strengths, could identify her unique value proposition, and knew how to differentiate herself from others to stand out. Embedded in their leadership journeys were challenges they confronted; their navigation of the mazes of life; the decisions made at various crossroads that led them to outcomes they could never have imagined. The words of wisdom I collected inspired me to share their expertise with others. Initially, I thought it would be captured in a book, but after my repeated rejection from publishing companies, I had soured on that notion. Finding myself wedded to the idea that tapping into girls' passion at a formative age could profoundly shape their experiences of power and leadership, I decided to try something different.

Once I had a vision, I knew I had to learn firsthand what girls this age are passionate about, their interests, how they experience the world, and what might engage them in a leadership program. Focus groups seemed like the most logical approach. On Sunday mornings, I began hosting twelve to twenty girls at my apartment for breakfast. In a protocol similar to that employed by market-research firms, they filled out questionnaires and participated in group discussions about their favorite causes, what made them angry, and what would motivate them to make a change. By the end of the focus groups, I had met with sixty girls between the ages of ten and sixteen, and one response reverberated: animal welfare. "Animals don't have a voice," they would say. "They can't defend themselves and animals can't report abuse. It's not fair."

This made sense to me from both a personal and professional vantage point. I myself had been an animals' advocate from the age of eight. Growing up, I would save stray dogs and cats, feeding and stowing them in my parents' garage overnight and releasing them early in the morning before my mother woke up. Obviously, girls this age could empathize with the defenselessness and vulnerability of animals. Girls experienced an overriding urge to protect and advocate for animals that were suffering, visualizing themselves as a voice for those less powerful. They felt capable of supporting this cause, committed to creating change.

Throughout the focus groups, other important issues were raised. Girls shared how difficult they found it to be perceived as irresponsible and defiant by adults and society. Again and again, they spoke about the negative reputation teenage girls have in the media, and how that translates to people's beliefs and responses to them. Being dismissed from volunteer opportunities, having community-service projects owned entirely by teachers, and listening to their ideas being rejected, girls craved opportunities to make a significant difference. "We want to make a real impact," they said. "If we're going to work with the homeless, we want to serve them and talk with them, not just make sandwiches. Why do we hear we can do anything, but then aren't allowed?" Their frustration is warranted—as Her Royal Highness Queen Mathilde of Belgium, honorary chair of UNICEF Belgium, stated, "Adolescents do not consider themselves as 'future adults'; they want to be taken seriously now."[22] The statement that truly reflected an adolescent's experience of her world emerged as I was seeking feedback at the end of one focus group. "What did you like most about this meeting?" I asked. Rebekah, a down-to-earth seventh grader, bluntly replied, "You didn't tell us our ideas sucked."

The focus groups, the outcomes of Unleashed, the discussions I am privy to each week, in conjunction with the given challenges women continue to face as they circumvent barriers to reach their potential, provide a compelling argument warranting significant change. Not only do our girls need an environment that permits them to showcase their talents, applauds their success, and encourages them to persevere; they must be able to fail miserably without setting the women's movement back twenty years. Our society conveys the message "you can have it all" to our female population, then magnifies their flaws and punishes them for making any mistakes. "You can have it all" has a caveat: "You can have it all, but you must be perfect and modest; and don't flaunt it or it may be taken away very quickly."

Which factors combine to create a strong girl, and which threaten to sabotage her? A strong female regardless of age is one who has developed her own unique blueprint, capitalizing on her capabilities, skills, talents, and sense of purpose. The more opportunities and experiences she has to cultivate, embrace, and showcase, the more likely she will not hide or minimize them. What she needs most from the world around her is for it to recognize and applaud her assets rather than to narrow in on her deficits. It is impossible to fully capitalize on and leverage strengths, create a robust value proposition, and shatter gender bias without building resilience to overcome adversity. One is highly dependent on the other; strengths are the platform or springboard for girls to bounce off from, propelling them forward with a competitive advantage. The ability to recover equips a girl with confidence and mastery that she will rely on for the rest of her life.

Power Boost

1. When the middle school girls in your life are challenged by a difficult moment or task, give them permission to struggle. Coach them to continue independently, encouraging them to take a risk. You might need to sit in the same room or say, "I know it can feel uncomfortable when you can't figure it out right away, but I know you can do this." Be prepared to face resistance; they may want to give up or you may feel you want to jump in so they can avoid a struggle. Life is full of challenges; these early experiences will prepare them for the future. Navigating through difficulties will help them discover coping strategies, strengthen their confidence that they can do things autonomously, and shape their sense of mastery.

2. When a girl experiences a setback (a poor test grade, an argument with a friend, a missed goal on the soccer field, or an embarrassing moment), help her process what happened, looking at all the contributing factors. Remain neutral and calm while she talks about her experience; give her space to think aloud and gain insight into what happened. Without judgment, ask what she might have done differently if given another chance, and encourage her to identify the lessons she learned from her mistakes. Most important, reinforce the notion that mistakes are normal and necessary for anyone to learn; share a few of your own failures, how you felt and what you learned from them.

3. Observe the middle school girls you know, paying particular attention to their strengths, accomplishments, or even the ideas and thoughts they have on a particular subject. Stretch yourself to view their behaviors optimistically, focusing on the positive aspects rather than the negative ones. A girl's experience, determination, and learning are more important than the particular outcomes. When she tries hard in a subject that is difficult for her, acknowledge the effort rather than the grade. Recognize and highlight her triumphs, being as specific as you can so she can begin to identify her strengths. For example, say, "I love the way you worked things out with your brother. I was proud of you when you told him why you were angry rather than lashing out. That took such strength!" At times she might ignore or dismiss your compliment. This is an opportunity to explore why; what gets in the way of her accepting praise? What does it feel like to her when someone compliments her, and how can she begin to see herself as others do?

Chapter 3

Social-Emotional Intelligence

E mbedded in Unleashed is the strengthening of emotional intelligence (EQ) and empathy. The "IQ way of thinking," not
EQ, permeates our society; our younger generation is pushed to
achieve in school and master achievement tests and led to believe
that academic performance is the only route to success. Yet, contrary to popular belief, our complex, irrational world demands a
wide spectrum of intelligences, as humans cannot function purely by
logic. Emotions are central to evolution, psychological development,
brain functioning, and managing life's daily challenges. Renowned
psychologist Daniel Goleman says, "Ignoring the power of emotions
is shortsighted,"[1] and Karen Stone McCown, founder of the progressive, social-emotional-learning-based Nueva School, asserts, "Being
emotionally literate is as important for learning as instruction is in
math and science."[2]

How does EQ impact a girl's sense of self? It extends far beyond
labeling feelings: it encompasses her emotional awareness, her understanding of reactions and why they occur. Emotional intelligence

increases a girl's tolerance for negative feelings and the ability to manage them appropriately; it helps foster empathy toward others as well as herself, promotes conflict resolution, and reinforces collaboration within relationships. All of this has a positive effect on a girl's ability to establish a strong identity, to navigate the complexities of her social milieu, and to gain insight into who she is from her perspective and others.'

Emotionally intelligent girls and women are more assertive, confident enough to directly express their feelings, positive about themselves, searching for a deeper purpose in their lives. Adjusting the lens and reframing this for our young women, normalizing the integration of affect, and placing greater value on intelligence beyond the scope of achievement tests strengthen their confidence and self-esteem.

Deficits in social and emotional intelligence lay at the heart of modern problems plaguing schools, communities, and families. Over the past four decades, economic and social pressures have dramatically weakened the cultural institutions that once filled the psychological needs of its younger generation.[3] Today, the majority of children are being raised in a fast-paced environment that bombards them with constant stimulation, confusing and uncensored messages, immediate gratification, and a focus on materialism, while reinforcing a "quick fix" approach rather than introspection for coping with adversity.

Compounding matters, the United States is more divided now than it has been since the civil rights movement. Heated disputes about personal freedom, civil liberties, national security, public policies, and affirmative action permeate the media. The news is filled with stories showcasing abuse, terrorist acts, random shootings, and the unethical behavior of adults in leadership roles. Children sensitive to our country's instability are, as a result, experiencing higher levels of anxiety and duress. Yet, in the face of tragic incidents such as Sandy Hook or Columbine, the public scrutinizes only the superficial layers: inadequate gun control legislation, mental illness, faulty parenting, and the need for higher levels of security. What remains taboo is how undervalued empathy, compassion, self-awareness, and personal accountability are in our society. Failure to address the underlying roots of this pervasive violence is problematic.

Not surprisingly, research shows that psychological distress among adolescents and elementary-school children is rising; society is witnessing an increase in vulnerability and physical ailments due to a decline in emotional intelligence,[4] and statistics over the past decade indicate that failure to thrive in school is due to a combination of individual and academic factors. Forty percent of children are at risk of problems due to poverty, racial differences, immigration, single-parent households, and health problems.[5] Looking more closely, the variables that yield the greatest impact are poor self-esteem, lack of self-control, social alienation, and feeling as though teachers do not care.[6] Now more than ever, there needs to be a sense of urgency about safeguarding the welfare of future generations.

The conventional wisdom of politicians, educators, and academia emphatically advocates for advancements in education, viewing it as the key to economic growth.[7] Yet, the United States is gradually losing its educational advantage over other countries, posing a threat to our prosperity and vitality. The National Center for Education recently pinpointed a correlation between the rate of school dropouts and a lack of social-emotional competencies (failure to feel connected; feeling emotionally unsafe; conflicts with peers and staff).[8] "The direct intervention of the psychological determinants of learning promises the most effective avenues of reform."[9] However, the US

Department of Education fails to recognize that school is a primary social milieu offering children an opportunity to learn so much more than just traditional academics. Focusing solely on IQ, standardized-test scores, and academic achievement without integrating valuable softer skills is a serious mistake. Schools may believe in the emotional components of learning, but are reluctant to engage in any activities other than those directly impacting academic progress (i.e., test scores) because softer skills have been positioned as "fluff." Funding is given only to those schools that consistently demonstrate high standardized-test scores, overlooking the fundamental skills necessary for a child to achieve. But over the long term, scores do not predict academic or life success; social-emotional intelligence does.[10]

Salovey and Mayer coined the term *emotional intelligence*,[11] describing it as a form of social-intelligence ability to monitor one's own and others' feelings and emotions, to discriminate among them, and to use this information to guide one's thinking and actions. The framework for emotional competence is largely organized by four basic tenets: self-awareness, self-management/regulation, social awareness, and self-motivation. Since the publication of Daniel Goleman's groundbreaking book *Emotional Intelligence*, numerous theories, definitions, and applications have emerged. But for the most part, all are in agreement that EQ or EI is positively correlated to learning, leadership, emotional health, and adaptive functioning.

Emotional intelligence has been validated as an aptitude separate and distinct from IQ.[12] Early on, psychologists recognized that an individual had to have certain noncognitive aspects to function effectively. David Wechsler, who developed the IQ test, defined intelligence as the aggregate or global capacity of the individual to act purposefully, to think rationally, and to deal effectively with his environment[13]; in 1983, developmental psychologist Howard

Gardner argued that there was a wide spectrum of intelligences (intrapersonal and interpersonal, to name two)—not just that measured by traditional IQ assessments. Emotions, interpersonal skills, and cognitive abilities operate synergistically, guiding decision-making and behavior and helping one navigate the social landscape of life.

Social-emotional competence and academic achievement are largely intertwined, maximizing the potential to succeed in and out of school.[14] It is dangerously shortsighted to believe that education is merely about passing a test; our schools need to arm children with skills to excel in life. Out of the eleven most influential factors that impact learning, eight are based on social-emotional learning. The capacity to recognize and manage emotions, solve problems, establish positive interpersonal relationships, and develop a sense of empathy for others, as well as attitudes and motivation, contribute to a child's ability to navigate the intricacies of academic achievement.[15] New insights within the field of neuropsychology validate the correlation between social-emotional intelligence and learning. Learning is largely relational; thinking and emotion are significantly connected; memory is coded based on emotions and situations; negative feelings can thwart learning.[16] More important, unlike IQ, emotional intelligence is malleable, reversible, and can be developed and shaped by learning and experience.[17]

Analogous to EQ, *social-emotional learning* is a term used in the field of education. It refers to the capacity to recognize and manage emotions, solve problems effectively, and establish positive relationships with others. Social-emotional learning is an education unlike any other. Decades of research illustrate that harnessing emotions to facilitate thinking and problem-solving is critical to a child's ability to manage the complexities of school. Autonomy, self-discipline, and ethical behavior are more likely to emerge when an environment fosters mutual respect, cooperation, caring, and decision-making.[18]

An emotional map, if established early on, cultivates an empathic and compassionate society, developing ethical, engaged citizens. Emotions are hardwired into the evolution and survival of a culture: they are informational; follow specific patterns; are connected to biological and brain functioning; need to be expressed, normalized, and incorporated into universal social rules. Avoidance and suppression of feelings, and ignorance of the impact emotions have in socialization, learning, and the development of pro-social behavior, will only result in the manifestation of negative social actions and strife similar to the issues dominating the latest news headlines.

Social and emotional aptitude is interwoven into the fabric of a female's identity—why should she be coerced into relinquishing aspects of herself that can be used to excel? Unleashed is invested in establishing a blueprint of emotional intelligence, creating a culture based upon the fundamentals of social-emotional learning. From the launch of the program to graduation, a conscious attempt is made to construct a milieu that serves as a microcosm for a humane and empathic society. The intention is to provide girls with an education, unlike traditional academics, that can repeatedly be used to influence their lives and those of others. The informal learning that takes place within such a short time (twelve weeks) is transformational; girls adopt an empathic, compassionate, and insightful approach to the world and are then equipped to break the cycle of apathy and violence. Unleashed girls utilize their experiences to educate, engage, and morph the beliefs of those in their community. Their exposure to an environment that aligns moods with decision-making and problem-solving fosters healthy communication of feelings, and supports girls in understanding the emotional landscape of their world will no doubt propel them to become ambassadors of this paradigm.

Unleashed's model of social-emotional learning is process-oriented; embedded into the program is a developmental trajectory that is custom-designed based on the individual team and each participant. However, the universal philosophy and learning modality central throughout the entire organization is utilizing animal rights and welfare as the vehicle to ignite an emotional response, increase empathy and attunement, and foster respect, cooperation, and collaboration in interpersonal relationships. Unleashed emphasizes the significance of emotional literacy, using a girl's passion for vulnerable animals as the way to enter into her inner emotional life. What is it about animal rights and welfare that penetrates deep into the soul of a young girl? Is it the unconditional acceptance an animal provides? Is it the vulnerability of a voiceless animal? Or does she simply feel socially responsible to defend something helpless and dependent because it has even less power than she does?

The response may be different for every girl. But the commonality is how Unleashed leverages a middle school girl's passion for dogs—her concern about their welfare, experience, and the host of issues confronting the canines in our country—to launch her into discovery and experimentation. Staying in the realm of the dog's experience and emotional life poses little threat to a preteen. What begins as attunement to the suffering of and cruelty toward our animal companions leads to the development of empathy and compassion for humanity in general. The program challenges girls to transfer the emotional-intelligence competencies and social learning developed from their connection to the puppies to other girls and coaches on their team. Ultimately, they leave Unleashed more tolerant of others, whether it concerns differences in opinions, appearance, or family background. The final hurdle is the capacity to apply the unconventional wisdom they have acquired to satisfy their personal needs. By the twelfth week, when graduating members become expert panelists, speaking before an audience of school faculty, parents, and Unleashed board members and supporters, it is apparent that the learning has moved well beyond puppies.

Unleashed is not unique in its use of dogs to enhance the emotional and social well-being of people. Companion animals have been used in mental-health settings as early as 1792.[19] I always say, "I would like to think the outcomes are due to my clinical expertise . . . but the impact of playing with a puppy outweighs any therapy." The provision of unconditional acceptance, affection, and nonthreatening comfort encourages the development of empathy, social and interpersonal ability, and trust. The natural affinity a child has for a dog creates a spontaneous and instantaneous bond. Social psychologists deem animals an important component for a child's development of self; animals are perceived by children as sharing their subjective experience; their working models of human relationships correspond to those they have with their pets (a positive attachment with the family dog is a catalyst for the formation of other satisfying relationships), and a bond with a pet increases overall mental and physical health. Over the past few decades, research has validated animals as instrumental to society in numerous ways: rehabilitation among prisoners (recidivism is decreased, self-esteem increases, and empathy is depicted after participation in programs such as Puppy Behind Bars); stress reduction, measured by decreased blood pressure; a buffer from traumatic natural disasters or tragedies; and supplemental treatment to aid in the recovery of people across all ages and diagnoses (post-traumatic stress, learning disorders, depression, anxiety, surgery, terminal illness). Neurobiological studies show that the brain is hardwired with a predisposition to animals.[20] The chemical composition of the brain dramatically alters when one interacts with a dog: levels of oxytocin (an attachment-promoting neurotransmitter) rise and endorphins become elevated (creating a euphoria similar to a runner's high). Pleasure-inducing dopamine and nurture-evoking prolactin are also positively affected.

It is no surprise that the combination of girls and puppies produces an undeniably magical effect. Animal mistreatment and injustice often have great resonance with adolescent girls: they closely identify with the feelings of helplessness and voicelessness evoked by puppies and can empathize with the plight of animals and their vulnerability. When girls cry, "Puppies deserve to be protected," what they're really saying is, "*I* deserve to be protected." When they say, "Someone needs to speak up for them," they mean, "Someone needs to speak up for *me*." This phenomenon is not surprising, since people tend to adopt the role of interpreter, speaking for animals and attributing "mindfulness" to a dog.[21] Often, the boundaries between people and dogs are blurred; the animal acts as a reflection of self and its behavior is personified; human characteristics are typically attributed to him or her.

Animal welfare and rights is a passion of the majority of adolescent girls. As mentioned in chapter 2, when I conducted focus groups with girls between the ages of ten and sixteen, 80 percent of them stated that they would forgo their favorite hobby to get involved and create change for this cause. Since the inception of Unleashed, I have presented to hundreds of girls, fielded daily inquiries about the program from teens and their parents, and received dozens of e-mails from across the country with pleas to launch Unleashed in other regions, all substantiating this finding—puppies ignite a call to action, a deep-seated yearning to tackle an injustice girls find horrific and disturbing. Unleashed leverages the intensity of this compelling urge,

engaging girls in a transformational journey; puppies level the playing field among every one of our participants. The power of this connection to an animal (despite its not being their family pet) overrides
the influence of their peers, family, socioeconomic status, and history, creating an opportunity for them to reevaluate their world and
their role within it. Halfway through the program one girl will state
aloud, "This isn't really about the puppies, is it?"—sparking other girls
to think critically about the process they have experienced, learning
about their community through the eyes of a vulnerable animal that
is dependent on humans for security, love, and well-being.

The four emotional and social-intelligence competencies that
are critical for girls to develop are self-awareness, empathy, self-
management, and appropriately leveraging and using emotions.
Within each of these respective domains are numerous skills a girl
must master; the domains overlap, since many of the skills are inter-
dependent and serve to enhance the development of others.

Self-Awareness

Self-awareness and insight serve as a foundation, underlying the
three other competencies. Being able to identify emotions and values,
to recognize situations that trigger responses, to evaluate strengths,
and to take responsibility for who she is and the impact she might
have on others are all part of this learning process. The primary goal
is for girls to understand and accept who they are as individuals, exploring all aspects of themselves and experimenting with newfound
abilities. During the initial sessions, conversations stay within the
framework and perspective of the animal, providing girls with a less
threatening space to practice becoming aware of their affect, labeling feelings, and building their emotional vocabulary. Much like play

therapy in a child psychologist's office, the puppies serve as a vehicle for expression. The inner life of a girl becomes transparent when she vividly describes or relates to a particular issue or personality type of one of our rescue puppies. One exercise depicting this introspective process is "If I Were an Unleashed Puppy."

Halfway through the program, I ask the girls, "If you were a puppy, what type of home would you want Unleashed to find for you?" Simone raises her hand and reveals, "I want lots of exercise and need some-one to throw a ball around with me all day long until I am totally exhausted." Eve boasts to the group with a proud smile, "I'm small, sassy, and I need a lot of attention, so I want a home where there are no children and I can get all the attention." (Giggles all around: the group enjoys this response.) Genny proclaims, "I am so active and need a huge yard and a family of tons of children to play with." Often, the quiet girl will relate to a bashful breed; the class clown will empathize with the feisty pup; the socially awkward girl will identify with a dog that has repeatedly been turned down for adoption because he's not "cute enough." This is Unleashed's version of a Rorschach test, but the ink splotches have been replaced with dogs.

Using a puppy as an assessment tool provides a girl with an oppor-tunity to candidly express herself, revealing aspects of her personal-ity that would normally make her self-conscious. Girls have shared, "I'm the kind of puppy who doesn't want any other kids or pets in my family—I want to be the center of attention." Once, a particularly shy student admitted, "I wish I had owners who respected me for who I am and didn't try to change me." I often reveal to the teams (as a means of modeling the process), "I would be the hyper dog who would rip up the living-room couch if my family didn't get me to the dog park to socialize with others and run." Once girls verbalize their "self-perceptions," coaches can dig deeper, probe for greater insight, and make connections in the moment so each member of the team can gain clarity about how these fictitious puppy representations may resonate with her own self-image.

Building self-awareness and an emotional vocabulary starts with engaging girls in the cause, provoking a range of feelings about the dogs. From the outset, girls are presented with the horrific realities that animals experience each year. Hundreds of thousands of canines are abused, abandoned by their families, sold to dogfighting rings, and used in laboratory experiments. Nationwide, 5–7 million companion animals enter shelters every year, and approximately 3–4 million are euthanized (60 percent of dogs and 70 percent of cats).[22] Puppy mills and illegal kennels are pervasive, breeding dogs for quantity, not quality, in filthy, cramped, abhorrent conditions, with the sole purpose of making money. These animals are confined to cages, deprived of food, water, veterinary care, or proper socialization with other canines or humans.[23] Girls watch videos featuring raw footage of life inside a puppy mill. Up until this point, many of them mistakenly believe puppy mills are beautiful fields where dogs roam free, receive regular meals, and wait to be taken home by a loving family. Never have they imagined hundreds of dogs crowded into small spaces, barking incessantly, circling round and round their cages (referred to as "cage crazy") amid animal carcasses of those who could not survive such hopeless conditions. They learn about dog auctions—the illegal underground that exists among puppy-mill owners and pet stores—and begin analyzing the parallels between human and dog slavery. Before dimming the lights and starting the video, I gently warn, "These clips are shocking and disturbing. You might cry; you might get angry; this still makes me cry, and that's after watching this video many times. But we need to get angry or upset in order to fight for a cause; otherwise we might not do anything about it."

Self-insight and emotional literacy gained from experiencing a wide spectrum of feelings evoked by the puppies, and their issues prepares girls to advance—moving from awareness provoked by the animals to being cognizant of the interpersonal dynamics that exist with other girls on the team. The relationships among Unleashed participants offer a host of situational learning moments. As girls become attuned to their own internal states, the triggers of their reactions, what they need from their surroundings to persevere and be respected, self-observation and awareness become the norm across many different contexts. The team serves as a training ground increasing emotional and social intelligence.

Vanessa was a sixth grader attending a Manhattan public school. Physically, she appeared much older than her age; she was much taller than the eighth graders, her posture was different from that of her peers, and her hairstyle and facial features were more mature. But her emotional and social maturity did not correspond to her exterior. Vanessa acted much younger than twelve years old: she could not stop poking other girls; she would sit within inches of her teammates, touching them or putting her head on their shoulder or in their lap; throughout sessions she would laugh aloud or say something irrelevant strictly to capture attention. During the first few sessions, her childish behavior enraged her teammates; if she raised her hand to participate, the others would yell, "No," or beg me to ignore her. Outwardly, she pretended the group's rejection did not bother her, welcoming any form of attention, even if it was negative.

Despite all this, in understanding the puppies' emotional state, she was accurate, empathic, and took matters seriously. At the rescues, she was the one who remained calm and centered, focused on the needs of the dogs.

After a few sessions, I thought Vanessa was ready for the group to

serve as her mirror, allowing her to reflect on her behavior and promote self-insight. As usual, Vanessa was provoking the girls sitting
next to her during Check In (the transition from school to Unleashed)
when I decided to have the girls play an Unleashed version of charades.
Each would take a turn selecting one name of a teammate and act like
her; the entire group would have to determine whose name had been
pulled. Early in the game, Jessie pulled Vanessa's name and began acting uncontrollably silly, laughing and jumping out of her seat. Every
girl on the team immediately shouted, "Vanessa." When Jessie nodded
her head in agreement, I turned to Vanessa and asked, "What did you
think of Jessie's performance? Do you see yourself the same way she did?
If so, how? If not, how is it different?" At first, Vanessa smiled devilishly
because all eyes were on her, but slowly her face changed from happy to
sad. "Yes," she replied quietly. "I know that I act crazy. . . . I don't know
why because I can't control myself." The entire team was shocked that
Vanessa had acknowledged her behavior.

The following week, the girls were asked to assess the program and
morphed it into an evaluation of their own progress. I sat astounded
as Livi, a shy sixth grader, spoke honestly about the changes she'd noticed in herself and then followed with "That's what I think, but let me
throw that out to everyone here. Do you agree?" Everyone followed
Livi's lead, naming a change and asking for feedback. When it came
time for Vanessa to respond, the girls were expecting her normal demeanor: wild jumping up and down, yelling, fingers snapping in their
faces—and they had pulled back to guard themselves. However, this
time Vanessa surprised them, saying, "I know I am cuckoo like cuckoo
for Coco Puffs; and I am loud and I can't sit still, but I am smart, I am
an expert in the dogs, and I am committed. I am the only one who has
come to every rescue." The room fell silent and I commented on the excellent job Vanessa had done; she was accurate in her assessment of her

intelligence and commitment. I added, "This Vanessa seems to capture everyone's attention—in fact, it is silent in here!" The room filled with clapping and the girls jokingly said, "Are you not feeling well? Did you eat something that made you act like this?" Vanessa laughed and knew exactly what they were saying. From that session on, Vanessa's behavior shifted tremendously; gradually she formed close-knit friendships and was accepted as an integral part of the group.

Vanessa's increased awareness of herself was the culmination of a process. Her ability to be aware of the puppies' experiences and emotional lives gave her the confidence and proficiency to then examine her own behavior, using her team as a mirror. Ultimately, her ability to take accountability, recognize her value, and take ownership of her emotional reactions led to significant strides and intimacy with others (which is the outcome Vanessa wanted from the beginning).

The desired magnitude of self-awareness will never be reached without examining personal biases and stereotypes. It is human nature to "judge a book by its cover," making assumptions based on past experience, ethnic and religious beliefs, family values, and sociocultural influences. Every individual perceives the world according to what cognitive psychologists refer to as schemas—a preconceived framework used to decipher and process information. Consistent with our model of developing emotional intelligence, Unleashed begins with facts and discussions about the existing stereotypes of dogs—breed, size, color, pedigree—and encourages girls to question and dismantle these prejudices. Pit bulls have a reputation for being aggressive; Chihuahuas are viewed as temperamental and "yappy"; and pets with darker coats are perceived as evil and malevolent. "Black dog syndrome" is a nationwide phenomenon describing the prejudice against an animal because of the color of its fur; darker-coated animals are overlooked at adoption events and shelter visits, remaining homeless; the result is a high incidence of euthanasia. The dialogues that occur in deeply examining these biases spark highly sensitive conversations. Girls encounter their own prejudices and reflect on these ill-conceived "truths," revealing discrimination they have already experienced (on the basis of gender, age, race, appearance, or even financial status). As Unleashed teams reproach those that discriminate against an innocent animal, they slowly become adamant proponents of human rights also. The reverberating question is "If this is happening to dogs in our society, can you imagine what people are facing?"

The following illustration is commonplace: it depicts the girls' anger stemming from the exploitation of dogs based on appearance. Gradually the conversation evolves into a deeper outrage about the pressures and expectations society places on girls regarding beauty.

ERICA: What makes me angry is when they put dogs in clothes. Dogs aren't supposed to wear clothes—well, maybe for, like, five minutes at Halloween or Christmas. But dogs have fur; they don't need tutus and costumes.

ME: Some people do dye their dogs different colors, dress them in fancy outfits, and may even put makeup on them.

ERICA: I also don't like the dog shows [meaning the Westminster Dog Show, which judges each dog based on its breed and AKC standards]. They have to be trained to perform, stand in a certain way, and be perfect. My dog has a white spot on his eye so he wouldn't ever be allowed to be entered in a competition like that.

GISELE: Women put their dogs in beauty pageants.

ME: What do you think about that . . . does that make you upset?

ERICA: Yes. Those dog shows make me angry because of all the regulations and stuff. The only thing people care about is having a perfect dog.

HEIDI: That is just like the little girls' beauty pageants I see on TV—like *Toddlers and Tiaras* and *Honey Boo Boo*! One mother stuck a pin through her daughter's ear because she thought her ears needed to be pierced so she could win!

GISELE: They spray-tan the little girls, too! And they're only, like, five years old!

HEIDI: The girls are always crying and the moms get mad at them.

Conversations like these quickly grow heated because it "isn't really about the dog"; the animal is symbolic of each girl's individual image and representation of herself. I hear statements such as "Barbie would never exist in reality with her measurements"; "Why do magazines airbrush girls? Why can't they take pictures of real girls?"; "There's no way they can be that thin and look that good"; and "It's not fair that girls have to look perfect." They organically move to pinpoint other stereotypes: "Pretty girls cannot be smart"; "Popular girls have to be skinny and blond"; "Middle school girls are mean and irresponsible." Girls and women of all ages battle these prejudices in today's world.

Understanding and Identifying Biases and Stereotypes to Increase Self-Awareness

Some of the most poignant changes in self-awareness I have observed are in biases about racial and socioeconomic diversity. Living in New York City, a melting pot of ethnicities, religions, and races, the majority of our girls have had exposure to heterogeneous groups of people. However, they have not had the opportunity to work collaboratively together, combining efforts for one common purpose. As a result, girls enter Unleashed with preconceived notions of one another based on the neighborhoods of their respective schools and on socioeconomic status. In the beginning, the dichotomy of the teams is noticeable as the girls struggle to remain with others of their own "group," reluctant to converse with someone who looks different. Debriefs of rescue events provide ample opportunity to explore the divide and the level of discomfort. With permission to have an authentic dialogue, the content becomes rich, but layered with complexity. Girls will begin, "The other team is bossy and hogs the puppies." Upon further inquiry, statements reflect one group's image of the other. A team from a school in a poorer neighborhood may remark, "Those girls are snotty and they all have designer boots." Staying neutral and asking "And . . . ?" with a desire to understand always leads to a question of inequity: "Are we truly equal in this program?" Girls from affluent neighborhoods may experience teams from poorer neighborhoods as more powerful because of assumptions that a tough veneer or a direct communication style holds more weight. Regardless of which end of the spectrum girls lie on, powerful conversations that would otherwise not occur are brought to the forefront.

Empathy

Empathy is another social-emotional competency desperately in need of strengthening. The ability to show compassion for others; adopt another's perspective; feel a sense of citizenship; cooperate; engage in positive interpersonal relationships—these are paramount to personal and professional success. Yet, empathy is declining in today's world, and the younger generation is far from immune to this trend.

Unleashed's approach is to ignite a sense of empathy by leveraging a girl's attunement to puppies. When selecting participants, I speak to an audience of middle school girls during a school assembly and present the facts on the current welfare of our nation's animals. Only those girls with a passion for animal rights register for the program. In the first session, the goal is to educate and present a broad spectrum of information about numerous issues. Videos with graphic details about puppy mills, auctions, and exploitation are shown, and a panel of experts (composed of veterinarians, rescue-organization members, attorneys advocating for animal rights, and animal behaviorists) shares facts and statistics to transfer their expertise to the girls. Girls are imbued with knowledge that the majority of adults do not have: They learn that the epidemic of animal cruelty and inhumane treatment masks larger social issues, such as faulty government policies and legislation. They become aware of statistics and demographics indicating that poverty is higher, educational levels lower, and violence more prevalent in the regions of the country where animals suffer the most. By the end of the first session, they are well-versed in puppy mills and high-kill shelters and have a deep understanding of the unethical behavior within the system regulating animal welfare.

During the screening of the puppy-mill video, some girls bury their heads in their hands or on one another's shoulders; others quietly cry. Afterward, I explore the range of reactions: "What was it like to watch the footage? What did you feel? Were you sad? Angry? Surprised?" I want them to understand that it is appropriate and healthy to show their emotions, to feel sad, frustrated, or enraged. Our culture encourages women to minimize and control their feelings. Emotions are viewed as a sign of weakness or lack of power, as a sign of instability, irrationality, and even unprofessionalism. But what is happening is a foray into the ability to identify complex emotions, empathize, and openly express intense feelings without judgment. Adjusting the lens and normalizing the expression of affect, placing tremendous value on an intelligence that extends beyond the scope of achievement tests, boosts confidence and self-esteem.

The history and scope of these issues provokes girls to feel compassion toward animals at risk. Building on this, Unleashed encourages girls to "put themselves in a puppy's paws," imagining what a dog may have experienced prior to being rescued, predicting what it might have been thinking or feeling. This approach continues when girls participate in the community-service part of the program, conducting the temperament testing of puppies entering our rescue organization. The girls are stretched to think about what a puppy has experienced in a two-day cross-country journey, placing the dog's needs above their own (e.g., letting it run and play rather than picking it up and carrying it around). The girls learn how to understand another's perspective, act sensitively, and decipher nonverbal cues.

Empathy and leadership are highly correlated. It has been estimated that 67 percent of the abilities deemed necessary for leadership performance are related to emotional intelligence rather than business acumen and expertise.[24] The ability to influence others, resolve conflicts, communicate appropriately, establish and maintain interpersonal relationships, negotiate, compromise, and collaborate are characteristic of a powerful, transformational leader. The majority of my consulting clients are not struggling with leaders who underperform or who are ill equipped to manage the operational aspects of their roles; executives have most difficulty with those responsibilities that are not taught in business school—such as social and emotional intelligence, understanding and navigating social exchanges in business (a microcosm of life). So much of Unleashed is predicated on this undervalued competency.

It was a Saturday morning, and all of the teams were coming together for a rescue. They had gathered at a local dog "spa," waiting for me to arrive with seven pups I had just picked up from our transporter, who had driven ten and a half hours from South Carolina, bringing the dogs to safety. To prepare for a rescue, the ladies arrive about a half hour early—always on a weekend—to set up bowls of water and wee-wee pads. They break up into as many circles as there are pups arriving, so each group can assume responsibility for one dog. On this day, a few members from one circle were complaining that a duo of girls, Rae and Mary Carroll, were monopolizing that group's puppy, taking her into a corner of the room and refusing to let the others in. Their puppy-hogging was creating hostility and bitterness.

At the girls' next regular team meeting, I created a role-playing exercise, enabling girls to experiment with how to manage these types of situations, while gaining insight into one another's perspective. I assigned Rae, one of the girls who had difficulty sharing the puppy at the rescue, the role of the girl who felt left out. Tyrie, a teammate who had wanted to participate in the activity, assumed the role of the bossy girl, and A.J. volunteered to be the puppy. Tyrie began by wrapping her arms around A.J., shouting, "I want this puppy now! Only I can play with her!" Rae tried to reason with her, but no matter how hard she pleaded for puppy time, she was rebuffed. Rae grew visibly frustrated; a feeling of helplessness washed over her—she even turned to me a few times to ask for help, so I encouraged her to label her feelings, saying to her, "It's really maddening to not be able to get in some playtime, isn't it?" Meanwhile, A.J. looked torn to pieces as she explained how confused and insecure she felt to be in a strange place after two days of traveling in a crate, away from her parents, and have people fighting over her.

By the end of the exercise, the girls who had had difficulty giving up control were able to step outside themselves and see the impact of their actions on others. Those observing thought carefully about their own behavior at the rescue and wondered aloud if they had perhaps been alienating others. They also brainstormed strategies they could tap into in the future if they were feeling helpless when someone else assumed control (such as "I could tell her how I feel"; "I could just say that I would like to be involved in helping out, too"; "I can tell her to think about the dog and the reason we are all here: to make a difference together"). A.J.'s portrayal of the dog as feeling helpless and overstimulated as a result of Tyrie's behavior helped the girls imagine how stressful a rescue must be for the animal itself. They understood that when you try on someone (or something) else's shoes, even for five minutes, your perspective shifts. The next rescue was free of conflict; the girls focused on feeding and observing the puppies collaboratively, preparing them to meet their new foster families.

What transpires over the twelve weeks enables Unleashed participants to develop the empathy required to be an influential, powerful leader. As Daniel Goleman eloquently states, "Understanding the powerful role of emotions sets the best leaders apart from the rest—not just in tangibles such as better business results and the retention of talent, but also in the all-important intangibles, such as higher morale, motivation, and commitment."[25] The experience of working together, adopting the perspective of others, and recognizing the value of interpersonal relationships is advantageous to the girls—they are one step ahead of the rest.

Research shows that children between the ages of seven and twelve are naturally inclined to feel empathy for others, particularly those in pain.[26] But empathy has to be cultivated and reinforced. By the end of the program, the progression from compassion toward an animal to empathy for other people has been solidified.

Faith was a sixth grader who, on her Unleashed intake form, answered the question "Anything I should know about you as your coach?" with "I'm really, really shy and quiet." That proved to be an understatement: Faith was nervous, socially awkward, and had a history of significant speech impairments; if you asked her a question, she would shrink back, requiring a long time to respond.

As the sessions progressed, Faith slowly began to open up, bit by bit. She would sit next to me in our group, and every now and then I'd feel somebody touching my arm or hair in a gentle, unobtrusive way. I'd look over and there was Faith, rewarding me with this bashful little smile. From there, she grew more outspoken and began revealing glimpses into her personal life, such as that she sometimes thought her father hated her. During the second-to-last session of Unleashed, I asked the girls, "After animals, what cause is closest to your hearts?" Faith raised her hand: "Cancer." Her grandfather, with whom she had been especially close, had died of it. Another quiet girl in the group who also rarely spoke stood up, announced, "Faith, you need a hug," and walked across the circle to embrace her. Then, all the girls yelled, "Group hug!"—forming a huddle in the center of the room. Faith turned out to be the most honest, authentic person in the group; she taught the others that they didn't have to be scared to reveal intimate parts of themselves, that the reward outweighs the risk.

During our final meeting, I asked Faith what Unleashed had done for her. "I think it's given me more friends," she answered. So I stretched her: "You think? Or you know?" The other girls in the circle yelled out, "You know!" And Faith smiled and said, "I know."

If that's not empathy, what is?

Self-Management

Self-management in one's self and with others is a competency of emotional intelligence that is often overlooked or misunderstood. Regulating mood is a large part of self-mastery—one of the most significant outcomes of Unleashed. The ability to self-soothe, to implement effective coping strategies without becoming paralyzed when confronted with intense emotions such as fear, sadness, or anger, promotes adaptive functioning. Those who are resilient can weather emotional storms without being hijacked by them, and they are able to express and process their feelings appropriately. Regulation of emotions is an aptitude that enables individuals to incorporate emotions into their decision-making; it is an integration of heart and logic—the ability to use mood as a signal to process information and problem-solve. All people have their own emotional thermostats, a personal threshold for the intensity of their feelings serving as a filter guarding against becoming a "slave to passion."[27]

One of the hallmarks of Unleashed is the self-efficacy required to master the intense emotions inherent in animal rescue, taking accountability for one's feelings and actions, engaging others, and creating positive social change. Social activism not only requires the change-maker to sustain her own passion to overcome obstacles and defy the status quo, but she must also tap into the emotions of others, motivating them to take part in her cause. A healthy relationship with emotions is fostered as girls learn to accept whatever mood they are experiencing; refrain from suppressing or denying even the most negative ones; and constructively use them. As a result, their judgment improves, impulsivity decreases, and they can differentiate between the intensity levels of their feelings, avoiding exaggerated responses. They become aware that strong emotional reactions direct their attention to something meaningful, guiding and focusing their efforts to take a stand against (or for) a purpose they care deeply about. They can allow themselves to feel sad after learning a rescue puppy has gotten sick or died, mourning the loss, and then committing themselves to help prevent animals from being exposed to horrendous conditions; or to cry after selecting a dog in a pen-pal program, realizing that so many animals in the system may never have a family. Unleashed reinforces the norm that emotions are essential; it is no longer taboo to openly express them; any attempt to control moods will have the opposite effect, resulting in an inappropriate discharge of feelings or a void in critical information for finalizing a decision.

Using and Channeling Emotions

Ideally, our girls reach a point where they can use their social-emotional intelligence to create change—a fourth competency referred to as "utilizing emotions." Channeling moods to achieve a desired goal is one skill within this category. Girls enroll in Unleashed because they are enraged about the plight of our country's animals, particularly dogs. The intensity of their anger is reframed into passion, concern, and social responsibility, providing an opening for them to think broadly about the world at large. The Unleashed philosophy is that synergies exist between the animal and human rights movements. Animal welfare is an epic social problem with far-reaching implications, and most of our country has not yet recognized such. The issues faced by animals are symptomatic of those faced by humans in various communities across our nation: homelessness, aggression, illiteracy, limited resources, bigotry, and bias are among the issues highly correlated to animal abuse. The country's dysfunction trickles down, impacting pets; society's problems are not insular. Animals are dependent upon humans to survive; the communities that suffer the most, with high percentages of animal abuse, neglect, and euthanasia, are struggling with flawed educational systems, faulty local governance, and financial instability. Dogfighting is not exclusively a violent act against animals: its perpetrators are aggressive, their crime and unemployment rates high, and they pervasively abuse women and children.

One activity illustrates how Unleashed becomes an outlet for extreme emotions: a container encouraging physical release so girls can catapult into action using the energy of their feelings.

"I'm going to pass around slips of paper," I tell the girls midway through the program. "Take two pieces each and write down a few issues related to animal welfare that make you really angry. Don't write your name—just jot down the concern, then crumple it up like a snowball." When they're finished, I shout, "Ready, set . . . snowball fight!" The atmosphere quickly changes from quiet to frenzied as girls run around the room tossing their "snowballs," crumpled bits of paper hitting the walls, the ceiling, and sometimes even flying out the window. I want the girls to get riled up and then be able to channel that emotion into real change.

After the girls tire a bit, I ask them to push all the snowballs into a pile in the middle of the room, and I recruit a few volunteers to unravel them, read them out loud, and record them on a flip-chart. The volunteers open each snowball, calling out the issues that stirred up their Unleashed team members: "Puppy mills"; "Abuse"; "Starvation"; "Abandonment"; "Overpopulation"; "Lack of health care"; "Dogfight-

ing"; "Stereotyping"; "Sexual abuse." The list goes on and on, and as each problem is announced and recorded, it becomes increasingly apparent that the same dangers plaguing dogs are also hurting humans: people—usually women and children—are abused, neglected, and abandoned; our planet is overcrowded; countless numbers do not have proper health care; many have trouble regulating their anger and resort to violence; the majority of people fall victim to hurtful stereotypes.

"Okay, so if these things are happening to dogs, how does that translate to humans?" I pose. Michaela raises her hand: "Sometimes a dog will get sick with cancer. Maybe their owners can't afford health care, just like some people can't." Miranda offers, "I once saw a crazy person on the news who killed somebody, just like crazy people kill dogs." Claudia bravely reveals, "I knew someone once whose stepdad didn't like her and hit her, just like some people abuse their dog."

Ask any Unleashed alumna to name her favorite exercise of the program, and 99 percent will say, "Snowball." Overtly, the game is fun, but beneath the surface, the ability to release emotions, express anger and frustration (two feelings girls and women are socialized to suppress), and then leverage those feelings to create positive change are what matter most. Identifying issues the girls feel most compelled to change leads into the final phase of the program: the Unleashed social-change model (discussed in greater detail in chapter 8), utilizing emotions to enhance critical thinking, get to the root of the issue, and develop viable solutions to make a sustainable difference.

At Unleashed graduation, girls participate as a panel of experts moderated by a coach before an audience of teachers, school staff, Unleashed board members, parents, and peers. During one graduation, a teacher raised her hand and challenged the girls: "Why puppies? Why not cats?" Without even batting an eyelash, the girls started firing back

intelligent replies. Tamika explained, "Puppies are the immediate prob-
lem, but in the long term, it's humanity in general." Allie offered, "In
areas where dogs are treated badly, illiteracy is common and women
are often treated badly, too." Lauren pointed out, "Look at everything
dogs do for us—companionship, loyalty, service dogs, therapy dogs." My
personal favorite? When Alisha quipped, "Why dogs? Because there's
no such thing as kitten mills." It was reminiscent of a civil rights protest
or a feminist rally; the passion and emotional outcries that often ac-
company social activism pervaded the room.

The social-justice element embodied by Unleashed bridges theory into reality for each participant. Passion, outrage, frustration,
fear, hope, humor, and empathy are experienced by a social change-
maker throughout her journey to take a stand against an injustice
she is passionate about. Emotions shape an activist's attachment to
a cause; without these feelings, there is no fuel to protest, manage
resistance, and hold fast to values and ideals that may be perceived as
irrational or illogical. Indignation, despair, anxiety, and fear motivate
an advocate to act. But fighting to defy norms and undo archaic policies does not happen without disappointment, setbacks, and intense
emotional reactions from those with opposing views. Unleashed
girls experience activism while being supported; they are navigated
to address and acknowledge emotions, using their feelings to fight
collectively for something they believe in.

Emerging scientific research, neurobiology, progressive education, and psychologists all strongly adhere to the belief that emotional and social intelligence is imperative to the development and
achievement of our younger generation. The world is changing
dramatically; no longer is it enough to receive a perfect test score.
Cultural institutions that once provided the scaffolding to support

children are weakening at a time when they are needed more than ever. Budget cuts, unemployment, and the national deficit are diminishing available community resources; technology and a fast-paced environment are altering the landscape; currently life is much more complex for people of all ages; the world that was once dependent on logical, rational systems is faced with a need for individuals to think out of the box, tap into creativity, and infuse the "softer" skills into all contexts (business, politics, education, and personal relationships).

The time is ripe to reevaluate the value of empathy, respect for others, self-awareness, and regulation of affect. Society is a human system; people are unpredictable and more complicated than machinery, and the vast number of interpersonal exchanges that take place in one day provides ample opportunities for derailment. At the core of every interaction lies emotion; to ignore this is detrimental. Unfortunately, a tremendous void has been carved out by our traditional, IQ-based education. Cultivating self-awareness and insight, recognizing a broad spectrum of feelings, and providing tools to reinforce integration, expression, and use of them at an early age will equip girls with an advantage to successfully navigate their world. When EQ is fostered, empathy skyrockets, passion surges, and compassion spreads. It is unlike any education children receive in school, but necessary to prepare our next generation to manage the uncertainties and challenges of life.

Power Boost

1. Pay close attention to your perceptions of the young girls
   you encounter in your life. What adjectives come to mind
   when you observe a girl's behavior or her response to you?
   Are these adjectives conveyed to her either directly or indirectly? For example, do you refer to her as "feisty," "difficult," "shy," or "reserved" in her presence, in conversations with others, or even alone in your conversations with
   her? Rather than generalize her behavior, labeling it as a
   character trait, think of how you may reframe an observation so it has a positive effect on her. When you notice she
   is being a little oppositional, think of how this skill can be
   channeled to defy the status quo, advocate for herself, and
   dig deeper to find the answers she might be looking for in
   her quest for knowledge. Girls are highly sensitive to the
   messages they receive from the influential people in their
   lives; during adolescence they look for validation and will
   identify with those labels they repeatedly hear.

2. Encourage girls to express their anger, viewing it as a normal, healthy feeling versus a forbidden one. Adults send
   so many messages to girls this age to squelch their anger,
   move past it, or ignore it because it isn't helpful or "nice."
   On the contrary, girls need so desperately to vent both
   positive and negative emotions. When you notice an angry response or frustration, identify it as such and ask
   them to tell you what happened; e.g., "You seem frustrated, what's going on?" If they refuse to talk about it, let

them be. Simply labeling an emotion without judging it can be powerful. If a girl seems open to discussion, listen without interjecting advice. At this age, venting and having a safe space to express themselves is extremely important for girls.

3. Increasing self-awareness and empathy, guiding girls to put themselves in another person's shoes, can help them resolve conflicts effectively, strengthen interpersonal relationships, and promote healthy decision-making. Whether she is arguing with her best friend or sibling, or upset that a group of girls did not invite her to join in their social plans, ask her to think about what the situation may look like from the other person's perspective. In the case of an argument you might say, "Why do you think Jane got angry?" She may resist and say, "You don't care about me . . . you only care about Jane . . . I am the one who got hurt." Be sure to validate how upsetting a disagreement is for both parties, especially when between close friends. But gently stretch her to think about what Jane may have experienced and what circumstances led to the argument. If the conversation between the two of you grows tense, stick with a simple, "If I were Jane, I might feel disappointed and hurt because . . ."

Chapter 4

Power

The first time I use the word power *and ask who feels powerful,
I am always met with blank stares and total silence. Remember,
the girls easily throw out names of powerful women whom they admire, but they seem unable to apply the word to themselves. In fact, this
is most likely the first time they have even been asked this question. So
I wait, giving them time to reflect. Inevitably, the girls remain unable to
answer, so I switch gears. "Why is this question so hard to answer?" I
ask. "Why do girls as well as the grown-up women I work with struggle
so much when I say the P-word?"*

*That question unlocks Pandora's box and breaks the silence. "People
don't like powerful women," I hear. "People think powerful girls are
mean and bossy."*

*Cut to the graduation ceremony twelve weeks later. The microphone
slowly winds its way down the row of girls sitting on the panel as they
introduce themselves and share their experiences and challenges. Interestingly, the girls are not focusing on the puppies—the spotlight remains
on their journeys, individually and collectively. Through their stories*

and recollections, the girls reveal their power to make a difference; their ability to work collaboratively; the confidence they have developed to take risks, to provide feedback and support to others, and to stand up to injustices they are passionate about. They share triumphs, challenges, funny things that happened along the way, and the transformation they themselves have witnessed. It is magical to watch. One father told me that on the way home after graduation, he asked his eleven-year-old daughter if she had been nervous. "No, not at all," she told him. "When I had that microphone in my hand, I felt like I held such power." That same girl continues to speak at Unleashed events, writes for our newsletter, and is applying to sit on our junior advisory board. Her parents say she's caught "the bug." I couldn't agree more.

Simply mention the word *power* and women cringe. It is the elephant in the room. No matter how far we think we have come as a society, *power* remains a dirty word for the female half of society, provoking intense emotions and responses ranging from denial and avoidance to discomfort and even fear. Some women shun the word *power* because it does not resonate with them. Many still cling to a masculine perception of the concept, conjuring up images of physical force and aggression; others minimize its importance, pretending it doesn't exist and is not worthy of discussion, or they simply cannot fathom being considered powerful.

But power comes in many packages, and it starts out as a teeny, tiny grain hidden deep within a young girl's soul. That girl has the ability to make an impact and foster changes in our world, large or small, regardless of how old she is or what she looks like. We can set our girls up for an influential future by encouraging them to tap into their power at a young age.

The premise of Unleashed—social justice via animal rights—acts as a catalyst for broader issues such as female empowerment, self-esteem, leadership, and social change. Of course, the girls do not attend meetings and rescues thinking, "Today I'm going to learn what it means to feel powerful" or "Today I'm going to figure out how to work well with other women in a group"; rather, the discussions and activities as they pertain to animal welfare and its impact on our society, and the leadership roles they adopt as a result, are designed to subconsciously rev their mental engines in those specific directions.

As a fifth grader, Marina was among the youngest on her Unleashed team. In the very beginning, it is usually challenging to rein in our fifth graders—they tend to be more prone to giggling and off-topic conversations and are more easily distracted than the older girls. But Marina was adventurous, with a take-charge attitude. She had innovative ideas but was careful not to be perceived as bossy; she would say such things as "I want to make sure everyone else has time with the puppies" at a rescue before she herself interacted with them or made a conscious effort to acknowledge someone else's efforts rather than focus on what she contributed. It was easy to forget she was only ten years old! But despite her maturity, I wondered if she assumed this role because she thought it was expected. I hoped that Unleashed would provide her with the permission to accept the value she added to the group and encourage her to take the spotlight, that it wasn't "selfish" to do so.

One afternoon, about four weeks into Unleashed, I opened an unexpected e-mail: "I just met your girls down on 69th and 3rd at their bake sale and I'm interested in adopting a puppy," the man wrote. "What are the next steps?" I was surprised and confused—this was the first I had heard of a bake sale. Unbeknownst to me, Marina had rounded up her teammates and organized a fund-raiser, downloading puppy pictures to design posters, delegating baking, and making the clever decision to let buyers determine the prices they were willing to pay, figuring most adults would gladly pay more than $1 or $2 for a brownie if they knew *it was going to a worthwhile cause. Their efforts raised $260, plus they handed out numerous brochures spreading the word about animal rights and rescue.*

Based on the bake sale's location, I figured out which team was responsible and sent out a group e-mail; Marina replied back saying yes, it had been her idea. At our next team meeting, she spoke about how she thought hosting an event outside of school to educate adults would be more worthwhile than a student fund-raiser because they could then reach a larger audience and bring in more money for the dogs. Not only had she taken charge of a project and led without fear, she now felt comfortable owning her accomplishment and allowing others to compliment her on her initiative. Through Unleashed, Marina tapped into her innate strength, even at her young age. Her evolution as she united her teammates, kept them on track, and executed that Third Avenue bake sale demonstrates an impressive maturation of power. In recognition, I named a spaniel-mix puppy after her—an honor the girls work hard to receive.

Power is such a loaded concept that even my adult clients, colleagues, and friends have trouble owning it. At a recent Unleashed marketing-committee meeting, three high-level brand strategists and advertising executives gathered at my dining-room table to develop position statements intended to communicate our message and increase awareness about the organization. Again and again, they resisted using the word *power*, despite the fact that our mission is defined as "'unleashing' the power and potential in girls." The committee kept trying to substitute the words *influence* or *empower*. When I pointed this out, each of them spoke candidly about her reticence, echoing what I had witnessed in the interviews I conducted years ago discussing power or the current conversations I have with clients: Ask women about their power and I am met with silence and *um*s; substitute the word *influence* and they can speak for forty-five minutes about the impact they have created.

If a group of high-achieving women who advise a social-justice program designed to unleash the power in our younger generation find themselves stuck owning the word *power*, how can we expect anything more from our girls? That is why I integrate *power* into Unleashed's vocabulary, asking them, "What does a powerful girl look like?" and labeling certain behaviors or sentiments I observe as powerful. This helps desensitize them to the actual word, much like gradually exposing a patient with a fear of flying to photos of an aircraft, then the entrance to an airport, and then the inside of a grounded plane slowly helps them overcome their phobia. At the same time, this increases their awareness of what powerful behavior and thinking is, based on their experience and own definition.

A common refrain I hear from my girls: "Adults tell us we can do anything we want, but they don't give us the chance." Their generation is dedicated to service, but finds itself held back by reined-in opportunities. They feel judged by their parents, their peers, and society. "Nobody thinks we can actually do something meaningful," they rightfully protest. For instance, they might want to help feed the homeless, but shelters invite them only to prepare sandwiches; they are not allowed to actually come on-site and work with those they are servicing; their school will select community-service projects without asking for the students' input; the local humane society will allow girls this age to organize a food drive, but will not permit participation in higher-level responsibilities of which they are capable. For many of them, Unleashed is the first time they do not just hear the words *you can do anything* but are actually given permission to do so and the opportunity to drive the process. This environment, unlike most others, applauds determination, ambition, and autonomy.

The result? Whereas my early-on "Who feels powerful?" query is met with lowered eyelids or shifting bodies and maybe a single brave hand venturing into the air, by the twelfth week they understand exactly what it means and are proud to label their own and one another's actions as such. As the girls receive their diplomas at graduation, they symbolically grab hold of their power.

Regardless of their ability to accept or embrace it, women *do* possess a huge amount of power. Research abounds showing they hold tremendous sway over the economy, health care, and corporate America. Consider that women . . .

. . . control 83 percent of consumer purchasing, are responsible for 53 percent of stock market investments, 62 percent of new-car purchases, and 55 percent of all consumer-electronics purchases.[1]

. . . make 70–90 percent of household health-care decisions[2] and spend two of every three health-care dollars—approximately $500 billion annually.[3]

. . . boost company innovation, accountability, and profit: Fortune 500 companies with three or more women on their board show a 73 percent return on sales, an 83 percent return on equity, and a 112 percent return on invested capital.[4]

. . . when they sit on their company's board improve the company's ESG (Environmental, Social, and corporate Governance) performances—a measure of corporate sustainability that is recognized by the investment community as an indicator of risk management, opportunity recognition, and strong leadership.[5]

. . . open 89 percent of bank accounts.[6]

. . . account for 58 percent of all total online spending.[7]

. . . are opening their own businesses at twice the rate of men; one out of every eleven American women now owns her own business.[8]

. . . are starting to outearn their husbands: two in ten married women currently do,[9] and over a family's life, 90 percent of women will at one point control its wealth.[10]

"We've come a long way, baby!"—right? Not so fast. Power is a social issue, and while our society pats itself on the back for providing girls and women with countless opportunities to propel themselves forward, it is still stuck in the 1950s in terms of real sustainable change:

—Only eighteen women are currently running Fortune 500 companies—and of those who do, they make sixty-nine cents for every dollar a male CEO makes.[11]

—Less than 17 percent of our key decision-makers in Congress are women.[12]

—One in ten Fortune 500 companies does not have a single woman on its board, despite that studies show that companies with significant numbers of top female managers perform significantly better.[13] In one study of fifteen hundred companies, only three—Kimberly-Clark, General Motors, and Walmart—had at least three female board members.[14]

—Women are on track to make up no more than 6 percent of chief executive officers in 2016, based on statistics and the growth pattern of the last twenty-five years.[15]

—During a 2012 town hall event, Republican presidential candidate Mitt Romney infamously referenced the "binders full of women" he had considered as Massachusetts governor when searching for appointees—a comment that quickly went viral. Yet, the percentage of senior-level appointed positions held by women actually dropped during his administration; at his private alternative-asset management firm, Bain Capital, only seven women could be counted among eighty-seven managing directors and senior executives.[16]

—When budgets are slashed, women feel it first, in the form of cuts to high school athletics, women's initiatives within companies, and government spending on programs that largely impact women and children, such as child care, welfare, and health care.

These statistics are pathetic. Women are seen but not heard. President Barack Obama summed it up nicely when he observed, "Women are not a special interest group."[17] As Lifeway CEO Julie Smolyansky—who in 2002 became the youngest female CEO of a publicly traded company—has put it, "If we don't have a seat at the table, we risk losing our power."

> Our deepest fear is not that we are inadequate. Our deepest fear is that we are powerful beyond measure. It is our light, not our darkness, that frightens us most.
>
> —Marianne Williamson, spiritual activist, author,
>   and founder of the Peace Alliance

Men and women perceive power much differently. Women interpret it in terms of command and control—stereotypically male characteristics—and thus avoid labeling their behavior as such. That said, they are attached to the notion of impacting and influencing others with no regard for personal gain and will readily accept power when viewed in this context. (It's no coincidence that from Rosie the Riveter to Rosa Parks to Eleanor Roosevelt, women have been pioneers for social justice and reform.) That is why my marketing committee toiled with the word, attempting to substitute *influence* or *empower*. Those words are more palatable because they imply the user is spreading the wealth, rather than appearing greedy by reserving it in her bank account. One of the most significant findings of my research on powerful women was that women assert their power more and most effectively when attached to a cause; they take action to create impact for others. It could be advocating for her team at work or pushing for a school ordinance to be passed because it will favorably impact her children's education. That is why international organizations committed to developing third-world nations often target women to create societal changes—to tap into their allegiance and commitment to family and community.

This aspect of power forms the foundation of Unleashed. When creating the program, I hypothesized that this tendency to tap into power when passionate about a cause or an injustice would be as prevalent among girls as it was among the women I interviewed. An often-overlooked continuum exists between girls and women; female identity is fluid—it doesn't start at girlhood and end at adulthood—and growth and development occur over a lifetime. I thought adolescence—such a critical period, when identity development is at its peak—would be the optimal time to focus on developing a girl's power. My objective was to use social justice as a springboard to engage the girls. Encountering the injustice of animal mistreatment and learning how to create change would ignite the girls to experiment with power and thoughtfully reflect on being a strong female. For most females, discovering power comes much later in life, if at all. Knowing that social activism requires strength, determination, passion, and action, middle school seemed like the ideal opportunity to introduce the importance of power and pave the way for girls to see what they could do with it.

Nancy Tartaglino Richards is chairman of First Preston, one of the largest residential-asset firms in the United States. A well-recognized real estate entrepreneur, she also founded the HomeTelos technology company, which generates 12 million hits per month. During our interview, Nancy recalled meeting with a bank executive in an attempt to apply for a large government contract and generate financing to grow her business. She had been a valuable client of this bank for years and had made strides to prove her competence . . . yet the bank's chief officer resisted even granting her an appointment. When he finally did, he greeted her and her partner by kicking his feet up onto his desk and smoking a cigar while they spoke. He challenged their business model, giving them unsolicited "advice" on their current contracts; at one point, he actually said, "Hell, I don't even understand what you girls do."

Nancy's colleague, normally the more reserved of the two, actually got up out of her chair and started to lean across the desk, getting in the CEO's face. But Nancy calmed her down and coolly replied, "Listen to me. We are going to win those contracts, and we will have twelve million dollars to put through to another bank." They wound up receiving their financing from out of state, securing a $12 million government contract that provided a huge surge in growth for the business, then moved all their money to a bank run by a woman. "I'm fine with rules unless they don't work for me," she told me. "I am constantly asking, 'Why do we do things this way?' I think outside of the box—I know there is always a better way to do things."

After more than a decade of consulting with women, guiding companies in developing their female leadership workforce, and helping them grasp the importance of a diverse environment, it still baffles me that women continue to be underrepresented in executive leadership positions, are not granted partnership opportunities in law firms, and are paid lower salaries, even in predominantly female fields such as teaching and social work. It does not make sense: Today's woman is flooded with equal opportunities, isn't she? Companies provide mentoring programs; women's sports are championed by Title IX; legislation prohibits sexual harassment. In many ways, women have broken the glass ceiling and paved a new, theoretically powerful way for themselves. So what is thwarting them from gaining an edge in powerful positions?

Put simply, *power* is a dirty word. As a society, we are still wedded to archaic stereotypes, be they subconscious or overt. Our culture has historically feared powerful women and is still reluctant to embrace this concept. In many ways our culture demands gender equality and promotes respect for women's power, yet it acts in ways to subvert them. From the moment the ultrasound technician proclaims, "It's a girl," that baby will be treated far differently from a little boy. She will be showered with dolls, clothed in pink, and spoken to in tones that are softer than those her brother may have heard. As a toddler—or even as an adult—if she acts in a way that is somehow perceived as more masculine (excelling at athletics or holding fast to a decision during a classroom discussion), she is seen as aggressive or labeled a tomboy. In high school, she is encouraged to try out for softball or volleyball, yet the girls' teams are the first to be cut when budget troubles loom. In college, she is advised to take charge of her sexuality and reproductive health, but then labeled a "slut" by Rush Limbaugh for testifying before Congress in support of birth control. She is lauded for juggling work and family, then silently judged for leaving her kids with the nanny; or praised for being a stay-at-home mom, but derided behind her back for deserting her career.

Whether we admit it or not, we are still extremely tied to gender stereotypes that subvert women's power. Many decisions come with a compromise and a dilemma: females are continually faced with situations where they feel there is no real win. The women's movement is still relatively fresh; for thousands of years, powerful women were scorned at best, murdered at worst. Susan B. Anthony was fined $100 for trying to vote; Joan of Arc was burned at the stake; Indira Gandhi was assassinated. True, women such as Abigail Adams, Doro-

thea Dix, Lucretia Mott, and Harriet Tubman have been celebrated
for their influence, but men have the spotlight in our history books,
largely credited with everything from fostering an independent nation to advancing medicine and solving the world's crises. Women
have historically been dissuaded from academics or purged of political power—men were afraid of their becoming educated because
educated women want to create change and we as a culture fear the
unknown. In 1967, Kathrine Switzer dared to challenge the Boston
Marathon's all-male tradition by entering and running, only to have
a male race official physically charge her in an effort to remove her
from the race. Women's rights icon Gloria Feldt was unable to get
a car loan without her then husband's cosigning in 1974, just after
she had assumed the role of CEO of Planned Parenthood,[18] and not
until 2012 was the first woman admitted as a member at Augusta
National Golf Club. Female powerhouses such as Oprah Winfrey,
Gloria Steinem, Hillary Rodham Clinton, and Condoleezza Rice,
along with pop culture superstars such as Madonna and Lady Gaga,
are constantly scrutinized for acting like men when, in fact, they are
simply individuals asserting their power.

Overtly, many strides and advances have been made: the Equal Pay
Act, sexual harassment legislation, *Roe v. Wade* . . . yet gender stereotypes continue to thrive "underground." As Katie Orenstein, founder
of the OpEd Project, whose mission is to boost the number of female
thought leaders in key public debates, has put it, "It's not enough to
have the right to choose; women must choose power."[19] Unless the
lens is shifted and the root cause is identified and addressed, scenarios like what happened at my recent marketing-committee meeting will continue to repeat themselves. It is important to reflect on
and recognize all of the advances in gender equality, but at the same
time we must realize that the revolution is far from over. By examin-

ing our own biases and behavior, by posing the questions "*Why* are powerful women feared? *Why* is *power* still such a dirty word?" we can begin a real dialogue about the issues at hand.

Today's girls are the next generation of women who will be grappling with these same dilemmas if things remain the same. Already, they are craving a forum to discuss gender bias and stereotypes and unable to find one; they are being exposed to male-centric textbooks and school curricula that leave out women's influence in history; being raised in a culture where their reproductive freedom is under threat; and wondering if a woman will ever be elected president in the next few decades.

And we *all* need to ask ourselves these questions—men and women alike. The advancement of women and girls is not just a women's issue; it is a societal one. Much as the Holocaust was not just a Jewish issue, and civil rights was not just an African-American issue, animal welfare is indicative of so much more than the treatment of animals. The issues that, on the outside, appear to affect just one subgroup of beings are symptomatic of a larger malaise. Right now, we need to challenge the implicit gender beliefs and norms that continue to exist, moving away from the assumption that the male POV is the norm, and that powerful women are some sort of aberration.[20]

The United States is a nation built by "our founding forefathers," but blame for the disparity of power does not rest solely on this patriarchal structure. Deeply embedded in our unconsciousness, women and girls, as well as men and boys, adhere to gender stereotypes, acting out roles that have been established as the norm and not fully leveraging or recognizing their own power. Think about Mindy, the global investment banking SVP who successfully reorganized her Finance and Technology Division, but was unable to name a single strength while preparing for her performance review; or Faith, the shy sixth grader who told the group, "I *think* Unleashed has given me more friends," before being encouraged to use the more powerful statement "I *know* Unleashed has given me more friends." Not all women are ready to champion this issue—some are fearful, some do not think the concern still exists (I've even heard younger women say about their older counterparts, "I understand they had to fight to make changes for us, but we do not have to fight anymore; things are different now"), and others fear being stigmatized as the Norma Raes of their environment, be it personally or professionally. If women remain wedded to cultural norms that dictate their choices and behavior and do not question the unspoken rules, sustainable change remains unthinkable.

To say that women are vital to any society's development is an understatement. From the work of the international poverty-fighting organization CARE, which partners with women to increase access to health care and expand economic opportunity, to the United Nations, with a mission to improve women's global standards of living, female education and empowerment are the building blocks for lasting community change.

Power is a critical component of the leadership equation. What was astounding to me was how many of the professional women I encountered were struggling with it—it was the proverbial elephant in the room. In an effort to work more effectively as a consultant, I pored through leadership books and articles written for and about women and was shocked to find barely any discussion of the subject. Power's absence from the literature was conspicuous and alarming; I realized that I would need to talk to powerful women to figure out the answers myself.

Based on two years of research, interviewing hundreds of women in powerful positions, I developed a three-dimensional model of power. This integrative model examines three aspects of power both in isolation and in relation to one another: personal power, which is defined as self-awareness, incorporating values into work, and personal life; relational power, which encompasses communication style and skills and talent for collaborating, engaging, and influencing; and assertive power—the take-action component. This power triumvirate is a system working in tandem to help women maximize their strengths and reach their potential. Picture a Venn diagram with three overlapping circles: the sweet spot lies in the region shared by all three. That zone represents each individual woman's true power. The consequences of an unbalanced sense of personal power are vast and reflect the struggle women frequently describe when they feel caught in a "no-win situation" or judged as "damned if you do and damned if you don't": one minute she is being told she is not assertive enough, and the next minute she is chastised for not being a team player or for acting like a bull in a china shop. Without the synthesis of all three, she will overcompensate, relying on one dimension more than others, compromising her full promise. A woman whose strength lies in her assertive power but lags in relational and personal power will experience trouble earning buy-in for her ideas at work or may even be branded as oppositional and difficult to work with. Similarly, a woman with remarkable relational power but with limited assertive power may be seen as "too nice" and risks not being taken seriously as a leader; when a possible promotion surfaces, she may be overlooked because management does not view her as capable of making bottom-line business decisions.

Although each woman's power style is as unique as her finger-prints, she needs elements of all three to experience, act, and effec-tively manage her power. An unequal distribution among the three types of power creates instability, causing a woman to wield her power ineffectively.

Personal power refers to the insights, behavior, and self-knowledge stemming from each individual girl or woman. A woman with a strong sense of personal power is self-confident enough to accurately identify her strengths as well as her blind spots, which she is continu-ally working to improve. She behaves in alignment with her values and beliefs and has a vision mapped out. These women take account-ability for their actions, are resilient, and can overcome adversity and challenges. They are also clear about who they are and what they contribute, recognizing the influence they have (or might not have) in various situations. In an adolescent, personal power translates into making a mistake and learning from it, or promising to do her homework—but not finishing—and then taking responsibility for it rather than making up an excuse. At Unleashed, she might acknowl-edge that she is better at writing than math and then take on the responsibility of creating a flyer rather than balancing the budget for a project. As a woman, she is cognizant of the value she adds to an organization and ensures that she receives recognition for her contri-butions, or she is willing to make a career change when she no longer feels passionate about her work.

In the beginning of Unleashed, I ask the girls, "What are your strengths?" Their responses provide me with insight about one piece of their personal power. Someone who can articulate her strong suits, even if a little encouragement is needed, and say "I am smart" or "I am outgoing" or "I am good at basketball" shows me she is con-fident enough to publicly share her abilities. The girl who struggles to name a single strength will need support to master this critical task. When I partner with a client to fortify her leadership skills, the underlying objective is often to amplify personal power, enabling her to leverage her assets, articulate goals based on her identified blind spots, and help her trust her instincts and judgment.

Relational power is measured by the capacity to engage and connect with others, encompassing the social and emotional skills that are critical to form and sustain healthy relationships across many contexts. Communication style, collaboration, negotiation, conflict resolution, and empathy all come into play. Women with relational power are proficient at building and leveraging social capital—they operate within multiple diverse networks and know how to tap into them to access resources (information, services, funding opportunities, to name a few) and influence others to achieve their goals. A strong sense of personal and professional community is a hallmark of the relationally powerful woman. An example of a middle schooler demonstrating relational power is a student offering support to a peer when she is struggling with an experiment in science class, or one Unleashed girl's sensing another's apprehension about traveling to a puppy rescue alone and offering to accompany her. A principal who is committed to developing her teachers' individual talents, a manager who sets clear expectations and guides others to meet them, or a friend who candidly shares how someone else's behavior has hurt her is in command of her relational power.

Assertive power encompasses creating impact and making a difference. Women who have cultivated their assertive power embrace and leverage their uniqueness and are at ease perceiving themselves as nonconformists—not because they are rebellious, but because they are innovative: defying norms, circumventing traditional approaches, and recognizing they do not fit into any one box. These women take calculated risks, experiment, and are not afraid to fail; rather, they perceive failures as learning lessons and necessary precursors to personal growth. Resiliency—the strength to bounce back and recover from adversity—provides them with the courage to tackle additional risks and understand that vulnerability is useful for moving forward. Remember when Gabriela inadvertently raised funds for the corrupt shelter? She processed what had happened, recognized and took accountability for her mistake, and amended the situation to right the wrong. That is the epitome of assertive power.

Two additional aspects of assertive power—advocacy and the ability to create impact—are embedded in the Unleashed program. Clearly, this is where the animal-welfare component of Unleashed plays out. We are teaching girls to assert their power by educating themselves about a cause they believe in, then using that knowledge to advocate and take action. Then they learn how to deal with pushback, fighting for an issue they are passionate about.

A team had designed a petition asking PetSmart to stop selling prong dog collars—collars lined with metal spikes that dig into the skin to help control movement. Men usually use them as a display of machismo, and fight promoters use them to induce pain and "toughen up" their animals. The girls had designed a dog wash, complete with raffles and a doggy-treat bake sale, to launch their petition, setting up shop on the sidewalk outside New York Dog Spa, Unleashed's home away from home. (The boarding and grooming center donates their space for rescues and events like Leads Day.)

A man and his friend who were angered by the petition confronted the team. He claimed that sometimes these spiked collars are necessary. They responded by presenting the research they'd conducted and maintained their stance that the collars are cruel and harmful. If he didn't agree, they said, he didn't have to sign the petition. The man approached me to complain: "How can you allow these girls to work for you on the street?" he wanted to know. I explained the premise of Unleashed and how the students had selected an issue they cared about, researched it, taken a position, and designed the petition—it wasn't my issue; it was theirs. He left but returned within thirty minutes to continue arguing—a situation that would intimidate many grown women. Yet the girls stood there, united and confident, repeating their reasoning and standing their ground.

In the Unleashed session following this incident, we discussed the ramifications of standing up for what you believe in, despite others' thoughts and behaviors. The girls never questioned their right to petition but were struck by how others might become angry in response. Their trust in me heightened as they saw how I managed myself in such a difficult situation, advocating for their right to have a position in our world. One of Unleashed's most powerful aspects is that it helps girls learn by experiencing situations in the moment, followed up by the opportunity to debrief, which consequently deepens their insights.

My goal is that, by the time she graduates, every Unleashed participant will have begun the journey of establishing an integrated identity as a powerful girl. No one style is valued over another; the objective is to fuse personal, relational, and assertive power in a way that feels right for each individual girl. Just as every child reaches growth milestones such as crawling, walking, and speech on her own timeline, a young girl gradually acquires her proficiency within each type of power at her own speed. From Check Ins and weekend rescues, to developing community awareness and leadership development, to understanding the impact they can have on their world, each component of the program was thoughtfully designed to strengthen girls' power at an early age.

Power has historically been—and still remains—taboo for both men and women. It is amorphous, the elephant in the room, forever being overestimated, denied, rejected, or ignored. But every leader, from the head of a household to a company CEO to the president of the United States, is required to exercise power in a way that is critical to themselves and those they lead. As a culture, though, we remain stuck, moving forward at a snail's pace when it comes to gender and power when compared with the progress made in science, medicine, technology, and education. Unfortunately, no simple answer exists; gender is a complex issue deeply embedded in our culture, how we have been raised and continue to raise our children, our individual experiences, *and* our biological constitution. Change will require collaboration, strategy, innovation, digging beneath the surface, evaluation, and reevaluation. Unleashed was designed to provide girls with unconventional wisdom and experiences based on my hypotheses of power . . . and it *is* working. The girls' transformation and development validates these hypotheses and provides a lens for others, regardless of age, to shift their thinking and assess their own potential for power.

Power Boost

(Ideally, these will be done in sequential order.)

1. Ask yourself how often you use the word *power* and in what context. How would you define it? What words do you typically use as substitutes (e.g., some use the word *influence* rather than *power*) and what might get in the way of using *power* instead? Try an exercise originally developed for Unleashed: Name two or three powerful women who have inspired you in your lifetime. What impact have they had on you and in their world? What characteristics and attributes would you use to describe them?

2. Look for women and girls who are headlined in the news due to their ability to use their power effectively. Present an article or video clip to the middle school girls in your life and engage them in a conversation about power. Explore the actions the girl or woman took, the challenges she must have faced, and the outcomes of her behavior. Ask the girls to think about the most inspiring aspects of the story and what they might have done in a similar situation.

3. Partnering with a teenage girl, encourage her to design a project, providing an opportunity to develop her assertive power (the take-action/innovation component). Start with the questions "What would you like to change in the community?" and "What are you passionate about?" Use her

responses to dig deeper, coaching her to think big (she can always make her plan more realistic). Take note of what excites her when she is speaking about her ideas; what pieces of her project spark the most interest for her and why? Guide her to create an action plan: (1) identifying the information and resources she will need; (2) creating a timeline; (3) listing challenges and possible setbacks (including how she will manage them); (4) establishing a specific and achievable first step. Set up brainstorming sessions with her so she can keep you posted on her progress, ask questions, and receive support. Make sure to refrain from stepping in and doing her project for her or instructing her on what to do or how to do things. You are the navigating system of the car and she is the driver.

Chapter 5

Leveraging Gender Differences

O ne classic Unleashed exercise begins with me asking the girls, "How is life different for boys and girls?" Regardless of the group, whenever I pose this question, hands immediately shoot up. "I spent the entire last weekend with a boy, and all he did was talk about how good he was at everything," Talia says. "No doubt," Gabriela agrees. "My cousin has no shame in telling me what to do and how awesome he is." The girls laugh at this, but it leads into a thoughtful discussion on how girls—and women—often feel the need to minimize their strengths or not call attention to them for fear that others might refute them or demand evidence, almost as if they were in court, standing trial against a judge and jury to prove their validity.

Getting back to the original question, Imani suggests, "If Unleashed was at an all-boys' school, there would be zero people on the team; boys would say they want to rescue puppies, but once they realize how hard it is, that you have to give up your free time, that it's more than just an after-school activity, they would get bored and lose interest." During one session, a girl named Bella shared that she played on a boys' soccer

team, and while her male teammates were accepting of her, the parents
all seemed enraged, as if having a girl on the team would doom them to
a losing season. Bella ultimately proved herself as one of the team's top
players, and the parents did eventually begin to treat her with respect.
"Can you believe I had to prove myself just because I'm a girl?" she
asked the group, her eyes wide with genuine disbelief.

From the moment of conception until their final breath, women
and men enjoy vastly different life experiences. Brain chemistry, hormonal fluctuations, emotions, communication styles, sociocultural
expectations, and more intersect to guide an individual's path and
shape his or her point of view and experience. By helping girls tap
into their innate abilities—the drive to engage in relationships, to be
empathic, and to collaborate, to name just a few—Unleashed facili-
tates an awakening as girls become aware of their value and skills,
start crystallizing their gender identity, and learn how to leverage
their DNA.

To gain an appreciation for a woman's inherent strengths, or to
really understand what it means to experience this world as a female,
one needs to grasp how her mind works on a biological level. It is
appalling to think that until as recently as the 1990s, researchers
had all but ignored the neuroanatomical differences between genders. In the twentieth century, scientists believed women were just
a smaller version of men—biologically, neurologically, and psychologically. In fact, women were typically excluded from most research
trials because their menstrual cycles would confound data. It was
just assumed that females and males were primarily similar except
for reproduction. And more than 99 percent of biological coding *is*
the same. Just one out of thirty thousand genes in the human body
differs—less than 1 percent. But that 1 percent carries momentous
potential, impacting every cell of a woman's body.

Today, we know that women's brains are distinct and influence everything from their relationships and connection to others to their styles of thinking, emotional development, and how they process information. In the nineteenth century people assumed that men were smarter because their brains are larger. In actuality, women's brains contain the same number of cells; they are just more densely packed.[1] Women's brains house ten times more white matter overall than men's[2]; these nerve fibers form connections between multiple processing centers, facilitating multitasking and a systemic way of thinking. Eleven percent more neurons in the language and hearing centers[3] means the "women are great listeners" stereotype is actually on target. (They also possess excellent vocabularies: women use about twenty thousand words in total per day while men stick with seven thousand or so.[4]) A flair for expressing feelings and an impressive ability to recall information are largely due to a more sizable hippocampus, the hub within the brain responsible for memory and emotion.

Neurologically speaking, women are not as static as men; women's hormonal fluctuations, beginning as early as three months of age and lasting through menopause, create peaks and valleys over the course of a month (and a lifetime). As these hormones flood the brain, they drive girls toward one another, promoting intense bonding; studies have shown that when girls and women connect, pleasurable hormones such as dopamine and oxytocin rush in, as in a runner's high, activating pleasure centers in the brain. The adolescent torrent of estrogen leads to a higher level of sensitivity to emotional nuances; high school girls are also already noticing that they are more sensitive to and impacted by negative feedback or experiences with failure than boys are, which may hamper their willingness to take risks.[5]

Chapter 6 will highlight the differences between the genders on how and when they use their voice, but in nonverbal communication, women carry tremendous advantages. They smile more than men,[6] leading to a boost in self-confidence for those on the receiving end.[7] (Unfortunately, that same asset can prove detrimental to a woman who is *not* smiling: A feminine neutral face tends to be perceived by others as fearful, sad, or angry.)[8] Women maintain strong eye contact in conversations,[9] and listeners respond with more direct gazing,[10] translating into stronger interpersonal connections and a sense of being heard. On a related note, females have excellent perception, excelling at reading other people's behavior,[11] knowing how to decode emotion in voice (especially sadness, fear, and happiness),[12] and engaging in a greater self-disclosure than men.

Biology is the foundation of existence, and, yes, it is vital to educate ourselves on how these factors can prime a young girl for life. But the human brain is incredibly malleable and is influenced by its environment, socialization, gender-role stereotypes, and more. Which is to say, biology does not "lock in" a person's reality; individuals download cultural expectations with information on how to operate—a lens with which to interpret events, situations, and each other, establishing both gender-role expectations as well as stereotypes. Every time we meet someone new, we subconsciously construct a snapshot of the person based on our prior experiences, beliefs, social interactions, and values. Many people encounter a beautiful woman and automatically assume she is not exceptionally smart; or they might presume a woman is unfriendly if she doesn't smile and prefers a firm handshake over a hug. People believe that gender equality prevails in this day and age, that archaic stereotypes have been obliterated, yet one look below the surface and it is evident that women and men still struggle with preconceived notions about one another that have been deeply chiseled into our culture and reinforced by tradition.

My hope is that books such as *Brave Girls* and programs such as Unleashed foster a sense of gender bilingualism, helping girls, boys, women, and men master their own language while fluently understanding one another—their inherent and complementary strengths, as well as the commonalities and differences that exist between them. Imagine traveling to a foreign country and knowing only a few key phrases of the native language: communication would be difficult; navigating a city impossible; and nuances of the culture would be lost. Being bilingual opens up a world of possibilities: the ability to connect, to create a shared experience, to foster appreciation of differences, and to learn from the diversity. Gender bilingualism would be just as beneficial, maximizing the quality of interactions between men and women and deepening each gender's understanding of the advantages of being fluent in the other's "language."

Middle school girls are ensconced in the journey of finding themselves. To crystallize this process of self-discovery, girls begin to explore and experiment with their gender identity. In this context, gender identity refers not to sexual orientation but to their own definition of what it is like to be female and what resonates most—their own stereotypes and experiences, perceptions, values, and beliefs. Bodies are changing; certain relationships are ending while others blossom; philosophies morph with developing reasoning and critical-thinking abilities—all of which leads to further exploration of what it truly is like to be female.

As young children, girls are aware that they are physically different from boys. But now, the level of awareness heightens as they grow more cognizant of how they are treated differently. As girls begin to physically mature, they experience the "benefit" of being treated more like adults; the presence of breasts, hips, and their height as they tower over boys of a similar age conspire to unfairly age them, compounding gender expectations. Rapidly developing brains enable them to reason at a more sophisticated level; "Wait a minute. People talk to me in a certain way because I'm a girl" or "People think I'm X, Y, Z, just because I'm a girl" are common insights girls express as they move into adolescence—like Bella, who was shocked that the parents of her male soccer teammates didn't want her competing. Because adolescence is a time when teens are sensitive to injustice, from homelessness to world hunger to curfews and homework-induced TV restrictions, they are questioning how others—and they themselves—are treated. They start to get riled up about cultural phenomena, such as Barbie dolls and the sexist image they portray, and grow attuned to how being female might lead to particular challenges that boys never confront.

In Unleashed's environment, they are surrounded by other girls maneuvering this same intricate web. Whether sharing anger, disbelief, and frustration about the gender stereotypes that still exist despite decades of gender reformation, or supporting one another through the trials and tribulations of figuring out "What does it mean to *me* to be a girl in this day and age?" Unleashed shadows the girls during this process. Girls embrace the motto "Once an Unleashed girl, always an Unleashed girl." No matter when the twelve-week program comes to an end, these girls forever consider themselves part of the Unleashed community. The program assumes the form of what psychologists call a transitional object, like a teddy bear or security blanket—something to carry with them for a sense of comfort as they traverse the rocky terrain of adolescence. The lessons they learn become ingrained in their psyche, within reach at all times throughout finding their identity, adapting to newly formed beliefs and values, and even experimenting with their outward appearance.

Boys think that because we're girls, we're quiet and mannered and calm, or that we don't think things through and just do whatever we feel like doing. Parents and teachers have their opinions, too. It's okay for them to have their own opinions, but I also have mine, so don't tell me who I am or how I should act. I like doing what I'm doing, and I think things through carefully. Unleashed helped me realize that women are more powerful than I thought we were. I used to be stereotypical and thought men were more powerful, but now I know that women can stand up for anything we want. Sometimes, we're even more powerful than boys; men think they need to use aggression to solve their problems. Girls know they can use words and talk it out.

   —Zhu, age twelve

What does it mean to be a girl? That is a complicated question.

For each young lady, the response is entirely different. What I tend to see most is denial of or embarrassment over anything that seems overly feminine or "too girlie." One of my roles is to offer permission to revel in traditional femininity if that's what feels relevant to the girls at that moment. It is perfectly normal to talk about the latest fashion trends, become obsessed with the color pink, or adorn their pencils with fuzzy pom-poms. None of these take away from their power. But I have repeatedly observed that when girls want to engage in behaviors that could be categorized as stereotypically girlie, adults—women in particular—grow fearful. It is an "all or none" philosophy wedded to our own stereotypes: if you wear pastel colors and play with dolls, you cannot be a powerful girl.

Acting more stereotypically male, embracing sports and academics as the only paths to being taken seriously and competitive in our patriarchal world—these are dangerous lines of thinking. They actually *perpetuate* stereotypes and sexism, indirectly reinforcing that the "male" style is the norm and anything else is substandard. It is exactly this line of thinking that dismantled the feminist movement starting in the 1980s. Women became alienated because they embraced their femininity and identified with those aspects of themselves. In doing so, they were thought to be setting the movement back. I, for one, have always loved fashion, grew up playing with Barbie dolls, and refused to cut my long hair. Yet, I am a feminist and believe in the power and equality of women. Gender identity must be predicated on the notion that every person's perception, DNA, history, values, and personal style is distinct.

Acting silly and laughing do not necessarily equate to being dumb and frivolous. In fact, my philosophy is "enjoyment fuels engagement." An overall sense of satisfaction—in work *and* life—stems from aligning your passion with your goals, actions, and choices.

We all need to delve beneath the surface and address the implicit stereotypes that are wedded within the fabric of our society. It is complex; much of this is still relatively unconscious, and most people are unaware of their own bias and behavior. Stereotypes remain stubbornly resistant to change because people tend to categorize others by gender; they remember attributes that are most consistent with a stereotype (e.g., blondes are dumb; girls are bad at math). This innate reaction exaggerates differences between the genders; it is hard to change because it has become habitual and automatic.

These types of discussions are critical to girls and shape their identities as young women. The earlier women can engage in conversations and learn that their experiences and perceptions are shared, the better off they will be later in life. The insights and learning that I was privy to while conducting interviews with powerful women are paramount to developing our next generation into strong women who align with and embrace their gender rather than reproach it. The wisdom collected throughout my two-year research project is an incredible gift that I share with the girls: the knowledge that powerful women have developed a strong feminine identity, refusing to put up a facade and mimic male behavior as a means to success. It may not register or resonate for a long time to come, but this information hopefully remains accessible to them moving forward.

Feminine and gender identity operate on a developmental continuum; girls grow up to be women, and women were once girls. Unleashed participants are continuously reminded, "Adult women struggle with similar things that you do, just in a different context. Plenty of them have trouble embracing those characteristics they feel are typically viewed as female and fear that others may be biased."

I highlight the fine line women walk—the proverbial tightrope they purposefully inch across as they figure out what is expected of them. Planting these seeds at this critical time may impact their evolution and identity as they grow older and are confronted with increasingly more frequent scenarios that will question their view of gender and power. Some women begin to believe male professionals are somehow superior to women. Or they reveal that outside of work, friends consider them funny and outgoing, but they don a "professional" persona—all business, no play—once inside the office in order to be taken seriously by male colleagues. "I'm worried that if I was to act like my real self or reveal my sense of humor, I'll be seen as less professional or incapable" is a common confession. In reality, trying to act "male" will lead to alienating herself from her colleagues.

This is a prototypical Fraud Factor mentality—a rampant phenomenon among women who believe they have to behave like a man to be successful. They misguidedly believe they need to disengage from aspects more associated with being female (displaying emotions; dressing in a feminine manner; being talkative) in order to thrive in a male-dominated world. But in the end, they achieve only a false sense of power and success that is temporary and superficial at best. Diana, a finance executive, shared with me during her interview that she behaves much differently at work than she does in her personal life. Her friends would be surprised how "buttoned up" she was with colleagues. Yet Diana was upset that her performance reviews consistently noted that she alienated herself from her team and did not appear connected. Diana admitted that she purposely hid her true personality so she could be perceived as professional and credible. (Six months after we spoke, I checked back in with Diana. Her firm had merged with another, and every partner had been brought on board the new staff . . . except for her.) It even happened to me. When I was in my late twenties and working as a trial consultant, a colleague took me into her office and said, "I think you're brilliant and really respect you and want you on my team, but I need you to cut your hair or wear it up in a bun. And you can't wear makeup [I wore only mascara at the time]. Oh, and could you stick with pants or below-the-knee skirts?" She herself had been indoctrinated into the Fraud Factor.

On the other hand, consider Ruby, a senior vice president of a tech company who was repeatedly criticized by senior management for being "too nice." (One example: sending handwritten holiday cards to her team members.) That may be, she told me, "but when there's a crisis and I need my team to work late or come in on the weekend, they are willing to give me their all. They know how much I value them, and it comes back full circle."

Ruby's success—and Diana's demise—are backed by research. When women utilize feminine leadership traits, such as individualized consideration for employees and an overall thoughtful, supportive mentality, they are considered more effective leaders than women who display masculine leadership characteristics.[13] (Men who exhibit these same feminine qualities rate higher as well; it's only women who fare worse when they attempt to adopt prototypically male traits of leadership.)[14] The glass ceiling is not only a myth; it is a self-fulfilling prophecy.

"You're a nurse, right?"

While earning my PsyD, I interned at a psychiatric hospital. Part of my daily routine included grand rounds, when doctors present intriguing cases to a group of psychiatrists, psychologists, and students and then open the floor to questions. Every week, one of the clinic's most prominent psychoanalysts, who was known for being a bit sexist—we'll call him Dr. S—would approach me as if he'd never seen me before and rhetorically ask, "You're a nurse, right?" He simply couldn't fathom that I, a young-looking woman with long auburn hair wearing feminine clothing, might be a doctor in training—despite that his own wife was a top child psychoanalyst. Finally, one week I replied, "Actually, Dr. S, I'm a psychology student earning my PsyD and I'm working really closely with your wife. She selected me to be the only psychology student to attend her weekly seminars." That was the last time he asked if I was a nurse.

Gender bias is prevalent whether admitted or not. Society has a desperate need to cling to the idea that equality prevails and people are not basing judgments solely on gender, but this is our culture burying its head in the sand and looking the other way. Women and men are both guilty of reinforcing traditional gender roles and making inherent assumptions. It often appears innocently: a five-year-old girl receiving a play kitchen instead of a basketball hoop;

enrolling a daughter in ballet versus karate. Moving along the continuum, it's a college football player assuming his team's cheerleaders
aren't smart, a waitress being called "sweetie" by her male customers, or a female psychologist-in-training constantly having to explain she is not a nurse. Even the use of the proverbial *he* in writing
or speaking is a result of centuries of habitual gender stereotyping,
unfair typecasting that pigeonholes women as invisible and inferior.
People rely on stereotypes because it is human nature to gravitate
toward organizing and processing information into categories. We
create internal buckets—"black or white"; "old or young"—because
it streamlines our processing of information. A baby dressed in blue
is assumed to be a boy; a redhead on the subway is automatically
labeled a fiery troublemaker. But just because something is simple
does not mean it's accurate: baby girls wear blue and shy redheads
exist. Most dangerous are the subtle, implied, subconscious stereotypes—those related to women's competence, for instance—that
people such as Dr. S do not even recognize as flawed. Worst of all,
women take on these prescribed roles because these biases are *that*
embedded in our culture.

While Unleashed is dedicated to combating tired gender stereotypes and promoting gender bilingualism, our mission is to empower
girls to realize and tap into their inherent feminine power. Despite
all the doom-and-gloom studies, books and media highlights about
how women are at a disadvantage in the workforce and shackled to
oppressive cultural expectations, having XX chromosomes has true
advantages. We must begin speaking less about the salary differential
and lack of C-level positions held by women and start examining
the impact and influence women *do* have in our society. I liken it to
climbing Mount Everest: even an experienced climber might give up

if she only looks at how far she has to go rather than sees how much progress she has made. When the spotlight is shone on women's lack of accomplishments, it implies they are not thriving, which is absolutely false. On the contrary, women have been and continue to be tremendous change agents within every industry in our society. Their impact might not be obvious to the degree it should be, but the "invisible power" women possess in our society is omnipresent and proof that they are nearing the peak of their own Mount Everest.

Although I am not a political analyst, I am often asked to comment on Hillary Clinton's 2008 presidential campaign from a women's leadership perspective, where I can see how a different approach might have proven more successful. One of the most striking aspects of her campaign tactics is how she failed to embrace being a female candidate—in fact, Clinton did her best to minimize it, lending a decided "elephant in the room" quality to her operation. I kept waiting for her to issue a call to action for women across the country, proclaiming, "This is our time!"—but it never came. Instead, she projected the notion that she was a candidate who simply happened to be a woman, inadvertently sending the message that women need to cut off aspects of their identity and don a mask of masculinity to be successful. When Senator Barack Obama was running against Senator John McCain for president of the United States, the former's actions and words made it crystal clear that he felt *now* was the time for an African-American to lead the nation. I believe if Clinton had adopted a similar strategy, she could have won. Instead, she was so afraid of alienating male voters that she downplayed her feminine strengths, pushing female voters away instead.

How could Clinton have better leveraged her DNA? Let's first look at what I mean by "feminine fundamentals."

Women Know How to Navigate the Labyrinth

One of the fundamental strengths that my research with professional women demonstrated was that women are highly attuned to possibility and opportunity. They see openings in the maze of life where others see only dead ends: where a negative business situation might actually become a potential advancement, where a romantic breakup can pave the way for a truly satisfying relationship. When a client working at a Midwest bank receives a call from a recruiter to work in the international travel-check business—something her boss had labeled "a dying industry"—and accepts it because she foresees the potential to advance her career and increase her overall value proposition, she has tapped into an inherent strength of being a woman. She intuitively knows when to take the risk and move down a different path, knowing that it might not live up to her expectations, but also that she cannot afford to let it pass.

This same phenomenon occurs when I present to a sea of middle school girls, offering them the chance to engage in an innovative program. Some girls sign up because they are eager to move outside their comfort zone and try something new; some identify Unleashed as a chance to get involved with a cause they are passionate about; and some simply recognize a call to action. Whatever the reason, the program resonates with them, they request an application, explain it to their parents, get permission, and agree to dedicate hours every week to attend sessions and rescues and engage in projects they design to make a difference. Regardless of age, women and girls are attuned to experiences and situations that are available to them that could shape their lives in some way. They recognize the feeling that these opportunities might not arise again, resulting in an urgency to opt in.

I first interviewed Carolyn Everson, Facebook's vice president of global marketing solutions, when she was the COO and executive vice president of US ad sales at MTV Networks. She recounted to me how she had worked at a consulting firm right after college, then attended a five-day program at Wharton on strategic alliances, learning how to help companies work together. A fellow student worked for Walt Disney and offered her a job as manager of business development . . . miles away from her job, family, and home. Despite being happy with her career, she quickly decided to relocate, telling me, "I packed and moved to Orlando for one and a half years." Although she had attended the Wharton program to develop herself professionally, completely committed to her current company and role, the Disney position was an opportunity she felt she could not pass up. Carolyn's eventual decision to attend business school—a move that helped propel her career—was largely fueled by her experiences at Disney and the mentorship of her boss.

Carolyn, like other powerful women I interviewed, was not wedded to a "plan" and was willing to take the necessary risks because of that mind-set. Would she have accepted the offer and moved cross-country if she had a definitive niche already carved out for herself? I am not sure she would have ended up with the same opportunities if she had. You are more likely to successfully navigate the maze of life if you are not clinging to a definitive plan; the willingness to veer in differing directions that seem exciting or rewarding is more likely to lead to connections with well-suited opportunities.

Women Go Off-Ramp

Besides being positively opportunistic, successful, powerful females navigate the system with an internal GPS, sometimes moving left or right or even a few steps backward in order to advance in the long run. The opinions of others and how choices appear to the outside world are not of major concern. Trusting instincts, entertaining novel ideas, and employing nontraditional solutions—knowing this will make a difference in their personal and professional lives—override a need to protect their ego. Powerful women tend to be non-linear in their career decisions, going off-ramp as they navigate the labyrinth of life.

Sheree was working in the headquarters of a Fortune 500 organization until she was asked to transfer to a smaller division to head up its finance department. She jumped at the chance even though her male counterparts considered it a demotion and had turned down the same opportunity. Sheree viewed the job as an opening to shine and stand out in a smaller office—a clever strategy to advance her career. She was successful in her new role, and when the head of her new office was promoted to CEO and moved to headquarters, he brought her along . . . as CFO of the entire organization. How's that for a demotion?

A fifty-year-old emergency-room physician might decide to quit medicine and become a baker when years of punishing hours and battling the bureaucracy have left her frustrated and unsatisfied; an attorney may permit herself to take a hiatus from law and stay home with her kids; a librarian who discovers her passion for public policy may gradually take on administrative roles until finally she is elected Dallas city manager. Through Unleashed, I have watched girls change their minds in minutes; they might attend a session and report an entirely new idea they had because of an article they read, or they might walk in with a new haircut or style—and in all cases they are proud to showcase their transformation. I myself was supposed to be a musical-theater actress, studying with voice teachers from the Metropolitan Opera, but left my Juilliard aspirations behind when a volunteer position at a pediatric, inpatient psychiatric unit helped me see a new career light. In all of these situations, the woman's move may not overtly make sense to others and might not reflect advancement and success within a patriarchal system.

That is because men tend to adopt a more linear approach, viewing success as something that comes by moving from point A to point B. Women's flexibility and adaptability stems from both external and internal influences. On one hand, women have had to explore innovative approaches to get to their goals because most business cultures are predicated on the male model of success and achievement. At the same time, women are more internally driven and motivated by intrinsic factors such as passion and making an impact. In the absence of those motivators, they struggle until they can figure out a way to align their values with their purpose. A great example of this can be seen among my female clients during the 2008 recession. They adjusted fairly well and had an easier time moving into the mind-set of exploring new career opportunities, looking at their underlying core skills and how their expertise could be transferred to other industries. The men I worked with had more difficulty moving away from their previous titles and making the connection between their acquired skills and the new recession-elicited environment. Women were also more likely to see this time as an opening to reinvent themselves versus a significant loss and defeat.

Economist Sylvia Ann Hewlett, a well-recognized expert on gender and workplace issues, has conducted extensive research addressing women's willingness to go off-ramp. In the push-pull of work-life balance, career is the "push" and family is the "pull"; eventually, the pull wins out, with many women taking temporary breaks from their careers, joining flexible-work arrangements, or working virtually from home. Hewlett found that 37 percent of highly qualified women voluntarily leave their careers, for an average of 2.2 years[15]—

often during the same period that is considered the "advancement" years in a traditionally male culture. The majority cited child-care challenges, although caring for their own parents, lack of job satisfaction, or feeling underutilized or underappreciated at work were other motivations.

Over the years, I have heard clients express how they felt pushed out after having kids; their bosses assume they are not interested in a new project or will refuse to travel. As a result, these women feel stifled, unchallenged, and unengaged as they are assigned mundane tasks, leading to a plunge in career fulfillment. Combined with the pull of children at home, women reevaluate their conditions: "I am not happy at work; I want to be home with my children; I am paying a lot of money for child care—so it makes sense to take a hiatus." The catch 22? It will be that much more difficult to return to work if and when they choose to do so.

Women Are Highly Invested in Developing Others

"What is the greatest impact you have had in your lifetime?" While conducting my research, I would pose this question to powerful women. Nearly all of them perceived their biggest influence to be in developing others. Powerful women feel responsible for their teams, hold themselves accountable for developing new talent that will benefit the company, and are invested in retaining and motivating others. I listened to countless stories of how they were sought out for guidance, even by employees who were not on their team; how they stayed in contact with former mentees, even if they no longer worked at the same company; how they maintained their strong social networks, which could easily be accessed for business purposes. There is a business case for this philosophy: employees work harder for and are more committed to those they feel connected to; workers who feel engaged and motivated stay at a company longer; and their teams excel. Facebook's Everson recounted a story about a valuable junior associate making a sizable but honest mistake that could have jeopardized his career at the company. Instead, Everson assumed collective responsibility, telling higher-ups, "Our team made a mistake." *That's* effective leadership—motivating your team, understanding what makes them tick, advocating for them within the organization, cultivating their strengths for them to advance.

Similarly, women tend to assume the role of relationship manager of their family; typically it is the wife who creates social plans for the couple and play dates for the children, volunteers at school, or serves on committees for their neighborhood organization. These relational assets are often downplayed by women, who deem them "soft," "too emotional," or simply not all that important. But the extreme opposite is true. Cultivating and maintaining relationships—at work, at home, among friends, and within the community—is extraordinarily valuable. Life does not occur in a vacuum; collaboration with others is a necessity, not a luxury. The African proverb "It takes a village to raise a child" can be applied to much more than child rearing. So much of life depends on interpersonal connections. Unleashed itself, for example, would not exist without my strong social network: the think tank of friends, colleagues, clients, and women interviewed for the book who provided hours of consultation and guidance; the attorney friend who convinced her top international law firm to accept us as a pro bono client, saving us thousands of dollars; the friend-of-a-friend graphic designer who created our logo without charging us. No matter if it is personal or professional, the inherent female fundamental of being relationship oriented should be reframed as advantageous rather than insignificant.

Women Are Passionate

Sixty-one percent of gentiles who risked their own lives to save Jews from the Holocaust were women.[16] Females are more likely than males to be living organ donors.[17] Those statistics don't surprise me: women are more likely to take risks when it comes to serving others and sacrificing themselves (whereas men are more apt to act heroically when physical prowess is needed, such as pulling an accident survivor from a car wreck). That risk taking comes from an inherent passion that I have witnessed among countless female clients and interview subjects. Women are wedded to making an impact personally and professionally, and if they are not effecting change, or if they feel their passion dipping, they will take the necessary steps to recapture it. You know the saying "Do what you love and you'll never work a day"? That fits most women to a tee. I work ninety hours a week, but it never feels like a job because I am so energized and fulfilled by the cause. But if I'm speaking to a man at a cocktail party and ask if he loves what he does, the answer is almost always "It pays the bills" or "It's just a job." If you are not passionate or engaged, you are just going through the motions.

Alisa, a credit-card marketing executive with an Ivy League MBA, was suffering from a lack of passion in her work. When a friend tried to pick her brain, asking her what field she thought she might be interested in, education sprang to mind. Alisa's friend connected her with the director of human resources for the NYC Department of Education; shortly thereafter, she quit her marketing job and switched fields, strategizing about teacher hiring, monitoring and managing thousands of employees, creating employee HR packages, and working toward getting the Board of Ed to run more efficiently. "It was a huge risk to go

from [a major credit-card conglomerate] to the NYC Board of Ed," Alisa
told me. *"New York was undergoing the biggest reform in education at
the time [this was in 2002, when Mayor Bloomberg had appointed Joel
Klein, a progressive, corporate-minded lawyer, as chancellor in an effort to revamp the entire NYC school system]; I moved from a very
effective organization to one of the most inefficient ones in the country.
I veered from the VP path to one that wasn't guaranteed and certainly
did not pay well; I followed my passion."* Eventually, Alisa moved to a
charter-school management company out West, where she was able to
blend her business skills with her interest in education, reporting she
now felt more fulfilled than ever before.

I would like to think that if Diana had been in a program like Unleashed when she was younger, she wouldn't have felt the same pressure to mask her identity in her twenties, thirties, and forties. That is
why the various feminine fundamentals are built into the Unleashed
program—to help girls leverage their assets now and in the future.

After interviewing the Pru Bushnells and Carolyn Eversons of the
world, I brainstormed about how to pass the knowledge I had acquired along to middle school girls. Powerful women have honed a
strong identity of being female and embrace this, using it to their advantage. They perceive the differentiating characteristics of being female as attributes, not handicaps, leveraging them to place themselves
in a unique position that cannot be filled by anyone else—especially
a man. I wanted to infuse girls with these concepts, like a life-altering
treatment in an IV drip in the form of leadership and power.

To eradicate gender norms and stereotypes, women and girls
must begin to leverage and embrace those unique aspects that differentiate them from men. Diversity is not only a proven catalyst for
sparking innovation and creativity; it positively impacts society as a

whole, affecting economics, health, education, and more. Decades ago, feminists set out to shift the nation away from a mind-set that viewed men as the norm and women as abnormal to one that perceives the genders as equal. Unfortunately, progress has grown stagnant, signifying a need for further action and philosophies. Women must be the first to initiate the change, and they can start by recognizing that their inherent distinctions are valuable, not a curse or even a handicap.

Women who neglect to leverage their DNA place themselves at a tremendous disadvantage. The characteristics they are trying so hard to minimize would in reality give them an edge, not handicap them. Attempting to hide one's gender by purposefully acting like the opposite sex often backfires, as Diana's work situation so clearly demonstrated. It is similar to when people in their forties and fifties try to "act young" by wearing teenage clothes and getting plastic surgery and Botox as antiaging treatments. The effect is often the exact opposite of what they had hoped for, and the consequences are profound—low self-esteem and preoccupation with forces out of their control. In their careers, women who adopt a male veneer often inadvertently alienate those around them or report feeling fraudulent, as if they are living on the verge of being "found out." (Remember, that is precisely what Mindy, the SVP who couldn't name her strengths when preparing for her performance review, expressed to me.) Instead of denouncing their fundamental differences, powerful women capitalize on them.

Power Boost

1. Ask a young girl, "What stereotypes exist for girls your age, even in 2015?" Be prepared for answers you may not have imagined. Girls this age don't have a forum to talk about the biases they are observing in class, on sports teams, and even in relationships with friends and family. Give her permission to advocate for herself, providing accurate information when she hears or sees someone adhering to gender stereotypes. For example, when a classmate says he won't pick her or her friends for his team in gym because "girls can't play sports as good as a boy can," she may want to point out talented female athletes or simply say, "That's a stereotype; there are plenty of girls who are good in sports."

2. Think about your own belief system and expectations related to gender roles for men and women, boys and girls. How do these impact your interaction, behavior, and relationships with children of both genders? Do you tend to select gender-specific toys and clothing for girls? Or at the other extreme, do you discourage the color pink and playing with dolls because you fear it is sexist? Challenge yourself to allow girls to select their own toys and clothing without judgment. Observe their choices and encourage them to experiment with many different styles and types as part of healthy self-discovery.

3. Young women may appear indecisive and unwedded to a position or an idea during adolescence: One minute they are passionate about a community-service project at school, the next minute they detest it and want to change their volunteer placement. As women veer off paths to experiment with different life choices, so does the younger female generation. Encourage this. For example, when you notice a teen struggling with choices about her after-school activities, ask her, "What initially attracted you to that program? What did you hope you would be doing? What is missing for you now that you tried it?" It is important that girls begin to evaluate and clarify what it is they are most passionate about. Adults can guide them, applauding their efforts for taking a risk and trying something new. As girls veer off paths and experiment, they may begin to trace back to a starting point and see how they landed at their final decision.

Chapter 6

Fearless Communication

I *remember the first time I met Lacey, a friendly but shy fifth grader at an all-girls school. She had attended an Unleashed informational meeting and was huddled between two classmates in the group circle. Clearly she was not confident about speaking up like the other girls, and she continued to hold back for the first few weeks.*

Little by little, I noticed her blossoming, speaking out more and being rewarded by encouragement and applause from the other Unleashed girls. When Lacey spoke, she was funny, engaging, and left you feeling as if you wanted to hear more from her. After twelve weeks, she volunteered to speak at our anniversary event. I gave her just one directive: "Talk about Unleashed and what it means to you." The evening of the event, she showed up in her Unleashed T-shirt and jeans without any note cards. After I addressed the audience of more than a hundred people, I handed the microphone to Lacey. She placed one hand on the mike and the other on her hip, looking like a seasoned NBC broadcaster. Lacey blew us all away—she was articulate, engaging, and held the audience's attention as she described her journey, going into detail

about how she learned to be powerful and make a difference, and how
she's no longer afraid to speak her mind. Afterward, her mother ap-
proached and asked me what, exactly, had I done to her daughter.

At the tender age of ten, Lacey found her voice. She was lucky—
for most girls, that is approximately the time they begin to struggle
with speaking their minds. Prior to adolescence, plenty of girls feel
comfortable articulating their feelings and making their needs and
opinions known.[1] A third grader swinging on the playground has
no problem informing someone who wants to get on, "I'm using this
swing, it's my turn now. You have to wait." I have a video recording
of my daughter, Jordyn, at her third birthday party walking up to her
best friend, who was jumping up and down, drawing a lot of attention from others, declaring, "Stop that. This is my party, so you can't
do that."

With the onset of puberty, girls are flooded with changes—physiological, emotional, cognitive, and social. From preadolescence to
adolescence proper, a girl's brain develops at an unprecedented rate—
unlike in any other stage of her life (except for infancy). At the same
time, the pituitary gland releases cells that set an endocrinological
system in motion, prompting monthly hormonal surges of estrogen
and progesterone. This cycle spurs the brain to develop female-
specific neurons and circuitry that were programmed in fetal development to be activated during this stage. In many ways, a girl's brain
undergoes an awakening between the ages of ten to twelve, reaching
its biological predisposition. Brain regions such as the hippocampus
(memory and learning), hypothalamus (organ control and functioning), and amygdalae (emotions) are all impacted by estrogen.

The female brain matures two to three years earlier than that of
a boy. The language centers and the corpus callosum (the cells connecting the language area of the brain to the emotional processing

center) in a girl's brain are larger than in a male's. At the age of ten, a girl's frontal lobe (the area of the brain responsible for cognition and processing information) doubles in gray matter.[2] Simultaneous with this heightened growth is the change in neuronal circuits; during adolescence the brain begins to prune itself, extinguishing pathways that are underutilized and strengthening those that are frequently used. This enables the brain to be more efficient, increasing its capacity for higher-order cognition such as abstract reasoning, synthesis of complex thoughts and ideas, and the deciphering of more sophisticated information.

Psychologically, adolescence is akin to toddlerhood; the push-pull between adult and child resurges, a girl's sense of defiance creating boundaries and fostering separation and individuation so she can have the freedom to explore who she is, distinct from her parents' values and ideals. Complicating matters is that girls this age are biologically programmed to seek connection, particularly when under stress. Estrogen increases dopamine (a neurochemical that regulates pleasure centers in the brain) and oxytocin (a neurohormone that triggers bonding and attachment), resulting in an increased drive for attachment and intimacy. No wonder a teen girl is heavily invested in seeking and maintaining close relationships with her peers; as she tests out independence, she still needs to bond with others, substituting friends for family. That is why girls experience much more stress than boys when a conflict or any threat to the integrity of a relationship emerges. Biologically and psychologically, they are programmed to attach and connect, possessing a high sensitivity to anything that might endanger affiliations with others. *Tend and befriend* is a term used to describe how females respond to stress; they exhibit nurturing behavior toward others (tend) and build a supportive network (befriend) to reduce anxiety. Men, on the other hand, are more likely to fight or flee under duress—becoming aggressive or attempting to escape stress.

Physiological changes and hormonal influx contribute to an adolescent girl's inner disequilibrium. Her body is adjusting to a newly formed biochemistry that is vastly distinct from that of any previous developmental period. She feels a lack of control of her own body as well as her moods. Her estrogen cycle now significantly impacts her behavior, perceptions, sensitivity, attention span, memory, how she copes with stress, body image, and self-esteem. A girl can appear remarkably different from one day to the next, depending upon where she is in her cycle, her levels of estrogen and progesterone, and the neural activity caused by her quickly morphing brain. These biochemical shifts have a large impact on her emotions, which, in turn, influence her behavior. No wonder girls vacillate from calm to irritable, have outbursts of anger after being happy just moments earlier, or become preoccupied with their bodies after recently feeling euphoric that they are maturing; they are riding the proverbial emotional roller coaster, searching for homeostasis, or at least some relief from the erratic motion. What an adolescent girl craves most is acceptance and emotional security, and she will shift back and forth, from seeking connection to peers to desiring unconditional love and affection from parents, in an effort to maintain connection.

Nothing feels familiar anymore—these girls' minds and bodies and identities are in such intense, simultaneous flux—yet the majority of them fear discussing aloud this ambivalence and apprehension. Girls this age feel they are the only ones experiencing this phenomenon and do not want to risk being seen as unique, differentiated from peers. As a result, they grapple with these feelings alone. Silence is perceived as a less threatening alternative, enabling them to feel secure without any repercussions. A middle schooler eager for acceptance would not be so quick to tell her fellow student to wait because "it's my turn now"; she is highly concerned about being accepted and fitting within the parameters of the norm versus being seen as out of the box relative to her peers.

Defiance, rebellion, and questioning are the hallmarks of female adolescence. Successful navigation through this rite of passage, transitioning from child to adult, is predicated on taking risks, defying the status quo, and experimenting and confronting. The developmental task at hand is to cultivate a newfound sense of autonomy and independence, ultimately shaping one's own identity. Adopting the position "I am now my own person, and this is what I think" is not only the norm but a prerequisite for healthy social and emotional development. Unleashed provides girls with permission to express their thoughts, feelings, and ideas, communicating a clear and powerful message that their words have value and significance; but we all have the power to create these safe spaces within our families, homes, and schools. At a time in their lives when ambivalence and lack of clarity prevail, girls need opportunities to shift their attention to an external issue, engaging in healthy distractions rather than remaining preoccupied with their internal struggles. It is important to allow girls to experiment with their budding voices; to serve as an outlet for them to express emotions and opinions; and to foster open and authentic communication that enhances interpersonal relationships. It is essential to convey to girls at this age that what they want to say—regardless of content, whether their beliefs are right or wrong—holds more weight than what they *think* they are supposed to say. Given the freedom to speak up, to articulate opinions authentically, to take a stand for or against an issue and experience being heard, enables girls to thrive and is paramount to future success. Once the template of fearless communication becomes ingrained, she will be able to use it repeatedly. Girls in today's world must be able to define, embrace, and articulate their beliefs and personal philosophies within many different contexts, including but not limited to their family, community, and school. Harnessing a middle school girl's need to question, challenge, and oppose the norm propels girls forward, easing self-doubt and self-consciousness.

It's not uncommon for me to ask the girls during a session, "What could we be doing better as a group?" Cora, a tall, introverted seventh grader prone to shrinking back during group discussions, suddenly piped up, "We're not allowing each other to voice our opinions." The room stopped—Cora rarely spoke, and now, here she was offering a provocative notion. She took a huge risk by stating her opinion, and I rewarded her by acknowledging it as such. "That was excellent! That was a big risk you just took." Cora beamed.

Toward the tail end of Unleashed, I give girls the opportunity to pair up, sit face-to-face, and offer constructive feedback on their evolution throughout the past twelve weeks. It is completely voluntary—no one has to participate, as it can be quite intense. Cora raised her hand to participate. Not only was I immensely proud of her courage in doing so—most grown women would be reluctant—but her partner rewarded her by sitting across from her and saying, "You're quiet, but we really respect you. When you speak, you say things that are thoughtful, and we all value your opinions."

Listen to Unleashed graduate Talia, thirteen, reflect on her transformation:

"Before, I felt like when I tried to offer my ideas in a larger group, I wasn't heard as well. Young girls aren't seen as being able to offer good suggestions. Now I feel more confident. It's transferred over into life outside of Unleashed, too. In history class. I never used to speak up. Now, I do."

Lacey grasps the change in her voice, too:

"When I started Unleashed, I was really shy. When my mom introduced me to people in her office—or anywhere, really—I was shy, hiding, scared. I talked in a low voice. Afterwards, I was able to give a speech in front of the entire school. I learned how to talk to people I'd never met before and interview them to see if they could take care of the puppies. It was a lot easier than I thought it would be. Last summer, at camp, I took riflery, and the teacher was the scariest person I've ever met—I mean, he's teaching children how to use guns. He yelled at one of my friends, but I couldn't see any reason why. I went up to him after class and asked why. He didn't have an answer. The next day, I went up again and asked him why, and he said, "I was irritated and tired." I was very, very proud of myself. A year later, I hadn't forgotten what I'd gone through in Unleashed to make me a stronger, bigger person."

Without a doubt, the most common sentiment I hear from girls when they leave Unleashed is "I can speak up now. I have a voice and I am not afraid to speak out anymore." I have witnessed girls like Lacey who, upon entering the program, barely utter a word in a group of fifteen, but later get up onstage and passionately speak before a large audience without being scripted or needing a single note card. Sydney, a bashful sixth grader who was small for her age and the quietest girl on her team, went from being barely audible in sessions to, on the last day, accepting my challenge for her to scream out loud—followed by applause and foot-stomping from the group, acknowledging her feat.

Defying Group Think

A girl's increased ability to advocate for herself leads to an emergence of bravery, self-respect, and the capacity to create appropriate boundaries. No longer will she accept behaviors that she feels are intolerable; she has a heightened sense of awareness, detecting when others are out of line. This proficiency aids in the development of healthy relationships. Now that a girl has clarity about what she expects from others, she can easily say no when she feels uncomfortable about a situation or when she doesn't agree, refusing to compromise her ethics, even if she fears the loss of a relationship. At the end of Unleashed, when girls are asked to share their observations of how they have changed, they will often say, "I can't look away when I don't like what people are doing anymore" or "Now I feel I have to stand up for things and not keep quiet." Girls will describe confronting a bully, holding their ground against a group of boys harassing their track team, or emphatically stating, "I like her," when hearing gossip about another girl.

How can girls and women become socialized to speak out, even when their opinion might not be popular? How can girls learn to crystallize their thoughts and perspectives to manage the inevitable pushback and resistance from others? Being scrutinized by a critical societal microscope makes it especially difficult—almost impossible—to go against the grain. After interviewing hundreds of women, I coined the term *social renegade* to describe those individuals who, when faced with moral and ethical dilemmas at different stages of their lives, were able to act with conviction because they felt it was their responsibility to do so, even when, instinctually, it feels uncomfortable or painful to do so. Whether it was leaving a job because the company's values did not align with their own, choosing to take a break from a lucrative career to stay home and raise their children (and being called "crazy" for doing so), or hiring a nanny so as to continue working at a fulfilling job, these powerful women stood their ground and did not veer from their beliefs. Girls and women need to find the power to cultivate the social renegade within, defining the "shoulds" for themselves without succumbing to external judgment.

The social renegade's biggest challenge is groupthink, a phenomenon that prevails in our world, from organizations to government to community. The dynamics of a group can be overpowering: aligned with Darwin's theory (survival of the fittest), members scapegoat and alienate one another to preserve collective strength and influence. Groupthink can be contagious, leading to poor decision-making and unethical behavior. From angry mobs to social cliques, and even boards that govern large corporations, individuals can be hard-pressed to speak their mind when it diverges from the majority's agenda. Quickly, the group can morph, dictating rules and values, reinforcing the notion that group members should accept the majority's belief system without any room for individual thought. Looking at our society as it stands today, we see that groupthink has ruined lives, destroyed businesses and our economy, putting our nation at great risk. (The most recent economic crisis in the United States was largely due to mortgage companies and investment banks being driven by profit, ignoring the inevitable excesses. Employees on all levels would lose their jobs if they did not conform, making it difficult to stop this powerful cycle.) People fear the consequences of questioning the majority and thus acquiesce in response.

The simple question "Why?" enables the nonconformist to look beneath the surface and challenge those ideas that do not make sense. To be a social renegade, a woman must speak her mind. She must be a truth-teller, which is valued far more than one might think. She must be brave.

Charlotte was the head of marketing at a large technology company, working for a boss whom everyone feared. Charlotte knew that her boss's reputation was getting in the way of the team's generating creative ideas, and she decided to take a risk and confront her boss. "People are fearful of you," she told her. "I think you need to hear that." Later, Charlotte spoke her mind a second time, as she felt her company was in disarray, acquiring new companies and launching new product lines in a hasty, disorganized manner. "I said to her, 'We just keep asking sales to sell more and more stuff. We need to come up with a better strategy.'" In both incidents, Charlotte was largely rewarded for her candor and ability to speak out. Her boss thanked Charlotte for sharing an outside perspective because she had been unaware of the impact she was having on others. Assuming the role of truth-teller was an example of how a powerful woman has a responsibility to be the messenger, asserting beliefs and sharing knowledge and expertise when necessary.

Look at Sherron Watkins, the former Enron Corporation vice president who confronted management about accounting irregularities, risking being ostracized from the rest of her team in order to stand up for what was right. Watkins brought the accounting problem to the attention of Enron CEO Ken Lay, informing him that the company "might implode in a wave of accounting scandals."[3] Watkins took a stand, even though doing so carried career risks and put her in an uncomfortable spotlight as a whistle-blower. Without risk takers like Charlotte or Sherron, costly mistakes may ensue. Defying conventional groupthink, the social renegade learns to challenge standard practices in order to overcome obstacles.

In my research, I observed that successful women exercise power, take risks, and become social renegades more often when attached to a cause. That cause can be large or small and may be relevant to their industry, career, or even personal lives. Regardless of whether or not it is a social cause, advocating for others is usually a central theme; it could involve protecting the rights of her team at work, challenging her religious organization's policies and procedures, or even developing a committee to welcome new families for her children's school. Powerful women leverage their talents and strengths to create impact and change for themselves and their organizations, communities, and families.

Unleashed taps into this innate desire to advocate by tying it to something many girls are passionate about: animal welfare. The program's methodology then enables them to grow adept at defying the status quo: They learn how to campaign for animal rights; how to confidently respond to resistance, such as the inevitable "Why help animals when so many humans are suffering right now?" pushback; and how to self-assuredly back their position, even if it is different from everyone else's. Over the twelve weeks, the girls begin to recognize the power of their voice—both the words they speak and the behavior that is aligned with their spoken messages. Their confidence soars, and they assert themselves with conviction unlike ever before. A girl does not need to rescue a dog in order to assert, advocate, or defend her position; attaching to any cause she is passionate about, taking a stand for or against something important to her, or even questioning a policy she cannot understand contributes to the development of these critical tools.

Remember Gabriela—the longtime animal-rights advocate who was horrified to learn she had unwittingly fund-raised for a PETA-investigated shelter? Listen to her father recount a subsequent encounter with a substandard facility:

"Ever since Gabriela was a little girl, we would pop into pet stores and play with the puppies. About halfway through Unleashed, we were out of town, visiting her grandparents, when we happened to pass by a shop where a bunch of kittens were in the window. They didn't look

like they were in good shape. One was curled up in the corner, seeming to be ignored. Her eyes looked unfocused and crossed. A bunch of other cats were there, too, all in a small, cramped space. The mama kitten was nowhere to be seen. Gabriela described what she experienced as an 'uh-oh' feeling. We went home and she started looking up rescue organizations, called Dr. Stacey for advice, and suggested we buy the kittens and personally find them safe homes. We returned the next day, and Gabriela was downright confrontational, asking the store manager about the kittens and their health. She asked to see their medical records. We were told that the mother had to be removed to receive some medical treatment, and that's why the kittens were stumbling and seemed so badly off (she had since been returned). Gabby described the previous day's scenario to the manager and asked for assurance that the mother would now remain with her babies.

"Every time we go back to visit my parents, my daughter wants to go back and audit that pet shop. She's also planning a big rescue there because it's one of the worst states for puppy mills. Even though Unleashed is over, Gabby continues to attend rescues and charity events. It's been a round-trip experience for us as a family: You actually see the effects as opposed to just hearing about them."

Gabriela later told me she was "a little scared" about confronting the pet store manager:

"It was my first time using my voice without Unleashed backing me up. But I felt prepared. Without Unleashed, I wouldn't have been able to speak up; I might not even have known to be curious about something I thought might not be right. I wasn't completely terrified because I realized all I had to do was ask the lady about the kittens. I was happy that I asked and that I had been able to employ the things that Unleashed had taught me, so that instead of just wondering about if the kittens were safe, I was able to find out for myself."

Confident individuals do not accept the status quo; they ask questions, dig deeper, defy the norm. In turn, they can be deemed troublemakers. Some in positions of authority may dismiss women who question their decisions or ideas, silencing them in an effort to maintain control. A past investment-banking client of mine was reprimanded by her male manager for asking questions—smart, insightful inquiries—about business strategies and initiatives during meetings. She wanted to understand the logic behind certain decisions, but was literally pulled aside by her boss and ordered, "Stop asking questions." She was in her midtwenties but was treated like a child.

Unleashed serves as a springboard, giving girls a platform to speak out and act authentically in accordance with their beliefs and values. This skill will be called upon repeatedly throughout their lives, across many situations, some less complex than others. But having a deep understanding that it is possible is empowering on many fronts.

During graduate school, I took a job as a behavior specialist and counselor for mildly to moderately developmentally delayed adults living in supportive apartments. My roles included helping clients with adjustments to work and life and referring them to psychiatrists if I thought medication was necessary. Alice was a high-functioning woman in her thirties with a clerical job, earning about $10 an hour. Rather than following protocol and allowing the staff to manage her money, Alice was hiding her wages; she told me people were trying to steal from her. She also complained of being perpetually hungry and claimed she was being starved. The head apartment supervisor—a master's-level psychologist in his late forties—labeled Alice "paranoid" without even having evaluated her and ordered me to refer her for a psychiatric evaluation to receive medication. Essentially, he wanted to quiet her.

But after meeting with Alice, I believed her: certain individuals were threatening to take control of her income without explaining their reasons or plans. But like so many women, myself included, she was deemed a "big mouth" and was being threatened with physical silence in the form of powerful antipsychotic medicine. The higher-ups would rather deal with a quiet, drugged resident than one who called attention to deficits in her care. I refused to allow her to be put needlessly on meds. My decision was met with hostility from my male supervisor; shortly thereafter, during an annual audit (when psychologists' records are inspected to ensure proper protocol has been followed), I was notified that all of my notes had mysteriously disappeared. In my heart, I knew the head supervisor took them in an effort to derail my efforts and get me fired. Thankfully, the rest of the staff supported my decision. I'd kept copies of my notes in multiple locations so I was able to replace them; the auditor later told the supervisor my work was "the best I have ever seen written by any of your clinicians." Alice was never forced to take the medicine, and I, a twenty-three-year-old grad school student, received major organization-wide kudos, all because I had a voice and refused to back down.

Sugar and spice and everything nice—these are the ideal values dictated to girls and women by society. Sensitive to this, our females, consciously and unconsciously, strive to meet these unrealistic expectations. They squelch negative emotions such as anger, frustration, and sadness and avoid conflict, at any cost, to preserve a positive image. But this silent, stifling space has severe consequences deleterious and counterproductive to a girl's development and overall functioning. As mentioned earlier in chapter 3 with regards to emotional intelligence, understanding and embracing our emotions is necessary for effective decision-making, conflict management, and navigating the labyrinth of life. Emotions, both positive and negative, are signals that alert an individual to changes in their surroundings and act as a guide to decision-making and behavior. Emotional responses, innate and automatic, are often perceived as "intuition" or "gut reactions." Emotional intelligence is highly correlated with success, life satisfaction, and resilience. Decades of research in sociobiology illustrate the importance of emotions in evolution and show that having a broad emotional repertoire is a crucial form of intellect not provided or reinforced by traditional education. What is most disturbing is that girls are inadvertently led down the wrong path. If research repeatedly shows that emotional intelligence and information are paramount to survival, then why is the female population negatively reinforced when leveraging this aptitude?

Unfortunately, society instills in us that women who exercise their voices and communicate powerfully are mean, bitchy, and aggressive. The public at large is living in the Dark Ages, still attached to the notion that assertive women are inappropriate and problematic, whereas the same behavior in men is construed as powerful, courageous, and assertive. Look no further than Hillary Rodham Clinton's 2008 presidential run. Headlines blared, "The 'Bitch' Is Back!";[4] Glenn Beck snarled, "There's something about her voice that just drives me—it's not what she says, it's how she says it. She is like . . . the stereotypical bitch. . . . There is a range in women's voices that experts say is just the chalk, I mean, the fingernails on the blackboard."[5] No wonder girls (and women) feel pressure to conceal aspects of themselves and hide behind the "good girl" veneer—not even the world's most powerful women can speak up without being chastised or humiliated.

As they enter puberty, girls increasingly grow more aware of the pressure to conform to gender stereotypes. Newly acquired abstract-reasoning and language abilities (including deciphering nonverbal cues), in addition to hormone surges leading to heightened sensitivity, contribute to their capacity to recognize the nuances and signals embedded in their world. When asked, "What challenges do girls today face?" my teams openly discuss the double standard surrounding voice: "People think you are mean if you talk about how you really feel or if you disagree"; "If you speak up and say you want to take the lead on a project, people think you are bossy." The biggest insult of all is to be labeled a girl who "thinks she is all that and more." One eighth grader remarked, "The feminist movement is really not over; there is still a long way to go."

The fear of voicing thoughts or exhibiting negative emotions, and succumbing to "nice-girl syndrome," ultimately leads to inappropriate expression of affect. As I told my young daughter after she apologized for being mad at her brother, "It's okay to feel angry; it's a feeling. Everyone feels angry sometimes. It will go away." Unless, that is, it is left unexpressed and repressed. Then the consequences are huge.

Bullying is one example of how a female expresses her anger. A girl suppressing her emotions may engage in psychological warfare, attempting to destroy other girls' relationships, thus impacting her self-esteem and causing her to be alienated from her social milieu. Rather than openly express her own feelings appropriately, she subverts them. As a result, she never learns how to cope with negative feelings, setting herself up for many more situations when she may be overwhelmed and at a loss for how to be candid and authentic. Avoidance of aggression is an ineffective strategy to manage emotions. In fact, the intensity builds and eventually erupts given the lack of an appropriate outlet. Girls may attempt to express true feelings but then quickly rescind their words, texting *JK* (shorthand for "just kidding"); they aren't *really* joking, but they have a profound fear of the possible social consequences of saying anything that can be misconstrued as unpopular. More serious implications of distancing from emotions are a proclivity for depression (anger turned inward), disorders that serve to reestablish control (anorexia, bulimia, drug and alcohol use), or an overall sense of dissatisfaction and disengagement.

Women who refrain from exercising their voices are more likely to act out. Or else they expend enormous amounts of energy trying to fit in, keeping quiet instead of speaking up, and trying not to upset the proverbial applecart. As bystanders on the sidelines, they keep silent, even when they secretly wish they could be more courageous and more powerful. As a result, they become increasingly resentful.

In my experience, women who stay shackled by the status quo suppress their emotions and overanalyze their behavior. Blindly playing by other people's rules and squelching aspects of oneself come at a tremendous price to individual advancement, the viability of a business, and overall satisfaction in life. Women who do not use their power effectively become angry, disengaged, and inappropriately competitive. To counteract feeling powerless, they resort to micromanaging, withholding important information from others, and not working collaboratively. Or worse, some sabotage others and strike back with anger, earning themselves the label *bitch*.

Women who communicate fearlessly, exercising their power to speak their minds and aligning their voice with behavior according to beliefs, report the exact opposite. Their energy level is high because they do not deny aspects of themselves or struggle to be someone else. They don't bully and judge, either in the office or at the playground with other moms. Even their appearance exudes confidence—poised to handle the complexity of their professional and personal roles, refusing to play games, manipulate others, or ignore the realities of being a woman.

The Social Renegade

Social renegades are a spectrum of women from the outspoken firebrands to the quietly self-aware. Some have blazed trails and marched for women's equality; others have taken a stand in a subtler way, going up against the status quo in a company to embrace new thinking, or impacting corporate culture by purposefully creating a more inclusive, sustainable environment. Women and girls discover and express themselves in many ways; the key is providing opportunities for them to practice their communication skills early on, so they become ingrained and automatic.

Opportunities for girls to learn to leverage their strengths and find a style of communication that reflects their unique personalities are desperately needed. The goal is not to force quieter introverts to be gregarious and boisterous; it is to empower girls to stand up for what they believe in, express their views with strength and clarity, and experience being heard. They must be encouraged to communicate authentically, whether that's in an outspoken and extroverted manner or with quiet passion. When girls and women discover their "true" voices, regardless of decibel, they become equipped to challenge traditional thoughts and behavior, leading the way for others to follow suit, and opening doors of possibility to create change. The earlier girls are exposed to situations requiring them to communicate fearlessly, the more likely they are to mature into women who are unafraid to have a voice even when faced with resistance from others. Renée, one of my clients, was a prime example. She'd climbed the corporate ladder from an administrative position at a well-known global investment bank and securities trading firm to managing director of fixed income. Renée strongly believed the bank needed a women's network, as the men in her company tended to eclipse everyone else in visibility and networking. Despite knowing she would encounter apprehension and resistance from male managers, she made a case for her initiative and received backing from her department head. She assembled a small committee that spent months identifying specific goals and objectives based on need and interest; for a year and a half they sponsored networking events, hosted a lecture series featuring influential keynote speakers, developed a leadership-development mentorship program, spearheaded charity work, and connected women who didn't know one another despite having worked just a few desks apart for years. Her concept was wildly successful, and soon her model expanded to other areas of the investment firm; not long after that, branches from all over the world were calling to inquire about starting a chapter. A year later when she asked for a raise—something many female professionals are hesitant to do—her request was approved.

Stifling authentic voices also thwarts communication skills, compromising the chances of a girl or a woman being taken seriously by others. All along the age spectrum, females tend to soften their statements, qualifying statements with "I think" or inserting the proverbial "like" or "um," diluting the power of their ideas. They respond to questions with "I know this sounds silly, but . . ." or "I'm sure this isn't right, but . . ." These qualifiers are not outgrown as girls mature: a 2011 study found that female executives are four times more likely than men to be self-deprecating or to speak indirectly or apologetically when approaching difficult subjects with board members, dropping phrases like "I know it's not my turn, but . . ."[6] The lead researcher labeled this phenomenon "linguistic second-guessing."[7]

Girls often do not realize how frequently they do this until an Unleashed coach points it out. At times we might create a game, instructing girls to stop when they hear themselves say "like" or "um."

Girls pick up on this quickly and have fun counting the number of times the words are used, challenging themselves and their peers to avoid those two omnipresent fillers. Laughter ensues, but it leads to a larger discussion of how we position our words and the importance of powerful, fearless communication.

Unfortunately, this pattern continues as they grow older. Even the most successful women soften their communication, seeking consensus and validation, pausing to hear a response, and ending sentences with a question so they can morph their statements if needed. Rather than adopt a style that balances likability and authority, women use many more disclaimers than men, such as "I might be wrong" or "I'm sorry" in an effort to avoid criticism or conflict. Women's communication styles are typically more relationship focused compared to those of men, who tend to be goal and task oriented, thus appearing more results driven. Subconsciously, women adhere to the gender stereotypes and expectations that have been laid before them: girls and women are expected to be affectionate, emotional, and friendly and to communicate accordingly. Women use influential tactics such as inspiration, appealing to the emotional component of a decision, and consultation (partnering with others), or make a personal plea to those they are trying to get on board. Men tend to use these tactics with other men but also integrate logical arguments, referencing policies and procedures and creating incentives for others to agree with them.

Thus, a culture trap establishes a cyclic chain of events: stereotypes impact a woman's mind-set and ultimately her behavior, which then affects her communication style, leading to how she is perceived, her status and position in multiple settings, and the power and influence she might have. This is problematic as the cycle is perpetuated and rarely broken; women and girls continually confront external situations that place tremendous value on confidence, assertiveness, power, and influence (even if superficial) in order to be taken seriously and heard.

When coaching clients in leadership roles, I reinforce this concept, visibly outlining the chain of reactions that start with their own perceptions and unspoken bias. This might be in the form of thought-provoking questions, such as, "What are you afraid will happen if you stand up for something you believe in?" or "What are the consequences to you and others if you choose to stay silent, don't act on your ideas, or agree to do something you don't agree with?" One way to break the cycle of unproductive, fearful communication is to encourage women to reexamine their communication patterns, paying attention to how they impact others and what will be needed to overcome stereotypes and bias. Exercising her voice, being outspoken about her inspirations and opinions, and leveraging her power and influence are critical for a woman to begin unhinging society (both males and females) from the gender stereotypes that still exist. Fearless communication will prove critical in her career when she seeks a promotion or negotiates her salary, and personally, in making relationships, parenting, or personal choices. Regardless of what type of decision or situation a woman confronts, suppressing her voice, ideas, emotions, and opinions is dangerous. An idea may be viewed as irrational, crazy, or foolish, but the risks of staying silent outweigh those of speaking out. Women need to consider that being a social renegade can lead to innovative, effective, life-altering solutions.

A few years ago, I interviewed American diplomat Prudence Bushnell. Her visionary leadership as ambassador to Kenya and to Guatemala has been recognized through numerous Department of State awards, the Service to America Career Achievement medal, and three honorary doctoral degrees. It's not just governmental agencies that have taken notice: Glamour *magazine has included her in their Top Ten Women of the Year list and* Vanity Fair *featured her in its Hall of Fame.*

Pru recounted the following story to me: While she was serving as ambassador to Kenya in 1998, the US embassy in the capital city of Nairobi was bombed by Al Qaeda. This came after repeated complaints from her office over the US embassy compound's unsafe location and its lax security, which she believed left it vulnerable to an attack. Pru was knocked unconscious during the blast. (Forty-four embassy staff were killed in the bombing; five thousand people were injured.)

The US secretary of state initiated a visit to assess the damage; despite her injuries, Pru was concerned that her staff would be unable to accommodate the political clutter and media frenzy that would likely ensue. "First, I needed to get everyone situated and safe and install the proper measures in this volatile environment," she told me. "We couldn't overtax ourselves by preparing to receive the secretary of state when we needed to piece things back together." And so she spoke out, even though she knew the decision would be unpopular and perhaps even seen as insulting. In place of preparing for the visit, she quickly assembled a trustworthy operational team to help rebuild the community—which included her encouraging key players to "go home and cry, that we needed to take care of ourselves physically and spiritually if we were going to get through this." Pru was also criticized by the Kenyan press for refusing to include civilians in search-and-rescue operations; rather than sit by and allow the media to bad-mouth her, she took to state television to emphasize the dangers of permitting untrained searchers to wander the treacherous terrain and the need to protect key evidence.

Most people wouldn't speak up against political protocol or media scrutiny in such a chaotic situation. But Pru trusted her gut and was rewarded with incredible accolades from around the world. Her decision was highly regarded by her peers, she helped a nation heal from tragedy and trauma, and her voice helped get a serious situation in check quite quickly. She is now regarded as a poster child for leadership and disaster coordination.

At times I can sense that my girls are trying so desperately to be "good"; they sit quietly with their legs folded, assuming the role of passive listener. It is disheartening to witness a group of eighteen middle schoolers paralyzed by their perception of society's expectations (or by what they think an adult may expect), unable to act authentically, suppressing their intelligence, humor, and enthusiasm until given the signal that it is acceptable to express them. Providing a corrective learning experience, stretching them out of their comfort zones, I will comment, "It really is quiet in here. I am wondering what's on everyone's minds." Silence provides a false sense of security. Not one girl dares to speak; the room remains quiet.

So I invite them to mix things up a little bit, to be loud and playful, but in a way that feels safe for them. I will grab a yellow tennis ball and announce, "Let's play a game. I am going to throw this ball to someone. If it's you, when you catch it, you have to answer a question asked." Sample questions might include "What is something you like to do when you're not in school?" or "What is your favorite class?" "Once you answer," I say, "you have to follow my lead and toss the ball to someone else, asking your own question." I'm giving them permission to speak, literally putting the ball in their court.

Then, something powerful happens. After a few throws, some girls will miss the ball and start laughing; one might shout out a quick response and shoot the ball across the circle, while another coyly holds it for fifteen seconds while considering her next question. As the ball's momentum picks up, so do the girls' voices. When we are finished, I ask, "What was that like for you? It wasn't that hard, was it?" I know that for them, talking out loud and challenging one another might have felt incredibly daunting at first, but soon they see that they have, in fact, survived! As they nod in agreement, I notice a shift in their demeanor: they are realizing they have a voice that deserves to be heard; that their peers will not judge them; that it is actually exhilarating and rewarding to be able to speak out loud.

The paragraph above illustrates the unfolding and development of fearless communication. Initially, girls are reluctant to voice their opinions, and they hold back, waiting for permission to share their thoughts and ideas. Unconsciously, they remain highly vigilant for any signal that will confirm that their preconceived notions align with society's expectations of how girls and women communicate. But as they receive positive reinforcement and support from their family, teachers, and mentors, they venture out of their comfort zones, expressing themselves, using styles unique to their personalities and budding identities. Gradually, they discover their potential to be either the outspoken firebrand or the quiet leader who makes herself heard without fear of social alienation or withdrawal. After experimenting early on with powerful communication, challenging the status quo, and channeling negative emotions to create change, the girls will no doubt use these across the span of their adult lives. Partnering with girls in an effort to hone these skills will equip them with a solid template, affecting self-esteem, confidence, and respect. No longer will they shy away from being unique; they will embrace it.

⋰ *Power Boost* ⋱

1. When you observe girls who continuously use *like* and *um* in their conversations or end declarative statements with a question, call attention to their speech patterns. Most of the time, they are unaware of how frequently they use these qualifiers and can't fully grasp the impact this has on their message. You can make a game out of this, encouraging the girls to look out for anyone saying *like* or *um*. Often girls think it's funny to point it out and end up catching themselves when they do it. To address the ending of sentences questioningly, explore the reasons a girl might be unsure of herself. Does she do it to avoid being wrong? Does she desire consensus or approval from others before speaking her mind? Have her imagine the worst thing that might happen if she was either wrong or the lone voice in the room, reinforcing the notion that everyone makes mistakes. You may also want to discuss with her the consequences of remaining silent and how she would feel if she never expressed her opinions.

2. Regularly encourage girls to speak their minds and advocate for themselves. If your daughter brings home a B- on a paper but feels the grade isn't deserved, suggest that she schedule a meeting with her teacher and ask for feedback. She may feel more comfortable preparing for the conversation by role-playing with you beforehand, adopting the role of both herself and her teacher to gain perspective from each. As she becomes more skilled at advocating for

herself, she may begin to transfer this mind-set to all relationships in her life, including yours. Her questioning,
assertion, and even pushback will require you to maintain
an objective stance, not taking it personally. This may at
times feel stressful or like a never-ending battle, so it is
always best to avoid these interactions when you are too
tired to remain centered and calm.

3. Coach girls to articulate their messages in powerful, con-
   cise ways. Often girls circumvent the main point, adding
   extraneous details or providing a rationale for every piece
   of their story, diluting the meaning of their words. When
   I witness this pattern, I may say, "Tell me the same story
   in three sentences?" or "Try to hit the bull's-eye . . . what
   is it that you want to say?" I will explain the concept of an
   "elevator pitch" (being able to tell someone a story in the
   time it takes an elevator to go from the lobby to the tenth
   floor) and how most people have a short attention span.
   This technique helps the girls to be more direct in their
   communication.

Chapter 7

Sisterhood

*There is a special place in hell for women
who don't help other women.*

—Madeleine Albright

*F*or many of our Unleashed girls, the rescues are the driving force,
the days they look forward to throughout the entire twelve weeks
*and the incentive to engage in the program. At 9:45 a.m. on a Saturday
they arrive at our Unleashed office or one of the many dog-boarding
kennels that donate space, wearing their sweats or jeans, maybe topped
with their Unleashed T-shirts. (In addition to being showered with
puppy breath and licks on their faces, most of them will inevitably get
pooped and peed on.) Adult volunteers are on hand to check girls in
and encourage them to form small groups—one per expected puppy.
Each cluster is purposefully composed of girls from different schools or,
if from the same school, the volunteers make an effort to separate close
friends. Prior to attending a rescue, girls are prepared for participation, gaining an understanding of their role and responsibilities and
what the puppies will need after a long transport, so they can properly*

provide information to the foster families, who will arrive at the end of the socialization time for pickup.

Armed with wee-wee pads, bowls of food and water, tennis balls, and stuffed chew toys, the girls wait with bated breath for me to arrive with the new adoptees. These dogs have traveled from states where overpopulation is a problem and many animals are at risk of being euthanized. (The majority of the time, we are simultaneously rescuing one to two litters from South Carolina, North Carolina, Georgia, Kentucky, and West Virginia.) When I do arrive, structured chaos breaks out. The girls are instructed not to scream, keeping the atmosphere calm for frightened pups, and are reminded that all dogs need to keep four paws on the ground and are not to be picked up (after being in transport for hours, the puppies want to run and play and could easily jump out of a girl's hands and get injured).

When first assigned a puppy, a team takes it into an area they have designated as their socialization space, covering the floor with wee-wee pads and scattering a few toys. Girls surround each puppy and observe how it responds to being separated from its littermates. They attempt to engage the puppy in play, squeaking a toy, rolling a ball, or dangling a rope toy for the dog to grab on to for a game of tug-of-war. Sometimes a puppy wants to be cuddled and crawls into a lap; others chase a ball, looking back to see who might be running after them.

After a little while, girls fill bowls with water and take them back to their puppies to hydrate them. Once a puppy has enough water, girls are asked if their puppy is ready for food; if so, they head to a table, filling a bowl with an appropriate amount based on size and age. Rescue responsibilities also include cleaning up after their pups. Girls may balk at wiping up accidents but come to realize both the positive and negative aspects of taking care of a puppy eight to fourteen weeks old. After a few hours, girls share observations of the puppies' personalities so they can provide as much information as possible to the foster families who will soon arrive.

Unlike what happens during the school day—or in circles of grown women everywhere—there are no cliques, colors, or castes here. "Athletes," "A students," and "queen bees" work side by side, asking each other, "Can you watch Emmett for me while I grab some more water for him?" or "Geraldine won't stay still—she's running into the other circles! Please hold on to her while I get more paper towels." The girls are no longer conscious of their differences—or of themselves (there is no time to worry about hair and clothing when running after the canine equivalent of a rambunctious toddler). Nobody can guess which girl is from a public school and which girl has a $40,000 middle school tuition, or who is an eighth grader versus who was just in grade school last year. Popularity no longer matters; the greater purpose of rescuing and caring for animals and helping them adjust after a long drive to safety unites them all. This is Unleashed sisterhood at its finest. Witnessing this magical interlude always leaves me wondering, "Why can't our world function more like these girls?"

In 2012, a YouTube video featuring an Ohio high school track meet made the rounds. Runner Arden McMath stumbled on the thirty-two-hundred-meter course and fell just before reaching the finish line. What did rival Meghan Vogel do? Rather than race by, Vogel stopped and helped her up, slinging her fallen competitor's arm over her own shoulders and carrying her the final fifty meters—pushing her across the finish line ahead of herself.

That video went viral not only because it was heartwarming and emotional, but for a far more important reason: it displayed a relatively rare occurrence of empathy among young women. Sisterhood—the notion that "we are all in this together," regardless of age, ethnic background, religious belief, or generation—has become virtually obsolete; today's girls and women are devoid of a sense of community. Its absence is detrimental in a multitude of ways, its effects far-reaching.

Sisterhood is a unique interpersonal network that creates a common bond and attachment, fostering intimacy, connectedness, and camaraderie. Biologically and psychologically, women and girls are prone to seek, develop, and maintain relationships within a larger community. Females thrive in supportive environments that provide opportunities to express a wide spectrum of emotions, gain unconditional acceptance, and align with those who share their XX chromosomal constitution. Additionally, sisterhood galvanizes our world's females to organize around a cause and pool their resources for a common purpose. The energy can be electrifying.

Women throughout the nineteenth and twentieth centuries united to fight for voting rights, equality, reproductive freedom, and more, and a sense of sisterhood spread far and wide. For decades, feminism was the epitome of sisterhood, exemplifying what is possible when women and girls are not polarized or fragmented. These movements were successful because of their reliance on sisterhood: women of all ages, ethnicities, and socioeconomic backgrounds created a common platform, fueled by passion and commitment. However, the twenty-first century has yet to see a powerful collective wave bringing all females together for one cause. Devoid of these types of movements, emphasis is placed on the personal (an individual's own battle to have certain rights) versus a collective. With the strong desire for sisterhood left unsatisfied, cliques often develop to satisfy the quest for intimacy and serve as a substitute (albeit an unhealthy one) for a vibrant, powerful female community. Bullying—a modern-day social disease—sustains the integrity of the clique. Girls and women alike will alienate others, engage in psychological warfare, or destroy another female's relationships in order to preserve their own social status and rank within a tightly formed exclusive group.

Change will happen, but transformation requires revolution, a total overhaul of society, and, with it, large numbers of activists. Unleashed is my modern-day version of a feminist movement because I want our younger generation to experience the power of the collective, discard the superficial barriers and fences that segregate one from the other, reconnect with issues that affect all females, and refuse to take equality for granted.

Life can be daunting for adolescent girls. As I detailed earlier, in middle school, their brains are vastly transforming, coinciding with the rapid growth and development of their bodies. Self-discovery and increased awareness of others' expectations are paramount at this stage; the girls' perspective of the world morphs dramatically as they form relationships beyond the family; and the need for acceptance from, and socialization with, peers grows increasingly important. Compounding matters, girl-on-girl bullying has escalated to an unprecedented high—74 percent of eight-to-eleven-year-old students and 86 percent of twelve-to-fifteen-year-olds have witnessed or experienced teasing or bullying at school[1] . . . and the phenomenon is notoriously *underreported*. All of this is happening at a time when sisterhood is desperately needed. Each girl thinks *she's* the only one getting (or not getting) her period, *she's* the only one who feels awkward or misunderstood, *she's* the only one who occasionally feels left out or disliked. In the midst of physical, emotional, and social fluctuations, young women are in dire need of authentic, intimate, healthy female relationships in order to feel valued and respected as members of their community.

The power of Unleashed is in uniting diverse groups of girls and providing them with the opportunity to build strong, collaborative relationships with one another. Their passion for the injustices animals face becomes a common platform; puppy rescue is the "reality" that fuels their passion and motivates them to continue the more difficult work of activism and leadership: learning about themselves and themselves in relation to others, researching issues, and stepping out of their comfort zones (speaking in front of larger audiences; stating things that may be jarring or shocking; not being popular or being a nonconformist) to become agents of real change. Leveraging this highly charged emotional component unifies girls and builds a strong community.

The wisdom gained by sharing meaningful purpose, passion, and values shapes our girls' experience of authentic interpersonal relationships and their individual social identities. Rather than remain shackled to their own biases, stereotypes, and perceptions of others who are different (race, religion, socioeconomic status, ethnicity), the girls break down barriers and ignore social pressures that may once have segregated them into subgroups. Girls have an opportunity to dismantle the hidden underground world that often categorizes their social and emotional lives. In doing so, they are liberated, free to make relational choices versus following the mandates and social orders of their respective groups. Participants gradually start to identify themselves as "Unleashed girls," fostering a greater sense of community and sisterhood. They participate in open dialogues about the stereotypes with which they now struggle ("She is from a private school, so she must be mean and snotty"; "She is from a bad neighborhood; she must be tough") because the girls who have now become part of their intimate network do not fit these images. Without a doubt, puppies level the playing field, aiding in the development of a new reality for all girls regardless of race, ethnicity, school, or even appearance.

To be rooted is perhaps the most important and least recognized need of the human soul.

—Simone Weil

Unleashed is predicated on the "it takes a village" philosophy, building a scaffolding of sisterhood early on. This instills a deep understanding of what it means to have a shared experience, cultivating connections that enable the girls to create a shared social commitment. Unfortunately, in a society that places so much emphasis on individual achievement, young women do not have many opportunities to build a coalition or to experience the support of a team standing behind them. Unleashed becomes a network of influence for all of our girls, enabling them to connect with others they might never have encountered, access resources they need to accomplish their goals, and learn firsthand that sisterhood is indeed powerful.

I became good friends with girls who were about to start high school, and I was just finishing fifth grade! It taught me to keep my eyes open, to be open-minded about things like friends and life. They're doing the exact same thing you're doing—helping puppies, meeting potential owners—so you know you're not alone.

—Lacey, age ten

Honestly, I think of us as a family; like sisters. That's how close we became. At first, I thought I'd be alone. Now, we're all best friends, hanging out and making a change for dogs. It's not just about working with your closest friends—we also have this major thing in common, which is a passion for dogs. I learned that women like to fight for change, together.

—Zhu, age twelve

Enabling girls to belong to a strong, cohesive female community is one of Unleashed's most powerful outcomes. Although teammates enter the program as strangers, the intimacy and closeness that develop over twelve weeks is profound. Girls repeatedly refer to one another as "sisters," authentically expressing how meaningful these newly formed relationships are to them and how dependent they are on the continual support they receive, regardless of whether the issue is related to Unleashed or not. This experience is transformative for multiple reasons. During adolescence, girls need positive peer relationships that serve as a sounding board, a glimpse of reality when clarity is a bit distorted. These exchanges validate self worth and increase self-esteem while illuminating the fact that the struggles of being female are indeed universal. Research conducted by the Girl Scouts has found that middle school girls appreciate and grasp the advantages of belonging to an exclusively female group,[2] and Unleashed girls are no different. For many of them, this is their first allegiance to a close-knit group with a shared purpose and values other than their own family. As the end of the program nears, they experience fear of losing these intimate connections and sisterhood. However, unbeknownst to them, this template has been deeply embedded within them, so that each of our Unleashed girls can re-create this type of kinship throughout her life, knowing firsthand that positive female networks (noncliques) can and do exist.

The benefits of this enhanced sense of solidarity are far-reaching, touching every area of a girl's—or woman's—life, including her physical and mental well-being. Social connectedness has been linked with everything from enhanced immunity[3] to a bigger brain size.[4] In 2004, longevity expert Dan Buettner partnered with National Geographic to identify locations around the world where people lived not only longer, but quantifiably better. Individuals in these locales, dubbed blue zones—such as Sardinia, Italy; Okinawa, Japan; Loma Linda, California; and Nicoya, Costa Rica—reach the age of one hundred at rates ten times greater than in the United States as a whole.[5] Residents of these places share a number of healthy characteristics, among them eating plenty of vegetables, moving daily . . . and maintaining a tight social network. Okinawans consider their *moais*—groups of lifelong friends who act as social, emotional, and financial support networks—a key to longevity.[6] In Loma Linda, Adventists gather for potluck socials,[7] and Sardinians endure less stress by getting together daily to laugh with friends.

Friendships have profound effects on health, creating an impact that may be as significant as avoiding cigarettes. An extensive research review of 148 studies on the topic, conducted by researchers at Brigham Young University and the University of North Carolina at Chapel Hill, found that women and men with poor social connections had a 50 percent higher chance of dying compared to people with more substantial social ties—about the same mortality difference as seen between smokers and nonsmokers.[8] One theory: people who feel connected, be it to a few best friends or a group of them, have stronger immune systems than those who feel alone.[9] The effect starts early on. In one study, researchers measured the cortisol (stress hormone) levels of 103 fifth and sixth graders multiple times a day for four days. They found that when kids are confronted alone with a negative event, their cortisol levels rise, but when they face the same event alongside their best friend, no increase occurs.[10]

There is even evidence that sisterhood promotes advanced cognitive abilities and brain size; teamwork requires cooperation, negotiation, reciprocity, patience, and forgiveness—behaviors known to be fueled by complex decision-making.

"I saw such a transition in Gabby. Her teachers tell me she assumes

a lot more of a leadership role in her classes, and I've seen her take more initiative in her friendships. She used to wait to be chosen as a friend, but now she thinks about what she wants from friendships. She put some distance between herself and some unhealthy relationships and found the confidence to go out and make friends with several other girls in her social circle's outer orbit. Now they study and organize activities together. It's as if she's blossomed right before our eyes."
—Gabriela's mom

"I didn't have many friends in Unleashed when we began. After we worked in small groups for projects, like making signs, brainstorming ways to publicize our events, deciding on our projects, I started to make friends. I got to know this girl named Rishi. We went to the same school and were in the same grade, but we didn't know each other. But while planning Unleashed Leads Day, we got to know each other better, working together as a team, and we realized we should be really good friends. We both love Unleashed and dogs; we love to sing and have the same favorite music. That happened with some other girls, too. I met new friends from different grades and different schools. Unleashed taught me that friends are everywhere." —Marina

At a critical time in their development, adolescent girls, as Carol Gilligan identified in her research, lack the ability to detect "relational violations,"[11] taking full accountability for derailments within their friendships. What role does this dynamic play in the social landscape of our young females? There is a crossroads, a social impasse, where a girl struggles with relinquishing her "voice" (ideas, thoughts, opinions), sacrificing it purely with the intent to preserve her connection to others. She will remain in friendships even if she is being mistreated, bullied, or threatened with the termination of the relationship ("You must do this or . . ."). Inevitably, she will idealize relationships because objective evaluation of the friendship may force her to confront the truth—and the stakes (the risk of being alone) are much too high. However, without real connections and unconditional acceptance, girls are trapped in a matrix, searching for coping strategies for navigation.

Unleashed serves as a relational laboratory for girls to practice healthy interpersonal skills. This culture was custom-designed to undo what society has unknowingly established—an intricate, complex underground social milieu with implicit rules that instantaneously change without any rationale. From the onset, Unleashed participants formulate their own rules for how they will interact with one another, given the message that "every rule contributed by a member is equally important." Respect, agreeing to disagree, listening without judgment, and voicing an opinion are not only encouraged but applauded. Each team session is similar to being part of a naturalistic observational study: dyads and small groups develop, conflicts emerge, outspoken leaders take the floor, some hang back and watch before participating, and the unspoken language, if detected, is more powerful than the spoken. Unleashed provides direction, coaching, and support; disintegrates cliques by facilitating inclusion versus exclusion; instills conflict-resolution skills, allowing girls to voice their feelings in the moment; and provides an outlet for them to openly discuss anger, sadness, and aggression. It is different from any other environment the girls have experienced. My intentions are for Unleashed to be the prototype, the microcosm, that becomes their reality so that our younger generation will be able to differentiate between healthy and damaging relationships, embracing those that align with their needs, boost self-esteem, and prevent the intentional concealment of their true identities.

Portia and Aurora got in a major fight at a weekend community-service event—there was yelling, foot-stomping, and tears. Through eyewitness accounts and a dramatic recounting from Portia (Aurora had stormed out), I pieced together that Portia felt Aurora was controlling the communal booth the team had designed together—a carnival game where guests gave a donation and tossed balls through a hole to win a prize. I soon found Aurora outside on the street, crying, begging her father to take her home. Her father looked relieved as he spotted me approaching and gave us privacy. After acknowledging the hurt and disappointment she was feeling, I stretched her a bit, saying, "You are a huge animal activist, Aurora. You worked so hard to help the team design this day. Are you willing to let this conflict prevent you from creating change for a cause you care so deeply about?" She shook her head no as she stopped crying and allowed me to escort her back to the event and assign her to a different booth.

Come Monday, both girls attended their afternoon Unleashed session in high spirits, chatting together as if nothing had ever happened. "We need to talk about something that happened at Unleashed Leads Day," I said after the entire group had gathered in a circle and checked in. "Do we still need to?" Portia and Aurora protested. Girls this age— or any age, really—tend to dislike confrontation and would rather have pretended the argument never existed. "Yes, we have to talk about it," I explained. "In a relationship, there will be disagreements. In fact, the more intimate your friendship, the more conflict you will experience. You don't get in fights with people you don't care about. It's okay—you can recover from it and come out with a stronger connection." I coached them to walk through what had preceded their argument, the roles each one had, and their highly charged feelings. In front of fifteen of her peers, Portia admitted she could be stubborn; Aurora owned up to trying to control the game. They each took accountability and realized it is possible to have an honest conversation with another girl—even if it's difficult and uncomfortable—and still emerge friends.

Accepting and Embracing Conflict

Conflict is healthy, much to the chagrin of the majority of girls and women who perceive it as threatening a relationship's integrity. Resolved and managed appropriately, conflict actually strengthens intimacy, enhances negotiation and problem-solving skills, increases self-knowledge and empathy, and has the potential to generate innovative solutions. Yet, to a girl (or woman) immersed in conflict, the thought of voicing one's anger is reproachable. Confrontations are avoided at all costs; aggression is subverted or exhibited covertly; alliances are built so a group can coalesce to dismantle another; and there is an overriding fear of retaliation. But denial and hidden agendas are ineffective—skirting upsetting issues has the opposite effect, turning mild disagreements into festering emotional wounds, often leading to passive aggression, resentment, even depression.

It is a disservice to our younger females to turn the other cheek, subsequently reinforcing the divide, perpetuating the underground culture that subjugates girls' healthy socioemotional development. Girls and women can free themselves from the chains that bind their social interactions by mastering the art of communication, becoming comfortable with emotional expression, and learning to openly address issues that occur in friendships. Life is full of unavoidable confrontational situations; being able to come to a resolution, de-escalate tension, and negotiate are skills that can be utilized across many contexts, in work, family, and other social relationships. Hopefully, this will spark others to follow suit, disentangling other women from the treacherous jungle otherwise known as conflict.

At a relatively young age, Marina, Lacey, Gabrielle, Zhu, Portia, and Aurora are experiencing breakthroughs that many grown women spend years in therapy trying to achieve. Unleashed is a

sisterhood—a vibrant community where girls revel in commonalities, yet can embrace their differences; share coping strategies and
have unconditional support readily accessible to them. Consider
Avery, a girl who was reluctant to disclose sensitive family information, but revealed her parents' divorce during the Stand Up exercise.
Debriefing the experience, she confessed to the group, "I wanted
to lie. I wanted to stay seated. But I didn't. I stood up. It made me
feel like there wasn't something wrong with me and I realized I am
not alone." Avery is not alone. Girls of all ages fear being alienated;
not until they undergo a corrective experience, partaking in healthy
female-centric environments, does this anxiety begin to diminish.

In her landmark book, *Odd Girl Out: The Hidden Culture of Aggression in Girls*, Rachel Simmons explores the epidemic of girl-on-girl
bullying, going so far as to categorize school as "a social minefield."[12]
Sadly, she is not being hyperbolic: it has been estimated that a girl
is bullied every seven minutes.[13] The problem is not always as obvious as a victim being cornered on the playground or pushed into
her locker. With girls, the bully's intention is to inflict psychological
pain, which can be just as damaging (if not more so) and triggers
longer-lasting effects than physical attacks.[14] Girl bullies threaten
and scare their target in countless insidious ways. They gossip and
spread rumors, publicly humiliate other girls for being different, and
control friendships using blackmail. Some become ringleaders of
their cliques and ostracize specific individuals. (The average clique
comprises five girls: one leader, two henchmen who carry out her
orders, and two other minions who are typically more reserved but
participate because they themselves fear being excluded.) Then there
is the peril of simply being ignored: as Simmons writes, "There is no
gesture more devastating than the back turning away."[15]

Technological innovations such as texting, Facebook, Twitter, blogs, instant messaging, e-mail, and more have given birth to a whole new echelon of torment known as cyberbullying. That means rather than glaring at a girl in the cafeteria and then whispering something to a group of friends, a bully might electronically send false rumors about a peer to a hundred people, post insults on a girl's Facebook wall for everyone to read, or visit an interactive website such as Spring.me or Ask to anonymously provide an opinion about someone. Girls can, and do, demolish one another in cyberspace, causing pain, humiliation, and isolation. Bouncing back is not so simple—girls have to walk into school the following day and face their invisible enemies, trying to determine who targeted them and who joined in (one insult often leads to others). Her confidence and self-esteem deteriorate—evidence that the bully has accomplished her mission.

Quite often, bullies are the most popular girls in school, well liked by adults, too. A mother might say to her daughter, "Why can't you be more like Janie? She seems so nice," having no clue that Janie, despite her polished nails and sweet smile, is the perpetrator of her daughter's misery. Aggression is often hidden and discreet (except to the person on its receiving end), so adults can easily miss a bully's disguised signals. Teachers, principals, parents, and even camp counselors who sleep in the same bunks as their campers are often clueless as to the severity of a bully's behavior. "I had no idea" and "Jamie would never do such a thing" are commonly heard refrains. It is not uncommon for a bully to wage warfare on a close friend, morphing from confidante to aggressor, using personal information to pull the trigger.

Why do girls bully? That is the million-dollar question. My philosophy centers on the lack of power. When a girl (or grown woman) feels powerless, regardless of the underlying reason, she will seek opportunities to regain it, no matter what the circumstances. Most think bullies suffer from low self-esteem, but what is more often the case is that the tormentor feels powerless in some way, whether it is due to family conflicts, a changing body, unhappiness in her peer relationships, academic troubles, or feeling less than when it comes to her looks, weight, or material possessions. An unconscious attempt is made to reverse these feelings, transferring them onto others in an attempt to regain control. Societal shoulds and don'ts (girls *should* be nice; girls *should* act selflessly; girls *should* be thin and beautiful; good girls *don't* assert themselves; polite girls *don't* speak up) are perpetually woven into the fabric of a girl's existence, and this pressure to live up to somebody else's idea of perfection can also fuel bullying.

American culture reinforces the stereotype that girls should subvert and squelch their anger. Earlier, I mentioned Nice Girl Syndrome: the propensity to mask negative emotions such as anger, sadness, vulnerability, and frustration, and to hide behind the veneer of the perfect girl. What makes Nice Girl Syndrome so toxic is that it contributes to the misperception that aggression is a deviant emotion, rather than a universally experienced phenomenon. As a result, girls fail to develop a normal, healthy spectrum of affect and are left with a limited emotional repertoire. Their anger becomes masked and integrated into "people pleasing" behaviors, preserving their image of perfection. Teen girls insult one another and immediately rescind with "Just kidding!"—but in reality, they are not joking nor is it funny; the feelings behind their comments are true and honest and reflect a realistic urge to release their anger. Bullying offers a similar outlet—it is one more way to discharge negative emotions. Girls desperately try to subvert this negativity because they fear both losing key relationships and relinquishing control. Yet, try as they may, it is virtually impossible.

Our culture reinforces the Mean Girl phenomenon, flooding our youth with television shows such as *Pretty Little Liars*, gossip magazines highlighting female celebrity catfights, and teen literature such as *The Clique*, which centers on the drama within the exclusive social groups of teenage girls. Parents and schools ignore or minimize the severity of the syndrome; their view tends to be that these behaviors (eye rolling, exclusion, alienation, covert aggression) are expected and the norm when it comes to raising girls. In the absence of physical aggression, emotional bullying is considered less damaging. The severity and consequences of a bully's actions are dismissed and denied, and the Blame Game (faulting the target rather than the aggressor) is played.

Moreover, adults have a sense of learned helplessness. Many professionals who work with large groups of adolescent girls have little confidence that they can alter or rectify the bullying, nor do they receive training on how to manage confrontations. Coaches, camp counselors, and teachers alike become frustrated, feel stuck, and look for guidance on how to intervene. Girls grow hyperattuned to the messages they receive from their environment (a strength identified in chapter 5). Adult tolerance or lack of appropriate intervention perpetuates the cycle, reinforcing the notion that bullying is a normal part of adolescent girl development, thus increasing the likelihood that it will continue.

Providing girls at this age with the experience of being powerful; facilitating the expression and venting of anger, frustration, and sadness; dismantling Nice Girl Syndrome; providing girls with conflict resolution skills; promoting accountability; and strengthening their ability to advocate for themselves and others are just a few options that can alter these damaging patterns. In an effort to build our next generation of powerful females, Unleashed was purposely designed to build a strong social and emotional foundation for girls based on development and the cultural influences that impact them. Consequentially and unintentionally, the program functions as a proactive antibullying initiative. By building a strong sense of community, creating common ground, fostering respect and diversity, increasing confidence, and enabling girls to have a voice and use their power in a positive way, we inadvertently eradicate potential bullying behavior among our teams, who then champion this intolerance in their respective communities and schools. Among the teams, there are no queen bees, bystanders, henchmen, or cliques. Power is equally distributed and leadership is shared, depending on the day and the activity. Based on my hypothesis that bullying is largely due to imbalances of and unhealthy relationships with power, Unleashed's mission is to restore homeostasis. Girls need a safe, supportive environment fostering growth and development, enabling them to take risks, widen their horizons, gain independence, experience common purpose, and learn how to advocate for themselves and others. Our goal is to channel young adults' energy in a direction that is appropriate, semistructured, and engaging. Their experiencing themselves as change agents indirectly, but effectively, minimizes bullying as would-be aggressors increase their power and girls at risk of being targeted gain confidence and strength to stand in their own defense. Bystander Syndrome—when girls remain silent as they witness bullying out of fear that they could become the next target—is also impacted by our program. As girls learn to rise above resistance, to defy group think, and to speak out even when their opinion might be unpopular, it becomes less threatening for them to speak out than they previously imagined.

The dynamics among women are not dramatically different from those of middle school girls. Grown-up girls fall prey to their own form of middle school bullying commonly known as relational aggression, a sophisticated umbrella term for behaviors intended to damage or threaten another woman's reputation, career, or social standing. Fighting friends give each other the silent treatment rather than attempt a difficult conversation; working moms judge stay-at-home mothers and vice versa. The workplace morphs into middle school as colleagues gossip about coworkers, discount one another's contributions, block access to resources and equipment, scrutinize e-mails, or exclude certain individuals from after-work events.[16] It's what I call "mean girls, all grown-up."

Relational aggression is due to the lack of a strong sense of sisterhood and the vast inability to create a powerful, cohesive one. Regardless of age, girls and women remain ill prepared to support one another and resolve conflicts productively. Women fearful of destroying relationships remain silent; rather than have a difficult conversation, they indirectly send messages and hope they are detected. Resentment and anger build until they explode, typically over something that seems irrelevant, which only confuses the person on the receiving end. As mentioned in chapter 5, women develop their identities in the context of relationships and are driven by connection and a sense of belonging. In this way, relational aggression serves as retaliation while symbolizing a true lack of power.

Why do women sabotage each other, personally and professionally? In my consulting and coaching engagements, and from listening to hundreds of women of all ages, I have identified a distinct polarization. On one end of the spectrum lie women who are highly invested in aligning with and advancing other females; on the opposite side are those who alienate other women, dismiss the importance of women's initiatives and associations, and openly state that gender equality is irrelevant. The former group—those who engage with other women—typically demonstrate integrated power, according to my model. They act with self-awareness, insight, authenticity, and in accordance with their values while simultaneously collaborating and recognizing the importance of teamwork both in and out of the office. These are the women who champion new ideas, feel comfortable socializing and working with others who surpass their expertise and skill, and bask in satisfaction stemming from others' happiness and success. Externally, these women exude confidence, are centered, and take accountability without becoming defensive; they can showcase their strengths and report feeling connected, optimistic, and energized.

Those that hover on the other end of the spectrum, however, exhibit just the opposite. Women who are judgmental, undermine and sabotage others, and gain satisfaction from others' duress or failure typically lack power and suffer from low self-esteem. One of my theories is that women who tend to rigidly evaluate others are usually equally self-critical. How can they applaud and recognize the efforts of another woman when they fail to see the positive aspects of themselves?

What is so disheartening about relational aggression is that it perpetuates the image that women are weak, unable to manage others, or "too emotional." These "mean girl, all grown-up" behaviors are highly visible, causing conflict and stress among others. Men refer to conflicts among women as "catfights" and are both fascinated and frightened by the friction that plays out, leaving them hesitant to hire and promote female candidates, fearing emotions will pervade and disrupt the office. Relational aggression not only damages those entangled in the power play, it indirectly reverses progress, setting women back a few notches.

When women use relationships as weapons and enlist others in their fight, they are no better than the eighth-grade bully hell-bent on threatening and harassing other girls. It is exactly the same phenomenon, only the stakes are larger because it slows advancements in gender equality. The conundrum is that relationships are so essential to women, biologically, socially, and emotionally, yet sabotaging them is the first recourse of females who feel rejected, threatened, or hurt. Sisterhood is not a luxury—it is a necessity. Same-sex friendships provide emotional support in life and at work; feeling connected to a group offers the opportunity to feel validated and experience a sense of belonging, understanding, and appreciation. Consciously or unconsciously, women partake in similar activities: rallying and organizing around family, community, religion, or social issues they care about or even working for the same company. Being female is the one commonality that levels the playing field. If women continue to perpetuate this "mean girl, all grown-up" phenomenon, the consequences are huge: they thwart gender reformation, they provide a negative role model for younger generations, and they perpetuate stereotypes.

> I was never a fan of all-girl environments. In college, I played field hockey and found it difficult being on an all-woman team. There was so much emotion, a lot of cattiness and backstabbing. I was immature and wasn't able to develop appropriate relationships with the other girls. So I've always just said, "I get along better with guys."
>
> Then I began volunteering as a coach with Unleashed. After five years of teaching middle school, I had watched as girls grew less assertive and more submissive as they moved from sixth to eighth grade. I loved the idea of empowering them, of teaching them to be fierce and strong, to refuse to be stereotypically submissive. I, too, wanted to learn how to be assertive and work

well with other girls. At the time I became a coach, I was in a transition—my relationships with my friends seemed superficial and unsupportive. I wanted to restore my faith in women and girls again.

We've been transformed together. From the exercises we've done, I've learned how to approach people; that it's okay to say what you're feeling instead of acting passive-aggressively or backstabbing them. Now I can look back at my field hockey team and appreciate some of the advantages, like the fact that I had a built-in family when I arrived at college. I have a renewed sense of faith that women are strong and don't have to be continuously judgmental of and competitive with one another. It's taught me that a woman's intuition speaks volumes, and the best thing in life is to follow your heart. My own power to reach my full potential has been unleashed.

—Unleashed coach Brittany Miaritis, thirty

Brittany's experience mirrors those of her Unleashed charges. I remember asking seventh-grader Anastasia during her graduation panel, "What was the biggest change you saw in yourself?" Her reply: "They're my sisters. I never had a good relationship with a girl before. I used to only hang out with boys. I didn't trust girls—they're mean, they talk behind my back. They judge me. But now, I have girlfriends—friends I can trust." Unleashed was a corrective experience for Anastasia. Working in a team at rescues helped her realize that she *does* have something in common with other girls. She was vocal about girls' rights in our discussions (she was an adamant women's rights advocate), inspiring her team with statements like "No matter what people tell you, remember you are all beautiful. Don't let anyone tell you otherwise." Her honesty about being taunted at lunchtime for having too many male friends brought her teammates to her defense, and she soon became respected for her strong leadership. Anastasia's experience changed her dramatically, as she learned firsthand that girls are trustworthy, that same-sex friendships can be powerful and rewarding.

Just as the word *power* remains a dirty word among women, so, too, does *feminism*. The media's use of the derogatory term *feminazi*, combined with the actions of a few small militant groups of women, has made it the new F-word, as the majority of the public succumbs to the stereotype that feminists are lesbian man-haters hell-bent on destroying tradition. In a recent CBS poll, 70 percent of women said they do not consider themselves feminists; 17 percent deem the label an insult.[17]

Yet, when read the dictionary definition of a feminist ("someone who believes in the social, political, and economic equality of the sexes"), 65 percent of women identify themselves as feminists![18] Once they realize that being a feminist simply means you believe women and men should be treated equally—once they realize the F-word is positive and not negative—they are on board. But without a dictionary on hand, the radical, bra-burning, male-hating stigma remains. This ambivalence (supporting feminist goals but resisting the label) has given birth to what is being called the "I'm not a feminist but . . ." generation.[19]

Feminism and sisterhood are largely aligned, fundamentally similar. During the feminist movement's heyday, the word was the epitome of "sisterhood," exemplifying what is possible when women and girls are not polarized or fragmented. In the beginning, being female was the defining factor; there was no right or wrong way to be a feminist. Despite divergences in opinion and approach, the bond created in the promotion of equality across social, economic, and political landscapes was powerful. An increased sense of responsibility for fellow women and future generations trumped an individual's personal quest, although it was all entwined. When spoken at protests, rallies, and grassroots meetings, *I* signified *us*.

Historically, feminism has been divided into three waves. The first wave began in the 1830s, when women began demanding the right to vote. At one of the first women's rights conventions, in 1848, suffragists outlined their platform. Besides wanting the ability to vote, they expected civil liberties such as the opportunity to own property, receive an education, and have a career. Once legislation permitting women to vote passed in the 1920s, the first wave's sense of activism diminished.

Then, in the 1960s, icons such as Betty Friedan and Gloria Steinem reactivated the women's rights movement, lobbying for gender parity in the workplace and family; paving the way for progress in sexual equality, reproductive health, and abating violence against women. Before subsiding in the 1980s during the Reagan-Bush era, critical legislative and judicial milestones such as Title IX and *Roe v. Wade* had been achieved and legacies such as *The Feminine Mystique* and the National Organization for Women had been created.

The third wave—the most controversial era of the feminist movement—began in the early 1990s and continues to the current day. Much contention exists because there is a huge divide. Some women feel we are in a "postfeminist" age, basking in our foremothers' success at creating true equality; others see a continued need for feminism because of vast differences from men in pay, health care, economic stability, and career advancement (in addition to the problems faced by women across the globe such as human trafficking, slavery, mutilation, and absence of all human rights); a third set has no idea what feminism is and remains completely alienated from discussions.

Modern feminism continues to fight for equality in health and

child care, self-esteem, media portrayals, and sexuality, encompassing everything from Naomi Wolf's *Beauty Myth* to the film *Thelma
and Louise*; from *The Vagina Monologues* to Jennifer Baumgardner
and Amy Richards's *Manifesta: Young Women, Feminism, and the
Future*. Yet, it lacks a "movement" and a leader. Radical strands have
alienated the everyday woman from this historically groundbreaking revolution. Girls and young women who were raised to believe
they could do and have anything are now turning their backs on the
ism that changed their world. Intergenerational conflicts are widening the wedge in the solidarity among women. Younger generations,
beneficiaries of past activism, and the "wavers" who sacrificed, do
not see eye to eye and are as a result plagued by inertia.

Many seem eager to pronounce feminism dead and irrelevant, yet
its primary goals remain unachieved.[20] Women receive less pay for
the same work as men; access to contraception and a woman's right
to control her own body remain politically contested; and sexual harassment, rape, and human trafficking remain problematic. In third-
world countries, females are considered property and can be traded
for cattle, raped in war, or killed for not wearing a burka. In the
United States, when a woman speaks out, as Sandra Fluke did when
lobbying House Democrats for insurance coverage of contraception
in 2012, or when Katherine Fenton asked about equal pay during a
presidential debate the same year, she is branded a slut[21] and has her
privacy invaded to the point where she is forced into hiding.[22]

Despite that some feel the battle is over and believe we have settled
into a postfeminism moratorium, in truth our society is in dire need
of gender equality and reformation. Suffragists and second wavers
alike were not exclusively fighting for women's rights; much of their
activism was collapsed into the human rights movement, advocating for equal treatment for all. In fact, the first wavers' summit, held

in 1848, assembled as an abolitionist movement, and the second wavers were heavily active in the civil rights movement of the 1960s (women began to realize they were being treated unfairly when grassroots organizations gave them secretarial duties and saved the leadership roles for the men). The feminist revolution integrated social activism and women's rights and unified a diverse female community for a common cause; Unleashed is a modern-day version of the movement. Animal welfare and rights are the platform, bridging our girls together as one "village." Passion for the humane treatment of animals incites a sense of injustice, appealing to the empathy the girls feel toward a vulnerable animal. This serves as a springboard to civic engagement, as girls begin to see the synergies between the human and animal rights movements. Throughout the twelve weeks of the program, a multitude of issues are presented and discussed at great length, launching dialogues that explore how each symptom is a reflection of broader social dysfunction in America. For example, when teams delve into how the stereotypes about certain breeds of dogs invariably lead to euthanasia, dogfighting, and abuse, discussions about gender, race, and ethnic biases organically ensue.

> Everyone thinks Asian girls have to be smart, quiet, serious, and respectful. Sometimes even my parents expect me to act like a "good Asian girl" and listen to everything I am told and get straight As. It just isn't fair. I want to be me and act like me. I am funny and I love to laugh out loud. Why are people always so surprised by that?!
>
> —Shelby, age ten

Just as feminists have taken on multiple advocacy roles (protesting the Vietnam War, advocating for mental health-care reform and poverty reduction) in addition to their primary agenda of gender reformation, Unleashed begins as a call to action for animal rights and welfare but evolves into a modern-day feminist movement. As Unleashed girls collaborate to improve conditions for animals, giving rise to a sense of solidarity, they begin to think critically about the issues affecting them personally as young women. Regardless of what is scheduled for each team session, sooner or later the concepts of feminine identity and gender reform are brought up. A meeting that begins with a discussion of pit bulls and dogfighting could easily end with a team member saying, "People think we are equal but we still have a long way to go." My initial prompt of "Who is a powerful woman you look up to?" might eventually result in a comment along the lines of "We need to stand up for our rights and cannot let other women think it's over—we have to join together."

Branding Unleashed as "my modern version of a feminist movement" does not translate into launching a "wave," radically protesting Barbie dolls, or promoting sexuality as a tool to exercise power. My philosophy is this: a feminist movement is a mind-set reinforcing a need for solidarity among women and girls. It is a primer that fosters the belief that equality should prevail, that all individuals have the right to freedom and choices without judgment or annihilation, and that respect, empathy, and diversity of thought (the DNA of this paradigm) enable one to occasionally put aside the "personal" for the sake of a larger cause or purpose. This framework allows women to embrace being female without worrying about others' expectations, perceptions, or biases.

Unleashed propels our tweens to identify the type of girl they want to be, based on their own beliefs and values, not those established by society. They have the chance to define what being female means to them, to see that it is possible to embrace their prototypical female characteristics alongside those that might be considered stereotypically "male." Involvement in a sisterhood without borders or fences enables them to realize that they are not alone in their fight, deepening this connection and providing a sense of community.

Decades ago, simply being female was enough to foster cohesiveness and create change by "a power in numbers" paradigm. Now, women and girls—as evidenced by the current state of the feminist movement—are generationally siloed, isolated from other women who are not within their specific age cohort. Sadly, a chasm exists between women of different generations; they have drifted apart and have lost a sense of universal connection. In corporate environments, leaders grapple with how to narrow the gap between the younger and older employees. The feminists of the sixties and seventies lament, "We worked so hard but *they* [the younger generation] don't appreciate it," while our youth, feeling unburdened and unlimited, counter, "We don't need feminism anymore." Tension among baby boomers, Gen X-ers, and Millennials flare up due to differences in values, communication styles, and attitudes toward work and life. Research shows that 48 percent of all women experience some form of intergenerational conflict.[23] Metaphorically, the hierarchies and power struggles that exist resemble those of mothers and daughters. Defiance, rebellion, and dismissal are used by the younger set as a way to communicate, "I am independent; I don't need your advice. You don't understand me. Things are not like they were when you were my age." Older generations wield power and can occasionally abuse it, attempting to claim expert status, but then cannot fathom why their messages are being ignored.

This divide has serious consequences. Creating sustainable change requires representation of all women (and men) in the room; intergenerational sisterhood is a prerequisite for gender reform.

Unleashed organically bridges the gap between multiple generations, from adolescence to young adulthood, extending to women
in their mid to late sixties. From the board to committee members
and volunteers, age is irrelevant—each shares a defining purpose: a
deep commitment to the organization, a conviction to investing in
the next generation of powerful female change-makers, and a passion for creating impact. Throughout the organization, sisterhood
prevails as differences are put aside in the shared belief system. Multiple generations collaborate as a means to obtain the optimal result:
gender equality. Much as the founding feminist mothers waged war
against the injustices about which they cared deeply, our Unleashed
"wavers" are in a passionate battle. Some of the older women involved identify with the plight of a pubescent girl. Often I hear, "I
wish I had Unleashed when I was in middle school; maybe I would
not have experienced the struggles I did as a teen and in college. It
would have helped me tremendously" or "I want to be an Unleashed
girl; when are you developing Unleashed for adults?" Others long for
the sense of community associated with an all-female organization,
whether they work in a male-dominated field and it fills a void or
because they want to strengthen their own networks of influence.
As my research demonstrated, women wield power more effectively
when attached to a passion or cause; in its absence, they lose energy,
reevaluating their choices in order to regain it.

When outsiders learn how Unleashed operates as a female-
driven environment, skepticism lurks in most people's eyes. I often
hear shocking statements such as "There must be so much drama
at meetings!"; "How do you manage all that estrogen?"; and "You
need to add males to the mix to deflate the tension . . . women don't
act catty in front of men"—all packaged as helpful feedback. Yet sys-
tematically, this formula of intergenerational sisterhood does prove

highly effective. Board members serve as peer mentors and advisers to one another, offering guidance in their individual areas of expertise. Volunteers and committee members share resources that are non–Unleashed-related, admitting "we receive as much as we give back." Recently, a woman searching for new employment revealed that she brought up Unleashed during a job interview, successfully changing the tone of her responses from guarded to positive. She said that the interviewer, who did not initially show interest, quickly became her champion. This volunteer's words of wisdom to me after the interview were "You are not just investing in the next generation of powerful female change-makers . . . you are investing in the current ones, too."

Society fails to recognize the profound influence sisterhood has on its female population. Our culture has become a social land mine for girls and women alike as they struggle to make sense of the implicit rules, tentatively navigating the labyrinths. Men and boys are inducted into "good old boy" networks, gaining access to role models who champion their professional and social advancement. "Who you know, not what you know" is not solely an adage; it is an undeniable reality.

Today's Role-Model Deficit

Our young women are suffering from a role-model deficit.[24] Where are the "old girls' clubs"? In 2015, many women balk at women's initiatives as if they were a handicap, yet struggle to find a sponsor or advocate in the workforce. Research institutions repeatedly point to a dearth of accessible female role models across many industries (not just the male-dominated fields), and psychologists argue that young girls need positive female role models even more than boys. Glance quickly at the media and it is no wonder—one is inundated with sexualized female images pervading television, films, and magazines, ultimately shaping our girls' identities. Positive role models are difficult to come by. More than eight in ten girls say they are interested in interacting with successful women, yet 40 percent of them report they have not had the opportunity to do so during the last school year.[25] Girls need access to powerful sisterhoods that will positively influence their lives, teaching them that there is more to womanhood than emulating Kim Kardashian.

Evidence of girls' limited breadth of inspirational women is illuminated early on in Unleashed. When I ask a group, "Name a powerful woman you admire and why?" I might hear, "Rosa Parks for her bravery" or "Michelle Obama because she supports causes and her husband" or "What about Alice Paul, because she did a lot to allow women to have the right to vote?" But it takes the girls a long time to generate these examples. Typically, silence permeates the room as they attempt to formulate ideas. Despite my going first, sharing my own role models to spark their thoughts, the circle remains relatively quiet with just a few hands going up. Boys, if posed the same question, would invariably shout out visible athletes, politicians, prominent business leaders, and even relatives. But their female counterparts have two strikes against them: not only do they suffer from a dearth of accessible role models, leaving their mental Rolodexes blank, but they are apprehensive about stating their opinions for fear they will be challenged or criticized. On one occasion, I allowed a girl to cite a character in a book as her role model, with the understanding that in future sessions only real women or girls would be permitted as examples. What does that say that today's female youth have so few real-life role models that they must look to fictitious characters for inspiration?

Adolescent girls are at the crux of feminine identity development, facing the challenge of determining who they are and want to be, and experimenting with different aspects of themselves in an attempt to integrate interests, beliefs, and values. Research is an element of this process, as they observe women and peers whom they respect and admire, emulating the characteristics that resonate with them, ignoring those that don't. During this critical rite of passage, girls desperately need positive female role models who are unique, powerful, confident, and authentic. As the girls venture into unfamiliar territory, having unconditional support and acceptance will enable them to take the necessary risks to crystallize their personal power (based on my model discussed in chapter 4).

Women-girl partnerships are a core Unleashed priority, influencing our philosophy and methodology. These relationships facilitate intergenerational dialogues and provide an opportunity to experience meaningful inclusion. Aware of what girls this age need in order to increase self-efficacy (mastery) and competence, we aim to validate and engage them rather than alienate or judge them. Cocoaches, guest speakers, panel presenters, and I are heavily invested in the development of our Unleashed girls. Staff and volunteers are trained to encourage experimentation, respect their younger partners' ideas and opinions, and support them as needed while they develop and manage their projects. Whether working side by side at rescues, community events, Unleashed Leads Day, or in team sessions, women and girls collaborate without a hierarchy (the message "adults are part of the team, not the leaders" is continuously reinforced). Autonomy and independence, two developmental milestones of adolescence, are cultivated, giving rise to an increased sense of trust and connection as the girls recognize that the adults are truly attuned to their needs. Within our microcosm of an intergenerational sisterhood, girls repeatedly encounter accomplished, passionate women who are a testament to the girls' potential to become influential change-makers. No matter what their profession, be it an animal behaviorist, lawyer, doctor, veterinarian, teacher, social worker, or volunteer, these women are proof that passion can be channeled to create purpose and meaning—for a social cause as well as personal rewards. And whereas Rosa Parks and Oprah live in the history books and on TV, Unleashed role models are within reach.

When I use the term *role model* in Unleashed, it signifies the responsibility women have in their relationship with the girls, recognizing their necessity to be highly available, to act authentically, and to be cognizant of messages sent indirectly and directly. Girls this age are forever testing the adults in their lives for trustworthiness, commitment, and ability to handle difficult situations. How a woman manages her emotions, interacts with others, and expresses her beliefs is constantly being scrutinized under the microscopic lens of a young girl, so potential role models must possess self-insight, awareness, and emotional intelligence. I have been through this rigorous assessment myself on many occasions.

Pearl was a Harlem eighth grader known among school staff for manipulating girls into following her orders. During a team brainstorming session, she gathered a small clique at one end of the circle and was pressuring them to endorse her idea. The girls leading the brainstorm looked to me, frustrated, as if to ask, "Are you going to do something or does Pearl have power over everyone?" So I said, "Girls, our group is not abiding by the pact we made on day one to respect one another. Remember, Unleashed is self-selecting—you have chosen to join in order to make a change in something you are passionate about. Everyone needs to think about if they want to be here and how committed they are to the team." Pearl's clique turned back to rejoin the circle, and even Pearl herself looked surprised, but also smiled. To the team, I became a trustworthy source who would make sure the group stayed intact; to Pearl, it was a relief, in some strange way, to have an adult stand up to her. (Ironically, teens—especially those who wield power over others—often worry about spinning out of control when testing the waters and hope for an adult to step in and set boundaries.) Later, I acknowledged Pearl directly, saying, "You have a lot of power and are definitely a leader. I wonder if you can channel that into our animal rights and activism so we can make a huge change together?" For the remainder of the sessions, Pearl proved to be a valuable team player. During Check Out one afternoon, I asked, "What goal do you have for yourself to become even more powerful?" Her response: "Stay focused and be part of the group."

Adults often underestimate the acuity of a girl's attention to detail. Girls are hypervigilant, analyzing every aspect of a social interaction, from outward appearances to how an adult manages and responds to conflict and stress. One Saturday following a rescue event, a co-coach called to inform me that I had been the topic of conversation on the train ride home that day. One of our new foster parents had been complaining to me that her pup was, essentially, not cute enough. After pulling her aside and calmly discussing our fostering protocol, I outlined two options for her: forgo fostering and volunteer another time, or give the puppy a chance. She walked away angry, but returned fifteen minutes later, agreeing to take the pup.

Unbeknownst to me, I was being watched. Even though my girls had seemed intently preoccupied with five other puppies during this conversation, their radar detected the tension, and they shifted their attention to observe what was transpiring. My co-coach relayed that the girls were shocked that a foster parent would care about a puppy's looks and were impressed and relieved that I had stayed calm and taken the time to try to understand the woman, rather than just asking her to leave. Hearing this reinforced my belief that adults must recognize that we are constantly offering templates of behavior for our younger generation. "Actions speak louder than words" is indeed relevant.

These types of interactions are endless and invaluable. Girls and women have a reciprocal influence on one another, and the intergenerational gap narrows as they partner in civic engagement and social action. Despite the age differential, learning and mobilization are shared for a powerful sense of sisterhood.

The health of any community is largely dependent on the vitality of these cross-generational exchanges. Younger cohorts contribute a fresh outlook that often leads to innovation; adults can transfer their expertise and knowledge to a population that absorbs information like a sponge, poised to take action when given the chance. The Unleashed experience fosters an increase of self-awareness for all who participate. Our board and coaches repeatedly report how the girls serve as reverse role models; the life lessons they experience hold true for their more seasoned counterparts. Girls have presented fund-raising strategies to the board, empowering it to reevaluate its own plan; provided feedback to the coaches, provoking self-insight; and modeled contagious passion and motivation, inspiring volunteers to join the organization. Learning and development are not limited by age nor capped at one's eighteenth birthday. I have gained so much from working alongside my teenage team. Endless times they have imparted valuable lessons to me that I would never have gleaned without them.

Carla was a twenty-seven-year-old co-coach who tended to apolo-

gize for everything, even when she had done nothing wrong. The words I'm sorry peppered her speech—if I was digging through my bag for pens and said, "Oh, I don't have a pen," Carla would reflexively say, "I'm sorry," even though it was my responsibility to supply my own pen. Similar to the likes, ums, and other qualifiers that need to be extinguished from female speech, I'm sorry only detracted from the power of Carla's statements.

One day, I mentioned it in front of the group and Carla agreed, "You're right. I always do that." Then she said to the girls, "See, that's my issue. I need to work on not apologizing all the time." She asked for our support in correcting the habit, and gradually its frequency lessened. Whether she realized it or not, Carla was living out Unleashed's principle of creating the next generation of powerful female leaders—and serving as a fabulous role model in the process.

> The connections between and among women are the most feared, the most problematic, and the most potentially transforming force on the planet.
>
> —Adrienne Rich, poet

Sisterhood's fragmentation and the lack of a strong universal female community remains a twenty-first-century social epidemic. Gone are the days when women and girls united for a common cause, putting individual differences aside for a larger purpose. Fences and walls stand strong, isolating one subgroup from the next, serving as rigid barriers that are virtually impossible to cross. Metaphorically, these clusters of women and girls are sophisticated cliques, dividing mothers and daughters, races, religions, the middle and upper class from the economically disadvantaged, working moms from those who stay at home. Here lies the conundrum: female relationships are a centralizing force of a girl's and a woman's identity; they long for connection; they will sacrifice their voices and authenticity to be an integral part of a homogeneous community; and their self-esteem and confidence are largely dependent on peer acceptance. Yet, there is a void; there is no longer a larger movement that is powerful enough to permeate the barriers, fusing these diverse circles of women and girls.

Historically, women bonded by a shared purpose have been instrumental in the advancement of human rights and civil liberties, extending far beyond those of their own gender. Sisterhood is powerful; it ignites change. Society, seemingly ready for this reformation, is inadvertently braking, resisting acceleration. This paradox of equality has left men and women in our country in a gender moratorium. Despite the uproar over pay parity, legislative amendments, the scarcity of leadership roles available to women, stereotypes, and bias, feminism is demonized, polarized, and invisible.

The prevalence and rise of bullying, intergenerational conflict, cliques, relational aggression, and the quest for visible role models are all symptomatic of women's failure to create the "village" they so desperately crave and need. There is no time like the present to reframe these cries for help into a call to action, filling the cavernous void that has been left behind from previous organized feminist movements. My hope is that Unleashed's philosophy of sisterhood, collective activism, diversity, and common ground, combined with the exposure to positive role models and intergenerational synthesis, will inspire future thought leaders to forge inclusive coalitions, revive the inherent values of feminism, dismantle the barriers, and pave the way for others to do the same.

Power Boost

1. Familiarize yourself with the female icons in today's pop culture (actresses, models, musicians, television and film characters, toy figurines). Ask girls to name a few of the women and girls they notice more often in the media, and pose questions about their appearance, attitude, values, and behavior: "How do the media portray girls and women?" "What stereotypes have you personally experienced or observed?" Prepare yourself for a long discussion that may get heated. Girls this age have definite opinions and are waiting to have this conversation.

2. What does *feminism* mean to you? How would *you* define it? Do you consider yourself a feminist? Be open with teen girls about your stance and beliefs and engage them in a dialogue about feminism. Identify a few current issues that have been and may still be controversial (reproductive rights, gender bias, or equal pay) and ask about the girls' position on each. Introduce them to intriguing current books, television programs, and documentaries that highlight women throughout history and in the present. Traditional education omits many historic women from textbooks, leaving girls unaware of the influences females have had on our past and present culture.

3. Bullying can cause a great deal of anxiety for both adults and teens. Most teenage girls keep bullying hidden (whether they are the target or the aggressor). Give

girls permission to have an honest conversation about how others are treated. Take note of girls' social relationships (cliques, intimate friendships, how they spend their free time) and don't be afraid to probe if you notice her not wanting to attend school or excluding herself from parties or group plans. When girls are together, pay close attention to their behavior—how they speak to each other and their gestures. Zeroing in on who sits next to whom, eye rolling, tone of voice, and more will show you the power dynamics of a girl's social milieu. The most important piece is not to become unraveled when you discover the truth. Stay calm, offer a safe space to discuss the situation, and problem-solve together. Allow a girl to cry, become angry, or vent her emotions about conflict with peers. If you do observe a girl treating another inappropriately, discuss the impact she is having on others. This is a wonderful opportunity to build empathy, explore ways to express anger appropriately, and help develop negotiation and resolution skills. Girls this age need an adult to provide a "mirror" for them so they can look closely at their actions and the consequences of them.

Chapter 8

Change-Makers

*O*ne *of the most inspiring women I met while conducting my interviews was Jennifer Goodman Linn, a fearless role model. An award-winning motivational speaker and marketing-strategy consultant for some of the world's most successful brands, Jennifer was a driving force behind* SpongeBob SquarePants *and* Dora the Explorer *while serving as senior vice president of consumer marketing at Nickelodeon. She helped propel Walmart, Coca-Cola, Samsung, and LEGO as managing director of the Geppetto Group/WPP Group USA and oversaw marketing strategy and media and public relations for Ann Taylor and LOFT . . . all before her thirties. The Harvard MBA was power personified.*

Just after getting married, she began suffering from uncontrollable night sweats and high fevers. At age thirty-three, Jenn was diagnosed with sarcoma, a rare and often fatal form of cancer. Her doctors gave her fifty-fifty odds of beating the disease.

But she refused to stop working and became even more driven to succeed. She created her own website, You Fearless, where she did everything from market her motivational talks (with titles such as "Becoming Your Own Best Hope" and "Sucker Punched") to blogging about appearing in public for the first time without her wig. She founded Cycle for Survival, the most successful patient-led fundraising event in the 125-year history of Memorial Sloan Kettering Cancer Center . . . and was later accepted into a new medical trial that stemmed from research financed through those fund-raising efforts. She refused to let cancer defeat her; instead it caused her to reflect on life, evoking a determination to create change for both herself and others. "My cancer helped me realize how to overcome fear," she told me. "I came to realize that you carve out your own life, and that fear prevents you from doing what you want. With Cycle for Survival, I had to ask people for money—that was always a fear I'd had. But cancer and chemo taught me not to be afraid, so I was just practicing what I learned. Cancer was the best thing that ever happened to me. It taught me to manage people better, to show my vulnerability, and recognize the value of relationships."

Jenn is exemplary of a woman who leveraged assertive power despite adversity, who refused to let obstacles deter her, even life-threatening ones, because her vision of creating a new reality and defying the tried-and-true outweighed everything else. Like our Unleashed girls, who are motivated by a calling larger than themselves (animal rights), Jenn successfully integrated her triumvirate of power. She was willing to take risks, integrating her values, beliefs, life experiences, and internal and external resources in an effort to engage, educate, and advocate. By publicly showcasing her own fight and resiliency, featured throughout the media from CNN and the Today *show to* Self *magazine and the* Wall Street Journal, *she inspired countless others to continue their battle despite fear or apprehension.*

After more than six years of chemotherapy, multiple surgeries, and five relapses, Jenn lost her battle in July 2011. But her legacy of courage, advocacy, and embracing assertive power has survived.

> The good we secure for ourselves is precarious and uncertain until it is secured for all of us and incorporated into our common life.
>
> —Jane Addams

Women are notoriously effective social reformists, challenging archaic norms of society and advocating for the rights and well-being of others. As mentioned in chapter 7, feminists were not exclusively fighting for women's rights; their cause was civil liberty for all, and their agenda included the abolition of slavery, mental health care and education reform, and the eradication of poverty. Globally, women are widely recognized as powerful change-makers—so much so that the United Nations considers investment in girls a societal health indicator.[1] UNICEF has specifically tapped adolescent girls as being poised to make waves, calling them instrumental in accelerating the fight against everything from poverty to gender discrimination.[2] Not only do young women bring a fresh perspective and an intense commitment, but they come armed with a diverse and extensive web of community and family connections, positioning them to create and disseminate innovative solutions to all types of complex problems.[3] "There is clear and convincing evidence, amassed over the past two decades, that investing in girl-specific resources in the areas of education, health services, reproductive health, and financial literacy leads to better educated, safer, healthier, and economically powerful adolescent girls," the UN says. "This can lead to a substantially better future not just for the individual girls, but for their families, communities, and our world."[4]

Over the past few decades, certain change-makers stand out, paving the way for younger generations, asserting their power to make a difference not merely as a personal cause but as a political one (revamping the system). Advocating for gender equality in women's sports in the seventies, Billie Jean King opened the courts to future generations of players; today, Venus Williams and Maria Sharapova are considered two of the greatest athletes in the world, and Venus has followed in King's footsteps, fighting for gender pay equality.[5] Sally Ride was one of eight thousand people to answer a newspaper advertisement seeking space-program applicants, and in 1983 she bravely launched herself into space, becoming the first US woman to orbit the earth;[6] since then, forty-four more female American astronauts have flown in space.[7] In 1993, Erin Brockovich refused to back down from Pacific Gas and Electric and, despite having no formal legal education, was instrumental in bringing justice—and $333 million,[8] the largest settlement ever paid in a direct-action lawsuit in US history—to many needlessly sick families.

Society is dependent upon courageous advocates with a social agenda such as Linn, King, Ride, and Brockovich in order to advance and evolve. Without these types of change-makers, our culture remains stagnant, irrelevant, archaic, and ineffective. Simply asking the question "Why?" paves the way to innovation.[9]

Unleashed invests heavily in the younger generation—our future leaders, the ones who will reform society, confronting biases and problems within their communities, challenging the tried-and-true and precipitating change. Our mission is to implant the seeds of social justice and civic engagement so they can be used as the springboard to tackle the many issues these girls will be presented with in the future. Among them may be the next King, the next Ride, or the next Brockovich. Regardless, I am confident that Unleashed is equipping our girls with the knowledge and belief that they indeed have the power to create impact.

> People think middle school girls are loud, irresponsible, reckless. If you walk into a store with glass and porcelain, employees in the store kind of tense up, like they're worried we won't pay attention and might break something. In high school, you look older so people think you're more trustworthy, but as a middle schooler, you're kind of expected to mess up. They just need to give us a chance; we could surprise them. We all have very vivid imaginations, so we never run out of ideas. You can fix any problem with imagination. And no offense to women who work in offices, but they're in offices with the same people every day. I go to sleepaway camp with people from Israel and Britain; I take a theater class with people from other areas of New York and New Jersey, both public and private schools. That gives me a chance to share my perspectives—the more people who have a chance to listen to your ideas, the more who will remember what you have to say. Unleashed taught me that you shouldn't leave the problems of the world to adults. We can help, too.
>
> —Lacey, age ten

It is no coincidence that Unleashed's tagline is "Investing in the next generation of powerful female change-makers." Social justice and activism, civic engagement and responsibility, and leadership development are all purposely integrated into the program as a means to strengthen assertive power (one of the three components of the model illustrated in chapter 4). Females who demonstrate assertive power defy the status quo; they advocate, innovate, execute strategies aligned with personal philosophies, take risks, experiment, and create impact. Faced with a dearth of ethical powerful leaders, our country is in dire need of creating a pipeline, empowering and engaging its younger cohorts to address complex social problems. Adolescence is an ideal time to introduce the philosophies of change, social justice, and community action because, developmentally, girls' cognitive functioning is rapidly maturing, evoking increased critical thinking and the reevaluation of values and beliefs. Ethical and moral reasoning is now more complex, and their identity and sense of self is morphing. The ability to weigh evidence, examine alternatives, and question assumptions are the building blocks of change, and girls this age eagerly await an opportunity to attach passionately to a cause, so they can exercise their newly formed abilities.

Assertive power cannot be maximized without the assimilation of both personal and relational power (previously discussed in chapter 4). The emotional intelligence and self-awareness that have been cultivated, the sense of sisterhood and community, the strong communication skills—they all become synthesized, transforming the lives of Unleashed teens. The juncture where the triumvirate of power intersects is a pivotal point in the program, underscoring the true meaning of the Unleashed vision (investing in the next generation of female change-makers). The moment girls begin to simultaneously recognize their capacity to create impact, develop a deeper understanding of their personal power, and experience being an integral member of a cohesive community, they are prepared to tackle any issue. This is empowerment at its best. At such a vulnerable age, the capacity to improve someone's or something else's life moves them away from overevaluating themselves, decreasing the insecurity, halting the reverberating "Am I good enough?" question that haunts girls this age. Redirecting their energy and attention toward advocating for animal rights and welfare is highly advantageous for girls this age. This mastery provides them with confidence and fosters a model for change, enabling them to transfer this line of thinking to manage issues in their own lives. Whether that means voicing an opinion in class, confronting a bully, or ending a negative friendship, these girls are no longer wedded to the belief that change is impossible and out of their reach.

Adolescents who are active in civic life have been found to be less likely to use drugs, make more informed decisions about sex, and be better able to navigate their way through the web of challenges that will be encountered en route to adulthood.[10] The opportunity to "create knowledge rather than merely receive it," as UNICEF puts it, spikes a surge in confidence as they take an active role in their environment rather than the passive one typically ascribed to younger children.[11]

Girls crave opportunities that foster a sense of responsibility and initiative. They overwhelmingly report wanting to effect change and be considered role models, yet only one in five girls believes she has the key qualities to be a good leader.[12] Often I hear girls remark, "This is the first time an adult told me I can do something and actually allowed me to do it—all by myself," "Everyone tells me I am not old enough to get involved," or "I have great ideas and I don't know who will really listen to them." Girls this age feel stuck; they are eager to get involved and urgently want to be part of an initiative that takes them seriously. Investing in girls produces the greatest return in economic development, social progress, and public health,[13] yet programs for girls receive a dismal 7.5 percent of philanthropic dollars.[14]

The Unleashed model of social change is a psychological framework based largely on systems theory. Central to this ideology is the need to gain a deep understanding of the problem, evaluate the interconnected factors contributing to the issue, and design solutions taking all variables into account. Simple solutions do not exist; every issue must be perceived as complex, a sum of its multiple parts, each one influencing the others. This philosophy fosters a sense of responsibility within the change agents, empowering a committed group to shape their world, taking on a participatory role versus an observing one. Unleashed's social-change paradigm assumes that humans are a critical factor; change must emanate from individuals, incorporating their needs and using their strengths and resources to create a sustainable difference. Critical to this approach is a deep awareness of how change happens. Change involves both progression and regression (at times solutions are moving full speed ahead, and at other times they stop or reverse). Girls look at a problem happening in our society with a microscopic lens, analyzing information, deconstructing the issue to gain insight into the whys and hows, and reflecting about the roots. For instance, when addressing pet overpopulation or dogfighting, their first step is to become experts in these areas: *Why* is this happening in certain communities? Are overcrowded shelters the result of a lack of education? Are religious beliefs or limited finances thwarting population-control (spay and neuter) efforts? Why do people place dogs in rings and incite them to fight? Is this an outlet for their own violence and rage? What do these phenomena say about society on a deeper level and what are the consequences if continued? (For example, animal abusers might be destined to eventually hurt children or women; the inability to provide health care to animals could be considered a reflection of the country's overall health-care system.) Getting to the roots of these issues and making the connections, the girls hone their critical and logical thinking, their diagnostic and problem-solving skills. They adopt a visionary mind-set.

As part of understanding the "system" (the context of the problem), after identifying the possible roots, our Unleashed change-makers move to identify the consequences that will continue to plague society if the underlying causes are not eliminated. This search for meaning provides them with critical information needed to establish a vision, an idea for what they imagine to be possible, and a detailed plan to execute. Education is an integral component of our theory of change, so every project must incorporate an educational awareness campaign. Girls craft powerful messages and explore vehicles of communication and the impact spreading the word will have on their efforts to improve the identified problems. Our philosophy is that changing even one mind or provoking someone to question his or her existing beliefs contributes to influencing and shaping the world. As Oliver Wendell Holmes Jr. said, "A mind that is stretched by a new experience can never go back to its old dimensions."

Civic responsibility and engagement are integral aspects of Unleashed. My view is that community service—having direct contact with the issues and the population the girls are advocating for—provides them with the insight and the sense of purpose necessary to activate. Typically perceived as volunteerism, community service focuses on an issue's symptoms—serving meals at a soup kitchen, on a Saturday afternoon collecting cans and recyclables littering Central Park, or buying a product that donates a percentage of its sales to a charity are a few examples. Even though we want to get to the roots of the problem, pressing needs must be addressed while working toward the ultimate solution. Dogs are in imminent danger of being euthanized and cannot afford to wait two years for a community to embrace spaying and neutering to decrease the number of animals without homes. The final outcome is imperative, but not without integrating these short-term life-altering objectives. Rescues keep our girls connected to their cause, fueling their efforts, and the girls tackle the cause with a dual mind-set, brainstorming ways to help in the here and now (stuffing pillowcases to make warm beds for shelter dogs) while implementing projects that work toward sustainable change in the future (collecting signatures to outlaw puppy mills; educating their peers about dogfighting).

Sustainable change, the ultimate objective of Unleashed, is a complicated, gradual process requiring a shift in cultural values, belief systems, and traditions. When creating viable solutions, the most imperative goal is to gain insight into the why, looking deeply at the underlying structures that continue to reinforce the dysfunctional patterns and maintain the status quo. Each symptom must be conceptualized as part of a larger system, knowing full well that if one symptom disappears, another will take its place unless the infrastructure improves. For example, combating homelessness requires more than soup kitchens and temporary housing; what if the government looked deeply at those requiring assistance and offered job training or educational programs? Change needs to start with inquiry ("*Why are Americans starving on the street?*"), an understanding of the patterns and dynamics that exist in certain communities, and how an issue may mask others (such as outdated educational systems, socioeconomic disparities, and limited employment opportunities). Essentially, reformists have to challenge the current realities and generate new patterns.

Tremendous experiential learning is embedded in Unleashed as a means of empowering our girls to take on the role of social activists. To develop the fundamental skills necessary for community reform (critical thinking, observation, reflection and experimentation, problem-solving, decision-making, and project management), one must have an opportunity to practice and experiment with them. These competencies enhance learning and development and are highly correlated with overall achievement and preparation for the future. The abilities to map out a problem's constituents, identify who might be invested in maintaining the status quo, and formulate ways to break a cycle of behavior prepare our younger leaders for much more than improving the rights of animals.

During twelve weeks, Unleashed members pinpoint problems in animal welfare, contemplate the roots of these issues, select two that are most meaningful to them, brainstorm ways to heighten awareness and educate others, and then implement their ideas. Since launching Unleashed, teams of girls have chosen issues such as dogfighting, breed stereotyping, abuse, overpopulation, improving shelter conditions, banning prong collars, euthanasia, the banning of puppy mills, and pet stores. The first step is gaining expertise about an issue, then understanding why it continues to be a problem. Next, the girls outline the consequences of not addressing the root causes and then design a project to dismantle the symptoms, educate the public, and work toward creating sustainable change. When teams have identified puppy mills as a problem, they have discovered that there is little regulation by the government; that farmers who were once prosperous can no longer exist solely by growing produce; that the irresponsible sale and breeding of animals is lucrative; and that most people are not aware of how local puppy stores obtain animals. This has led to girls creating Adopt Don't Shop campaigns or using Unleashed puppies to dispel the stereotype that shelter dogs are all "mangy mutts."

Unleashed Leads Day is another example of a programwide change initiative. Teams work collaboratively to design and implement a day of community service that fosters education and provides an opportunity for others to get involved. Each team contributes two booths to the event and is responsible for their idea, obtaining supplies and resources, and creating a budget and submitting it to their coaches if additional funding is needed; they then manage the setup and execution of their activity. The objective is to engage others, make the experience enjoyable for guests, educate, and create a difference. Booths have included toy making for homeless pups; crafting quilts to cover cold cement shelter floors; decorating dog bowls; and making T-shirts to provide warmth and security to dogs during transport.

A large part of any social justice movement is community involvement—the art of bringing others along. Girls learn how to identify communities they belong to (academic, neighborhood, religious, extracurricular, and more), map out their circles of influence, engage them, and work toward broadening their network to increase the impact of their efforts. The relational power they utilize as a means to better the lives of animals is profound. They leave Unleashed cognizant of the sustainable difference made as a result of their commitment and activism, eager to continue their foray as change-makers. During one of the final sessions, girls are asked, "What's next? Now that you have tackled animal welfare, what other causes will you adopt?" I hear a wide range of responses, including "cancer," "the environment," "politics," and "education." These girls are invigorated to continue the journey, armed with knowledge, power, and a deep understanding of how to implement change initiatives.

While activism for social justice fosters change, it is always met with some degree of resistance—our natural response is to fear the unknown and to be skeptical of the results. People find comfort in a familiar environment and are hesitant to let go. The creation of new norms can be painstakingly long, and agents of social change are routinely challenged, sometimes mocked or even scorned. Early explorers who wanted to prove the world wasn't flat were considered brazen and out of their minds. Einstein's intelligence was doubted early on. Not surprisingly, in interviews I conducted with powerful women, each recalled a time when she was labeled oppositional, rebellious, defiant, different, or "unique." For example, ABC's Marlene Sanders was called a "bad mother" for working and was warned her son would suffer emotional problems as a result of her ambition. Then there was the lesbian executive who left her high-level marketing position after experiencing prejudice at work.

But despite the hardships, each scenario led to a breakthrough. Sanders is widely recognized as the first female Vietnam War correspondent and was the first woman to anchor a nightly newscast for a major network (ABC);[15] the singled-out marketing executive went on to spearhead MTV's Logo channel. Ideas that are perceived as crazy and illogical are often the ones that lead to breakthroughs in technology, science, and education. (As recently as twenty years ago, few would have predicted the reliance on smartphones, the influence of the Internet, or how something called Facebook would absolutely revolutionize our world!) When it comes to breaking new ground, a large part of the learning curve is being fully aware of the potential obstacles.

The first step in any successful change initiative is to somehow unfreeze the status quo by helping participants see how the current system is no longer viable, opening their eyes to other possibilities. Resistance is almost guaranteed. Throughout their lives, girls will experience the social pressure to think differently about an issue, be coerced to go along with the group's mentality, or have their ideas challenged or dismissed. How they manage the resistance or pushback is preparation for their future—consider viewing the middle school generation as budding social renegades and nonconformists. They must hear, "There are times when you may feel alone as you fight to make a difference. It can be frustrating when others don't see things the same way you do. Some people may get angry if they hear you fighting for causes they don't believe in. I can promise you that there will be times you struggle to stay true to your values and feel scared about being unpopular. But if you don't take those risks, nothing will ever change."

Girls this age need reassurance that falling flat on their faces or feeling as if they have failed is perfectly acceptable and expected; they need to be told they are strong enough to weather the storms. Using examples of historical activists such as Rosa Parks and, more recently, Malala Yousafzai, a sixteen-year-old Pakistani schoolgirl who dared to speak out against a ban on female education, you can reinforce the notion that every action may have consequences, but the girls should always trust themselves and their instincts, never compromising their values or beliefs, no matter what others say or think.

I volunteered to take pictures at Unleashed Leads Day and write about it for my school newspaper. I photographed the dogs before being rescued and after being groomed, so everyone could see how scared they looked beforehand—some of them didn't even know how to play with the toys!—and how happy they were after. I wanted to educate the other students. I also told my friends about how horrible puppy mills are, and how we rescue and help dogs escape from high-kill shelters. They learned about animal welfare because I educated them about it.

At Unleashed Leads Day, we each had a lot of responsibility to make sure our booths did well, to fund-raise and to answer guests' questions. Adults were there, but none of them "bossed" us around, telling us what to do. For me, having the responsibility made me feel important and like I was part of something. It also made me feel that I can make a difference. I think it took a lot of courage for me to ask people if I could take pictures of them with their dogs or to answer their questions.

I graduated knowing that I can be really powerful, that I can step out of my shell. Through Unleashed, I "got socialized" just like the puppies. Before the rescue, the dogs don't know anything about the real world—all they know is life inside a shelter. But once we rescue them, they discover there's so much more to explore—cars and buildings and people. They realize there's a whole other world out there.

—Tomiko, age eleven

Coming Together: Narrowing the Divide

Despite the progress made in diversifying our country, it still remains somewhat segregated, even in 2015. Political parties, race, religion, sexual orientation, socioeconomic status, regions of the country, and gender continue to divide citizens, polarizing and segmenting them into small factions. Judgments, bias, and hatred spread like wildfire. In politics, parties struggle to unite, and the nation bears the brunt as politicians fail to leverage their mutual positions—the desire for prosperity, safety, and happiness.

If our nation wants to create sustainable social change, it needs to draw multiple groups of people together in the same room, encouraging them to focus on their fundamental similarities, offering a wide range of perspectives on solving complex problems. Leveraging commonality is the key to breaking down barriers and formulating effective, richer solutions.

Unleashed is committed to promoting social equality, creating an environment of respect, unity, and humanity. I made a conscious decision to develop an organization that values diversity and sanctifies common ground and parity among girls and women. The sisterhood and solidarity lacking in our world inspired me to identify and utilize our commonalities rather than accentuate our differences. My instinct was that at their core, middle school girls, regardless of clique, class, or color, were more similar than different. Being female in a society wedded to gender stereotypes, facing changes in body, identity, and relationships, are experiences all teen girls confront despite socioeconomic factors. My instincts were on target. Despite encountering criticism and skepticism, I decided to use the passion for animal rights as an example for eradicating stereotypes, precon- ceived notions, and bias that each distinct group may have held for others. Now when I witness Pearl, a student attending a school with minimal resources, and Cora, a seventh grader at a competitive pri- vate school, interacting during a Saturday-morning rescue, I have no doubt that barriers have been dismantled and differences set aside for a common purpose. It is possible to mobilize the younger female generation with a call to action, facilitating a commitment to shared responsibility so collectively they will be able to influence the future, creating new social policies and norms.

> The world is a dangerous place, not because people do bad things
> but because of those who look on and do nothing.

> —Albert Einstein

Becoming an Un-bystander

In today's world, apathy combined with learned helplessness pre- vails. For decades, psychological research has examined this phe- nomenon of "social conformity." Human nature propels individuals to model the behavior of the group rather than act independently. The Bystander Effect occurs because the pressure to do something is diffused by the group. The mind-set is, if nobody else is getting involved, maybe I shouldn't either. Fearful of judgment, individuals are more concerned about demonstrating "socially acceptable behavior" rather than following their intuition. Social conformity is also heavily influenced by the presence of authority, whether it is a person who holds tremendous power or a system of accepted norms. In the 1960s, Dr. Stanley Milgram, inspired by the Eichmann trial (Adolf Eichmann was a war criminal convicted of ordering the death of millions of Jews in Nazi Germany),[16] was eager to gain an understanding of the influences of obedience and authority on conformity. In his famous social experiments, subjects were ordered to deliver shocks to others. He found that people were compliant if the instructions came from those perceived to be experts or leaders. His conclusion: ordinary people can become agents in destructive behavior because most do not possess the resources needed to resist. Interestingly enough, in the presence of rebellious peers, the level of "obedience" decreased in subjects; people are inclined to engage and abide with the norms established by their respective groups.

More recently, the field of psychology has been interested in heroism. Dr. Philip Zimbardo, a leading psychologist who once studied evil, malevolent behavior, has refocused his attention on identifying those attributes that constitute a hero or what I call the un-bystander (one willing to take a stand against an injustice). His organization, the Heroic Imagination Project, is empowering teens and adults alike to develop pro-social behavior and attitudes necessary to create positive change.[17] With a philosophy much like that of Unleashed, the project integrates individual skill development, emotional intelligence, and a shared experience to promote the advancement of these budding change-makers. Dr. Zimbardo's belief is that heroes are made, not born. Wise and effective habits of heroism can be learned, encouraged, modeled, and achieved by anyone at any point in life.

Many of us will be called upon at some point to choose whether to be heroic.[18] Human twin studies suggest that genes explain about 50 percent of altruistic tendencies;[19] the remaining part comes from cultural or social effects.

According to Robert F. Kennedy, moral courage is "the one essential, vital quality for those who seek to change a world that yields most painfully to change"—every time a person stands up for a thought or tries to help the greater good, she sends forth "a tiny ripple of hope," which ripples, in aggregate, to "build a current that can sweep down the mightiest walls of oppression and resistance."[20] Developing heroism (being an un-bystander) enhances the welfare of others. Moral and physical courage are needed for individuals to defy the status quo, trust intuition, and refuse to veer from their moral compass. Study after study shows that those who are concerned with the well-being of others are empathic; possess high levels of competence and confidence; have a strong moral compass; persist despite being afraid or reluctant; and are generally optimistic and resilient. These are the defining characteristics of the un-bystander.

Our Unleashed heroines are empowered with critical tools they will employ throughout their lives in an effort to be powerful change-makers. The assertive power, cultivated in the program, incorporates many of the same attributes normally defined as physical and moral courage. Advocacy, challenging the status quo, resiliency, risk taking, charisma, and empathy are all outcomes of the Unleashed philosophy and model of change. The primary objective of the program is to instill a sense of urgency to act on something that is personally meaningful, using the girls' resources and compassion to be socially responsible. They do so without fearing the repercussions of their actions or worrying about safeguarding their own "image." Regardless of the "what," I want them to graduate from Unleashed with a deep understanding of the "how." The ability to advocate evokes a sense of power as girls learn how to become ambassadors of a cause serving as *the* voice for either the issue or those affected by it. Presented with the harsh realities of what is happening to animals, the impingement of their rights and well-being, the girls' sense of personal responsibility is ignited. But their journey as reformists and change agents has only just begun. Transferring their wisdom to their communities, they will serve as role models, influencing others to reject social conformity and minimizing the Bystander Effect.

Pho was trying to answer a question I had asked during an after-school session, but Colleen kept talking over her. Pho looked to me with frustration in her eyes, so I said, "Everyone, let's stop for a second. Pho, what would you like to say to Colleen? It's okay—you can tell her how you feel."

"Okay," Pho answered, turning to Colleen. "I'm trying to say something and you keep talk, talk, talking." (She drove her statement home with the perfect "blah blah blah" talking-hand gesture.) Fifteen minutes later, Colleen repeated the same behavior with another team member, Jasmine. Immediately, Mimi, a physically small sixth grader, called her out: "Colleen, Pho just asked you to stop interrupting. Now you are doing it again with Jasmine. You really have to stop!" Exercising her newly discovered advocacy skills, Mimi stood up for both Pho and Jasmine, glancing at me with a satisfied look that reflected a sense of power and responsibility.

Never underestimate the power of a small group of committed people to change the world. In fact, it is the only thing that ever has.

—Margaret Mead

Middle school girls are looking for adults' permission, directly and indirectly, to move out of the passenger seat and into the driver's position—to speak out, form opinions, and take risks. Advocating for animal rights and fighting passionately for their cause gives girls the freedom to speak their mind—and inspire change—across many domains of their life. I would prefer to have an Unleashed girl as a teammate rather than most adults, due to the girls' passion, deep commitment, and insight. If we are ever going to reshape women's roles in society in a sustainable way, our younger generation of females must be provided with an opportunity to create change—for others and themselves, constructing a new blueprint of power. At graduation, I ask the girls in front of an audience, "What did you personally get out of this experience?" Without hesitation, girls respond, "Now I know I can do what an adult can do"; "I *know* I can make a difference"; "I am powerful"; and "I learned a lot about myself and what I want to do in the world." This is a far cry from the initial focus groups that shaped Unleashed, when Rebekah told me I was the first grown-up who "didn't tell us our ideas sucked" or when I heard "adults think we [middle school girls] are incapable or irresponsible."

> I was an outgoing girl before Unleashed, but I didn't love taking criticism, especially from my peers. I felt I was a leader sort of figure, but in elementary school, people used to tell me I was too bossy, so I thought a leadership program would help me turn that into a good thing.
>
> Unleashed changed me so much as a person. I take in criticism without letting it hurt me unnecessarily, and I've grown a new strategy to help me with difficult decisions: I think about who would be impacted by my choice, and how. I also have always had an insight into the troubles of the world,

and this experience has inspired me to become active with a website called change.org, where you can make and sign on-line petitions. My new main concern is a girl who has become famous by posting the most outrageous, racist things to her Twitter account, angering thousands of people all over the United States. I have posted the petition on Google+ and I'm working to getting her off of Twitter to stop her terrible rages.

Every week, I remember what I've done in Unleashed and I use that to propel me to do other things that will impact my-self, my peers, or even the world. I've learned that I am my own person, and that anyone who tries hard to improve and make a change can do that!

—Aurora, age eleven

Aurora epitomizes the trajectory of the Unleashed social change process. It is not enough for a social activist to take a stand against an injustice; the political transformation of a society is highly dependent on the personal development of each change agent. The meaningful experience of leveraging assertive power shapes a female's identity, self-confidence, values, and belief system, giving rise to an individual who is invested in the manifestation of positive change. In 2015, we are greatly in need of genuine heroes—not celebrities, but ones who demonstrate moral courage and are willing to advocate for others, refusing to conform to outdated social norms solely because they fear the consequences of being criticized, judged, and alienated. The emotionally intelligent, self-aware activist who seeks partnerships and alliances is better equipped to advance her cause.

History repeats itself. For decades, women have been at the forefront of social reformation; statistics validate that women are instrumental in the economic and social stability of a community as well as in fostering the overall health, welfare, and education of its members. The investments we make in the next generation of powerful female change-makers will produce better dividends than investments made on Wall Street. Our country needs the 51-percent-and-rising to tackle faulty foreign policies, economic insecurity, the increase in violence, the countless natural disasters resulting from our declining environmental health, and the domestic divide caused by extreme differences of opinion and beliefs. Adolescent girls are waiting for the opportunity to take action; they are willing to take risks, defy the status quo, and engage in a journey to contribute to reshaping their world into one that is just, humane, and mindful.

Power Boost

1. What do you feel passionate about? What issues would you change if you could? What organizations and/or causes resonate most with you and why? Evaluation of your level of civic engagement will be useful when you coach an adolescent to develop hers. What has gotten in the way of your taking a stand against an injustice you care deeply about? What would you need to begin creating change in your own community?

2. You have the power to shape our next generation of female change-makers! The first step is to ask her what causes she feels passionate about; encourage her to research these issues, learn more about organizations that advocate for the population she is interested in serving, and listen to her ideas or plans that interest her the most and support her desire to get involved. Based on your answers to Power Boost #1, your interests may be compatible with hers, providing an opportunity to partner and volunteer as a team. Keep in mind, her motivation will be stronger when she designs the plan of action and you participate in the project she outlines.

3. Cultivate budding un-bystanders by creating hypothetical ethical dilemmas and asking girls how they would respond. What would they do if they overheard a student at school being teased for her weight? How would they

respond to observing a parent chastising his son for wanting to buy a "girl toy"? These discussions are beneficial
in weighing the pros and cons of advocating for someone
else, guiding teens to define social responsibility for themselves, and ultimately fostering the Un-bystander Effect
and genuine heroism.

Chapter 9

Building Her Entourage

I always considered myself to be a team player, but now I realize how important it is to be able to work with other people in life. Say you became a doctor. You don't just decide what to do with your patient—you interact with nurses, surgeons, even the patients themselves. You can't just tell them what to do; you have to talk to them, work together with them. In Unleashed, we have to talk to the school principal and ask for permission to set up an assembly; when we hold adoption interviews at a pet store, we have to discuss with the owner about where we can set up and how long we can stay there. Before, no one in our school knew anything about animal welfare, or how easily it can be to find your voice and stand up for what you believe in. Now, the whole school knows, because we educated them. Now they know Unleashed means effort. It means not giving up. It means teamwork.

—Lacey, age ten

Whether it's on a large or small scale, impact cannot occur without engaging a community of invested individuals. There is undeniable strength in numbers: dramatic societal shifts and sustainable change do not happen without support from others.

A change-maker needs a strong network to help shape and morph ideas, with the ultimate goal of executing her mission. Susan B. Anthony, Gloria Steinem, Erin Brockovich, Billie Jean King—each of these groundbreakers recognized her potential to build a personal entourage, unifying individuals with a common platform and tapping into the resources of their circles of influence to make a difference.

Social capital is a sophisticated term that refers to both the actual and potential resources available to a person (or an organization) because of the person's relationships and social networks. It is largely based on the fundamental principles of the financial market—creating a diversified portfolio, gaining a return on investment, pursuing valued resources. West Virginian education official Lyda Hanifan is credited with defining the concept; in 1916, he was working to bring neighborhoods together to improve the school system and defined *social capital* as the "tangible assets that count for most things in the daily lives of people: namely good will, fellowship, sympathy and social intercourse among individuals and families who make up a social unit."[1]

What are the benefits of social connections extending beyond personal fulfillment? A diversified social network increases the ability of one to have influence, achieve a mission, or contribute to her world (professionally or personally). It gives a person a wider reach, enabling the accomplishment of goals, improving access to information and resources, and increasing the likelihood of obtaining economic security and success. Seventy percent of learning accomplished within an organization is done through relationships;[2] 75 percent of new business development or ventures gain financing through informal networking.[3] Researchers have even discovered a direct link between having a robust network and physical health.[4]

Individualism is a myth. For centuries, people have been and remain interconnected, part of many different social clusters. Social capital is a lifelong endeavor built on trust, respect, and mutual support. For it to be productive, there must be reciprocity, a give-and-take among members. Genuine investment in others is made without the expectation that it will immediately be returned. The well-known phrase *six degrees of separation* refers to the small-world phenomenon of everyone's being within reach of one another and has been validated by scientific and mathematical research.[5] These networks of influence are centered around "linchpins," connectors belonging to multiple diverse groups that cross-pollinate, sharing ideas, information, and contacts. My intention is for Unleashed to transform hundreds of girls into future linchpins, enabling them to secure a position of power within their various circles of influence.

Adolescent girls crave a sense of community (previously highlighted in chapter 7), often pursuing inappropriate, unhealthy relationships to feel as though they belong. From an early age, boys are socialized to create circles of influence, participating on teams and growing accustomed to working fluidly side by side with one another without apprehension. This early training equips them to reap tremendous social and professional benefits. Unfortunately, the majority of the girls today are not outfitted with the tools or knowledge necessary to develop a strong network of influence and resort to developing cliques versus a powerful entourage. Business transactions, decisions, and introductions are often made informally, based largely on the relationships and resources people have access to because of their connections (i.e., "It's who you know, not what you know"). So today's girls mature into women who struggle to compete with their male peers for business and promotions, with their networks that are weaker or less accessible.

My goal is to leverage the sisterhood created in the program, using it as a social nucleus for the girls to build upon, expanding their networks. Walk into any school Unleashed partners with, and the program is highly visible, known not only to students, teachers, and principals but the security guards and cafeteria and support staff. Our presence permeates the building, from DO YOU WANT TO MAKE A DIFFERENCE? posters plastering the hallways, stairwells, and elevators to photos of puppies used to advertise foster-home recruitment and adoptions. For most teams, school is their core community, the center of their social networks, the ideal platform for experimenting with bringing others along and tapping into the resources of their circles of influence. They engage others in their mission by presenting issues in homeroom, writing newspaper articles, speaking to reporters, organizing fund-raising bake sales, and meeting with the principal to negotiate placement on the school assembly calendar. Some have integrated an emotional pull to educate and increase involvement, creating a slide show of dogs with a musical sound track showing the rescued pups saved from the lists of high-kill shelters. Regardless of the action taken, approach, or style of engagement, Unleashed girls are indoctrinated into a philosophy that deems relational power the cornerstone of creating impact.

The Unleashed team experientially serves as a social capital laboratory, providing girls with the skills needed to develop diverse, powerful circles of influence. They establish a small, vibrant community with common ground, using shared experience as a bridge leading to increased connections and access to additional resources and relationships. Addressing societal issues is more complex than they might imagine; it is advantageous for this next generation of powerful female change-makers to recognize the merit in developing a social network. Tangible outcomes are obtained via interpersonal relationships; the human component plays a role in any type of personal or professional interaction.

Despite legislation and politically correct policies, segregation remains rampant in society, in social cliques, country clubs, exclusive neighborhoods, and schools. This "birds of a feather" mentality will ultimately prove to be a thorn in our nation's side if changing the world and challenging the status quo is on the horizon. Relational power and being socially savvy propel Unleashed girls to narrow the gaps among diverse groups, enabling them to be at the helm of sustainable progress and cutting-edge solutions. Social justice is the core aspect of our program, narrowing the divides among socioeconomic status, race, ethnicity, religion, or even clique. This expertise and appreciation of diversity will enable the girls to continuously build their networks, diversify their relationship portfolios, and increase their social capital as a means to creating impact for themselves and others. Human relationships and networks intrinsically outweigh stocks and bonds.

Helen Keller said, "Alone we can do so little; together we can do so much," and that sentiment is inherent in Unleashed's paradigm. Many life lessons are embedded in healthy teamwork. It enables one to establish a strong connection to others, feel part of something profound and meaningful, learn and acquire new abilities, share information, and receive support. My goal for each team is to challenge their preconceived ideas and past experiences of being part of a group (whether it was a clique, conforming to norms, or squelching their ideas and thoughts), shifting expectations to incorporate this new way of thinking. Rather than perceive teamwork as a sacrifice of a girl's individuality, I want to emphasize the positive attributes of collaboration, establishing a prototype girls can use as a model for the rest of their lives. Based on the principles of group dynamics and organizational development, the Unleashed model of a powerful circle of influence has seven critical components: clear goals; defined roles and responsibilities for each member; a shared vision; effective communication; trust; proactive conflict resolution; and collaboration.

1. A Clear Goal

Regardless of its function—a book club, the PTA, or the board of a Fortune 500 company—a team needs clear expectations and objectives: The purpose for a group's existence (what it was designed to accomplish) must be transparent. Development of a collective identity that all participants align with and relate to, in addition to identifying priorities, enables a circle of influence to thrive and remain intact. This blueprint shapes a team's interaction while providing an overarching plan of action so no one veers too far off course. Membership criteria are largely dependent on this identity; it enables others to determine if they want to participate and in what capacity.

Prior to launching a new team, Unleashed shares its vision publicly to an audience of girls attending the middle school site being launched: we are investing in the next generation of powerful female change-makers. Girls hear firsthand that Unleashed was designed as a result of believing in girls' power and a desire to inspire them to take action, have a voice, and make a difference in the world. Then, armed with information, they can make an educated decision about whether this cause resonates with them and if it makes sense to enroll.

Martin Luther King is a great example of a visionary who stated his objectives clearly and definitively: "I have a dream that one day this nation will rise up and live out the true meaning of its creed . . .

that all men are created equal." His clarity and passion rang through, activating and engaging a nation, regardless of race. Occupy Wall Street, on the other hand, illustrates how an obscure mission can derail a network. The 2012 movement repeatedly headlined national newspapers and magazines, and what began as a grassroots, New York City–based effort soon spread worldwide. Yet many political experts consider the experiment a failure. Despite the WE ARE THE 99% posters and dollar-bill blindfolds, much of the country—myself included—remained confused about its message, priorities, and call to action. It is difficult to enlist others in a group when its identity or purpose is ambiguous. When girls are designing presentations, they are stretched to formulate headlines that answer the questions "What is Unleashed?"; "What are the benefits?"; "What do girls get out of the program?" Not only does this prepare them to speak publicly and recruit the help of others, it reassures them that they have selected a program that is meaningful to them.

2. Transparent Roles and Responsibilities

Any system is comprised of hierarchies, roles, and alliances. These are both explicit (an executive leads her team; parents manage the development of their children) and implicit (the vice president of the company is responsible for promotions; Mom is viewed as the mediator), but each role shapes the dynamics of a group. Responsibilities can be assigned to members based on natural fit (the publicist will manage communications; the outgoing teacher will be a parent liaison) or an individual can select a function based on interest or passion. The "function" a woman adopts becomes largely tied to her identity and adds to her perceived value. In fact, people are often reluctant to relinquish a responsibility because they are so attached to

this perception of themselves. (When women transition into mana-
gerial roles, I have observed how difficult it is for them to delegate
day-to-day operations to their staff because it feels uncomfortable
and is experienced as a loss.)

Unleashed girls are repeatedly encouraged to think about their
role, their value proposition, and how they contribute to their circle.
Embarking on a journey to strengthen both their personal and relational power, they need to have a clear perspective on who they
are and how they impact others. Throughout the program, girls are
encouraged to experiment with skills they want to develop, get involved in those activities that inspire them, and take action when
compelled. Individuals are encouraged to take a stand, spearheading
projects they feel most attached to and want to own. But at the same
time, everyone is highly aware that each teammate plays a meaningful role in the larger scheme of things. Unleashed Leads Day is a
prime example. Even though teams operate only two booths, overall success is measured by the cumulative results and outcomes of
the event. If another team needs support, girls will offer to help; the
Unleashed culture promotes collaboration. What's most important is
that people are placed in positions where they will thrive and remain
motivated, deepening their overall sense of commitment.

3. Shared Vision . . . Shared Ownership

A strong, effective team is the sum of many parts working synergistically, with no single element taking precedence over the rest.
Individuals share ownership, revel in success together, and assume
collective accountability for overall setbacks and failures. In chapter 5, Facebook executive Carolyn Everson refused to blame an
employee for the error he made, emphatically telling upper manage-

ment, "It was *our* mistake." Similarly, Unleashed girls learn firsthand not to deflect responsibility when something goes awry: "We are all in this together" is a reverberating theme. This type of shared ownership strengthens accountability and deepens commitment, fueling the group to continue striving toward its defined goal. In this way, shared vision is like a kaleidoscope, with each team member's perspective and contributions transforming the outcome with her own special twist.

At puppy rescues, most girls will inevitably be faced with cleaning up "accidents"—wiping up messes, throwing away soiled wee-wee pads, and possibly getting peed or pooped on. It comes with the territory. "This stinks!" they giggle-shriek, glancing at me to see if I will step in. "Do we have to clean this up?"

"Yes, it does stink," I answer, "and, yes, you do have to clean it up. You can't have the perks of puppy time without the negatives. And remember, Unleashed puppies are your responsibility, not the adults'." Understanding firsthand that the puppies are "theirs" deepens their sense of ownership and their investment in the cause. It fuels their commitment and levels the playing field among teams, as everyone has a common stake in the organization's successes as well as its failures.

4. Communication

Humans are unique in personality, background, and perception. As a result, teams are complex networks, brimming with unpredictable relationships and interpersonal exchanges. Emotions can easily override logic, effect decision-making, and push the group off course.

Five of us were charged with creating a marketing strategy for an event. Two women on the team became closely aligned (sometimes duos and trios align within one team), and they developed a subsys-

tem within the larger group. A meeting had been scheduled to discuss our overall plan and develop ideas. Right before the meeting, the two women e-mailed the rest of the group, objecting to the meeting, claiming it was unnecessary. The number of messages flying back and forth quickly grew overwhelming, and I could sense the rest of the team holding back or replying in resignation—disappointed but not up for a fight. As this was happening, I was entering an Unleashed graduation ceremony. After listening to the insights of eighteen middle school girls, seeing their collective self-awareness, ability to align, and respect for one another, I walked out of the ceremony in disbelief, baffled that my girls could accomplish what a group of mature, successful women could not.

I e-mailed the team stating, "We committed to meet and I will definitely be there. I am looking forward to working together. I am leaving a team graduation feeling inspired that girls and women have the capacity to work wonders together and am confident that we can accomplish what our girls have done so beautifully—teamwork." Privately, I e-mailed one party of the duo, "I don't know if you realize the impact your actions are having. Your e-mails are coming through, one on top of the next, and it feels like an attack, like the rest of us are being tagteamed. It is very overwhelming." The woman was genuinely surprised and apologetic. "I didn't mean it that way!" she assured me. "I was just making our case. I didn't feel that meeting together made sense. I never meant to make everyone else feel badly."

This is a typical communication derailment: one party has one perspective and another has a contradicting view. But effective communication is like a dance: partners must tune in to one another, follow each other's moves, and avoid stepping on toes. Despite any discrepancies in views, strong communication requires all parties to be sensitive to the impact they have on one another, fully cognizant of the messages they are sending and of the potential responses that might be elicited. When a person has insight about her audience, it enables her to share opinions and ideas without alienating her network. Powerful communicators are active listeners, focusing on their audience's spoken and unspoken language. Not only is it important to listen to what has literally been said, but attention to body language (gestures, posture, eye contact), paraphrasing to ensure accuracy, and knowing when to introduce an idea are equally critical.

Unleashed's philosophy is grounded in the psychological theory of group dynamics. That means coaches act as orchestral conductors, paying attention to each musician while keeping their eye on the overall group. When strong personalities clash or a quieter girl needs additional floor time without interruption, a coach is on hand to navigate the interpersonal dynamics. In business, this role is adopted by the manager; in life, it could be a mother with her children or a friend who knows how to serve as an effective mediator.

5. Unconditional Respect and Trust

Trust is the foundation of all relationships. Within a network, trust promotes creativity and critical thinking, increases energy and passion, and enables people to challenge the status quo, evoking an overall sense of security. Environments that foster emotional safety are liberating: women are more willing to take risks, learn from their mistakes, take accountability, and act intuitively versus remaining guarded and inflexible. Self-respect is a meaningful variable in this equation: to trust others, a woman must be confident about her own reliability and ability to manage uncertainty. She must also be able to extend this same belief to others: "I am optimistic that others are as trustworthy as I am." The ability to rely on others accumulates over time, deepening with each positive experience. Actions speak louder than words; trust and respect evolve when others meet expectations, honor agreements, show commitment, share resources, and provide continual support.

Unleashed fosters this mutual understanding, reliability, and appreciation. From the onset, girls develop a set of rules that guide the behavior of their team, proactively accounting for each member's needs and comfort level; this is the working agreement that shapes the team's interaction, tone, and culture. The relational power (one facet of the integrative model of power) developed throughout the twelve weeks of Unleashed is largely predicated upon the respect and trust that emerge among the girls and coaches. Everyone has faith that "whatever is shared in Unleashed, stays in Unleashed."

By the end of the program, an inspiring level of trust exists among group members and coaches. This is reflected by the authenticity, intimacy, and degree of personal information shared in each session. Girls rely on one another to take on certain responsibilities and trust that the coaches and the staff are invested in their development and growth. The consistency that is woven into the policies and procedures of the organization has a profound effect on the teams. During one of the last sessions, in an exercise that reflects the confidence and security within the group, girls take turns providing and receiving feedback. It must be "specific," "relevant," and meant to increase a teammate's power and effectiveness as a leader. One member faces another and is asked to share the growth she has noticed and to encourage her partner to take further steps to continue her leadership journey. When I observe this exercise, it always validates for me that a group has solidified and transformed into a strong circle of influence.

6. Healthy Conflict Leads to Better Solutions

One of the Unleashed doctrine's most valuable tenets is "agree to disagree." Conflict and friction over ideas and thoughts ultimately produce smarter, more innovative solutions. Robust, passionate discussions, differences of opinions, and diversity of thought all contribute to successful outcomes. Ideally, a safe environment where no idea is considered bad or stupid offers people the chance to have difficult conversations without fear of repercussions. Leveraging similarities and starting with commonalities (what is agreed upon) rather than differences is a productive negotiation tactic, ultimately leading to compromise. Avoidance of conflict reflects an overall lack of trust and, time after time, leads to an unhealthy climate resulting in anger, frustration, and passive aggression. The more readily a group can resolve conflict, the more engaged and productive they become, and the better able they are to solve problems efficiently, remaining focused on what is most important.[6] Remember Portia and Aurora? Their clash over running a booth at Unleashed Leads Day left one of them in tears, nearly derailed their fund-raising event, *and* risked destroying their relationship. But after working through the discord, both girls emerged with greater insight into their personal Achilles' heels, leaving the team able to approach future events without the interference of interpersonal conflicts.

The concept of agreeing to disagree fosters a climate that embraces differences of opinion. This normalizes and encourages conflict, providing an opportunity for learning "in the moment." Unleashed functions as a forum for practicing negotiation, engaging in an open dialogue without censorship. This strengthens the girls' assertive power as they begin to defy the tried-and-true, revel in being unique, and resist conforming to the majority opinion. Cultivating diversity of thought normalizes disparity among a group, validating the fact that it is necessary and expected.

7. Collaboration

When a team collaborates, working together in perfect harmony, it creates beautiful music. Teamwork's value is often underestimated; the assumption is that everyone should be able to effortlessly function as a whole. On the contrary, for a team to align, the foundation of effective communication, empathy, a willingness to compromise, and a leadership style that establishes clear expectations and boundaries must be in place. Without synchronicity, it is impossible to achieve significant outcomes. Personal agendas and individual achievement can easily override the collective ones; limited levels of trust prevent delegation and shared ownership; silos emerge, dividing a network, diffusing its power. Without synchronicity, it is impossible to achieve significant outcomes.

Group dynamics and the principles of collaboration are largely integrated into the Unleashed program. Huge emphasis is placed on how the team is a microcosm of the girls' world, enabling them to see firsthand the impact they have on one another; how a group goal supersedes a personal one; and what can be accomplished when they unite for a common purpose. Leadership is not only about command and control; it involves knowing when to sit back, follow, or share power. The project-management component of the program enables girls to understand the scope of a large plan; identify resources needed; proactively assess possible obstacles; and take on roles and responsibilities based upon interest and talent. Executing a project from planning to implementation, Unleashed teams experientially learn how to delegate and collaborate, reveling in the sisterhood that emerges when working side by side.

Together and in alignment with one another, these seven principles comprise the fundamental characteristics of an Unleashed team. Being an integral participant in a group that innovates, overcomes difficult challenges, operates with minimal resources, and aspires to achieve significant results offers girls a working model for healthy teamwork. Each team is the nucleus of a girl's Unleashed social network, her primary circle of influence. Later, when girls are ready to execute their project plans, lead educational-awareness campaigns, and build momentum for their cause, the group serves as a reliable source of reassurance, guidance, and support. It is an incubator of ideas and launches them into the next phase of social-network construction: widening the breadth of connections, expanding their reach. For the Unleashed girls, their purpose for cultivating this network is to advocate for animal welfare and rights, engaging others in their mission. For others, the purpose may be to start a business, form a parenting group, or explore new career opportunities. Regardless of the goal, social capital is vital in a world that is largely dependent upon people and human nature to thrive.

It takes drive, courage, and an entrepreneurial mind-set to blaze new trails for a social cause, personal change, career transition, or any unfamiliar terrain. Charismatic leaders' ambition, determination, and confidence are contagious, inspiring masses to get involved. Although Unleashed consciously empowers the younger generation of female leaders to be linchpins—the connectors within their social milieu—countless others want to be engaged but are stuck when it comes to initiating. People *do* want to be an integral part of changing the world in small and large ways, but most do not see themselves as pioneers; they are waiting for others to enroll them. It is unfair to say that our citizens have checked out, unconcerned or even inhumane; society's problems seem so far-reaching, out of the realm of improvement, and so tremendously time-consuming that people feel hopeless and eventually accept (and expect) a downfall. If given an opportunity, however, people do rise to the occasion. Civic engagement is at its best when others become swept up in the movement.

In his book *Citizen You: Doing Your Part to Change the World,* Loews Hotels CEO Jonathan Tisch highlights a concept called active citizenship.[7] Just as chapter 8 differentiates between community service and change, the well-known philanthropist issues a call to action for a shift from onetime volunteer activities, such as ladling out soup at a homeless shelter, to sustained civic engagement, such as Bangladesh's Grameen Bank, an organization that funds small businesses for the rural poor based on trust rather than collateral. Similar to Unleashed, he also encourages people to examine the root causes of those social issues that inspire them.[8]

Citizen You is Tisch's effort to bring others along, shifting people's mind-set from hopelessness/helplessness to a belief that everyone is capable of making an impact, even in a small way. Tisch's movement aims to inspire everybody, regardless of financial status or position—truck drivers, stay-at-home moms, artists, scientists, company CEOs—to fulfill their civic duty by serving their own community.[9] Truck drivers can use their rigs to transport food and water to flood victims; stay-at-home moms can organize a neighborhood 5K to raise money and awareness for juvenile diabetes or a carnival to support local schools; artists can volunteer their time in schools with no funding for arts programs or offer painting classes at local elder-care centers. The underlying belief is that all citizens are valuable members and contribute largely to transform their respective communities.

Our younger female generation is up for Tisch's challenge. Over the past three years I have witnessed this phenomenon firsthand. Today's girls yearn to take action, contribute, create change, and inspire people of all generations. Unleashed girls past and present serve as ambassadors for the organization and revel in the role, sharing their vision and purpose to pique the interest of others. Opportunities for inspiration are limitless—while on vacation, at sleepaway camp, waiting in line at the bus stop. Girls report standing outside pet stores while visiting relatives to educate potential customers; sharing puppy-mill facts in their camp bunk while away for the summer; sitting around holiday dinner tables and informing family members about faulty legislation. Outreach within their own schools and neighborhoods during the program may include presenting to homeroom students about an issue or two, writing for their school newspaper, designing a newsletter, scheduling time with their school principal to gain buy-in to publicize an event, and speaking to the media. Identifying which communities are readily accessible to them, the "low-hanging fruit" is the start, gradually stretching their reach to include those who could possibly be enlisted to join their movement.

Every program cycle, girls design and implement Unleashed Leads Day. Throughout the day, activities run the gamut from the girls' inviting attendees to appeal to local politicians to amend legislation, to selling black-and-white cause bracelets emblazoned with our logo and the words CHANGE AGENT. Education is a large component of Unleashed Leads Day: our teams provide data and statistics about various animal-welfare issues and how they reflect larger social problems plaguing humans; and the girls introduce guests to adopters who provide first-person accounts of the influence rescue organizations have on humans and dogs alike. A welcome team greets guests, registers them, and offers name tags and a description of the day's agenda. Past the welcome table, a sales booth is stocked with Unleashed T-shirts, bracelets, and a donation box, along with a large cardboard thermometer visibly charting the girls' fund-raising progress. As donations roll in, girls call out, "We're halfway to our goal of one thousand dollars! Who wants to help us get to the next level so we can rescue more puppies?" Adjacent to the sales-and-donation team is an information booth stacked with flyers, pamphlets, and petitions awaiting signatures. Next, guests enter a huge room outfitted with a glass window that enables them to view puppies rescued from past years. Upstairs, colorful booths are decorated with signs such as CREATE A QUILT SQUARE—LET'S COVER CEMENT SHELTER FLOORS! One girl sits on the floor surrounded by kids and adults alike, everyone's lap covered with fabric strips being braided into homemade rope toys that will be sent to the rural shelters we serve. The air is vibrant with excitement and hope as attendees get to experience what it feels like to make a difference, even for just one day.

Leads Day is a pivotal event in the twelve-week curriculum, planned entirely by the girls. Even after nine Leads Days, I am still floored by the energy, passion, camaraderie, and teamwork that go into preparing for the event. It is a snapshot of the entire Unleashed process: creating change, personal transformation, sisterhood, girls using their voices, embracing their power, and now bringing others along. Younger and older generations of all races, religions, and economic standing band together for a common cause. It is not uncommon to see a Muslim eighth grader in a hijab high-fiving a fifth grader wearing a tank top and shorts, or an Upper East Side adult sitting cross-legged on the floor, decorating a pillowcase doggy bed alongside a bohemian animal-rights activist from the Lower East Side.

Leads Day is symbolic of the dynamic that occurs within our program: a diverse set of people coming together for a common purpose (to support animal rights and the empowerment of girls). Guests include program officers from national foundations assessing our organization, Unleashed board members curious to see the girls in action, and families who want their children to participate in community service. This event is the culmination of the girls' Unleashed experience; only now does their work become public and highly visible as they engage dozens of budding animal-rights supporters in the community and guide them to make a difference.

My responsibility for Unleashed Leads Day was to help guests make dog beds. Visitors, adopters, and other girls would come to our booth and draw on pillowcases with fabric markers and decorate them with sparkles, pretty landscapes, or loving messages. Then we'd stuff them with filler and donate them to shelters so dogs had somewhere warm and soft to sleep instead of on the cold, hard cement floor.

But that wasn't always the plan. Originally, our team was brainstorming ideas, and some of the older girls came up with the idea to make blankets for the dogs. Then someone else suggested making pillows, which would be easier, and I turned it into "Let's stuff pillowcases and make beds." Everyone added on to the idea—if we had been just one person, it never would have become such a great idea. It shows that teamwork can get you a long way.

For every problem, you have to come up with a solution. Maybe other people have that solution—it's not always about you. Working in a team lets everyone be very creative. You can look to others to inspire you and then help change things for a dog, a community, or yourself.

—Marina, age ten

Widening the scope of influence, adopting the role of a linchpin, and engaging others are processes not unfamiliar in corporations. Prior to launching any new leadership initiative, an individual or small group invested in the idea must adopt the role of champion or sponsor. For investment banker Renée from chapter 6, securing her department head's approval enabled her to move forward, assembling a committee as a think tank to advance and develop women in the firm. As other divisions and offices nationwide heard of the success, Renée broadened her reach, growing into a mammoth women's network of more than two hundred. By strategically aligning with someone in a visible position of power, she was able to recruit women with large networks and then prompt them to spread the word, taking her idea viral and shaping the lives of women in finance across the globe.

Similar dynamics were observed when a large, international Fortune 500 company received low scores on an annual employee-satisfaction survey. Employee engagement and morale were rapidly declining, and management wanted to know why. A team of Human Resources executives was enlisted to spearhead the change desperately needed. As a consultant, I was hired to qualitatively assess the underlying causes and recommend solutions. This core group and I designed focus groups to enable staff to engage in high-level conversations, empowering them to be experts and improve the work environment. Rather than just allowing people to vent and complain, the focus groups blossomed into proactive work sessions. Employees were inspired to make a difference and actively laid out what needed to be done: they wanted the company to maintain its identity despite mergers and acquisitions with other organizations, craved powerful leadership and management effectiveness as the company grew, and felt that incentives such as career growth were being overlooked. These circles wanted to be brought along to be part of the solution, not the problem. My recommendation to the HR team: form a leadership circle consisting of the focus group participants who were willing to make a larger time investment. "Your employees feel powerless, unmotivated, and undervalued," I explained. "A leadership initiative will allow them to continue the process that we began, continually providing feedback, keeping you in touch with the needs of the employees and empowering them to take necessary action." A year later, the team was passing the baton to others they had recruited to sit on various committees formed throughout the year. This was a true embodiment of bringing others along, creating impact, and broadening the reach to those individuals affected most.

The art of widening the range of influence and broadening the reach of a network includes strategically aligning and partnering with other circles. The world is a very different place from what it was even a decade ago because of advances in technology; the advent of social media sites such as Facebook and LinkedIn have dramatically changed the landscape. Now people can connect across the globe with just one click of a button. The paradigm shift is from "living in little boxes to living in networked societies. Boundaries are more permeable, interactions occur with diverse others, linkages switch between multiple networks, and hierarchies are flatter."[10] The

impact this transformation has on a community is huge; the weight
of its influence will not be recognized for decades to come. However,
in the midst of this shift, our younger generation must learn how
to function in a world vastly different from the one in which their
parents were raised. Not only must they experiment with leveraging
this new technology they will have to develop the savvy to navigate
the challenges of having the world at their fingertips. Direct experience, affiliating with an organization, and having access to various
partnership models enable the younger set to gain insight into the
process. For Unleashed girls, the animal-rescue community is a powerful network to emulate. Every day, dozens of e-mails circulate from
multiple list serves, pleading for someone to save an animal or two
or ten. Facebook posts and tags come from all over the country, from
shelter managers desperate to avoid euthanasia, from rescue groups
soliciting the donated services of drivers and pilots to transport animals to safety, and from hundreds of volunteers looking for foster
families or donations to pay the bills. No single person's contribution
is more or less valuable than that of the next. An overriding sense of
urgency fuels these rescuers (the majority of whom are women),[11]
and each individual leads her cadre of volunteers as they save thousands of lives. It is remarkable to witness animal rescue in action;
rescuers from across the nation—poor, wealthy, Democrats, Repub-
licans, urbanites, and those living in more rural settings—who have
never met in person, form relationships and alliances due to their
common passion.

   *One night I was perusing Craigslist, South Carolina, as I do occa-
sionally to save animals from horrific situations (the state is rife with
animal abuse and "free to a good home" pets often end up in the hands
of laboratories or as bait in dogfighting rings). I clicked on a link advertising yellow Labrador puppies and saw a group of six adorable*

Lab mixes being sold for $20 apiece. I quickly went on Facebook and privately messaged April, a woman in South Carolina whom I know from the rescue world. April urged me to call the Craigslist poster while she issued a plea to her friends who lived near the advertiser's location. In less than half an hour, April had recruited Holly, a mother of two young boys—one of whom was battling a serious illness. Holly and I friended one another on Facebook and established a plan: I would wire her money, and she would buy at least one of the puppies. By that evening, despite the difficulty she was facing with her son, Holly had one of the Labs safely in her house. The pup had been living in an overcrowded, dilapidated trailer park with no running water, housed in a Rubbermaid container with her siblings. Within two weeks, that puppy was transferred to April, who made sure it received proper medical care, and then to Unleashed's transporter, Beth. Beth drove it to NYC. When the puppy arrived, it was desperately ill and required two weeks of around-the-clock care. Knowing it would be time-consuming and stressful, I fostered the puppy, nursed her back to health, and fell madly in love with her. Now Rowan is part of our family.

Like April, Kristin, an economic-development professor and consultant by trade, advocates for animals in her free time, using her expertise to tackle community government in some of the poorer areas across the country. She focuses on one community at a time, investing hours and hours of time and energy as she recruits thousands of people for different tasks, including shelter building, petition distribution, supply collection, and animal rescue. Her approach has been to create a central, unified group in which everyone is a partner, then to leverage the group by having it go out and recruit others. Kristin, like our Unleashed girls, addresses the immediate problem while working to create sustainable change, putting systems and processes in place and creating best practices while modifying legislation. Under her leadership, I have seen small, shacklike shelters festering with illness and saddled with a huge percentage of euthanized animals transform into community centers filled with volunteers and appropriately paid managers, with drastically reduced disease and newly constructed pens and dog runs. Kristin could never do this single-handedly, but she inspires thousands across the country to get on board and take her vision live.

Stories of everyday heroes like April, Holly, and Kristin are limitless, each highlighting a different tale of one person or a small group bringing others along; leveraging their charisma, passion, and clear vision of what needs to be accomplished; and enabling the everyday citizen to make a difference in the world.

Unleashed would not exist without the diverse networks and relational power of a small group of determined women: our original think tank of twenty women convened monthly for six months, brainstorming, sharing resources, and bridging their respective circles of influence. A fellow working mom at my daughter's nursery school took Unleashed on as a pro bono client in her prominent law firm; a wine aficionado who was married to a friend's boss donated space for the launch event to raise initial funding; a graphic-artist friend of a friend designed the logo for free; an advertising firm created our website as a professional favor; and a technology consultant managed the various IT components free of charge for our first year. Over the past three years, the cumulative social capital—my own and the board's—has more than doubled its investment.

Hundreds of puppies would have been euthanized, abused, neglected, or lived a life of despair rather than living with a loving family. Teams of preadolescent girls, at a critical time in their development, would be struggling to find their voice, attempting to find the support and acceptance they needed as their identities crystal-lized. As change-makers throughout history—from those in ancient African cultures to Hillary Clinton—have said, "It takes a village!

Anne-Marie was an eighth grader who had been cyberbullied to the point where she was begging to transfer to a new school. At her first Unleashed session, she insisted on sitting next to me in the circle, her chair scooted a few feet away from those of any of her peers. Anne-Marie was bigger than her peers, tall, but minimized her height by hunching her shoulders, and spoke in a barely audible voice, staring at the floor rather than making eye contact.

About three weeks in, I was speaking with the girls about some puppy crates we needed and casually mentioned that some pet stores throw them away. After the session, I was walking down Eighth Av-enue and stopped into a local pet store to inquire. Imagine my shock when I discovered that Anne-Marie had beaten me to the punch! She was already inside, inquiring about donations. She had approached a salesperson and asked to speak with the store manager, to whom she introduced herself as a member of a girls' leadership group that was committed to rescuing puppies. By the time I entered the conversa-tion, Anne-Marie already had two puppy playpens and six crates in her hands, had begun discussing donated puppy food, and was asking for permission to post foster-home recruitment posters. Her progress in communication and solicitation skills absolutely blew me away. Anne-Marie also helped recruit one of her neighbors—a successful businesswoman named Sage—whom she invited to Unleashed Leads Day. Within a year, Sage had become the chair of our annual Dia-monds in the Ruff gala and was instrumental in the planning and execution of two benefits.

Social capital enables a leader to fulfill her mission, make valuable contributions, and affect society in profound ways. Anne-Marie leveraged her relational power, building a personal entourage. Using the skills she acquired as a member of an intimate, highly connected team, she transferred her expertise, expanding her reach. Recruiting Sage into the Unleashed community was a testament to her ability to network and garner resources to advance her cause.

Social capital has a ripple affect: one relationship leads to others, one circle of influence is bridged to another by a linchpin. Interpersonal relationships are undervalued in nearly every facet of life (business, friendships, family, community). Throughout *Brave Girls*, I have highlighted the genetic, emotional, and psychological constitution of the female that propels her to develop personal connections. Socially, she thrives when experiencing a sense of sisterhood and belonging; she plummets with the threat of alienation. Yet, there is a dearth of accessible female mentors; men are socialized to and benefit from establishing good-old-boy networks, while women minimize their relational skills, afraid they are "too feminine." (Paradoxically, the opposite holds true: those with more entrepreneurial networks achieve greater levels of success.) My philosophy is that by empowering girls at an earlier age to build a robust entourage, position themselves as linchpins, and experiment with bringing others along, they will recognize the intrinsic and extrinsic worth of relationships. It is virtually impossible to revolutionize or transform a community or business alone; to solely promote the merit of individual achievement and autonomy would be a disservice to our future female leaders.

Power Boost

1. Assess your own social capital: List the "communities" to which you belong, drawing a circle representing each one. Examples might include your neighborhood, the company you work for, a gym or yoga studio, your child's school, a religious affiliation, and more. Next to the circle, name three people who also belong to that particular community. Looking at your social capital map, draw a line connecting one circle to another if there is some connection (other than you). Ideally, your map will show that some circles are linked in your network, while others remain unconnected. This provides you with an opportunity to be a linchpin, the person who can make introductions to those in your network. This exercise helps you to see how many different communities you are involved in and how you might leverage them or add to them in the future depending on your goals (finding a new job, starting a book club, exploring child-care options, becoming active in a nonprofit organization).

2. Building and strengthening your social capital requires investing in others. Look at your circles and the people listed in each and think about how you can contribute to their success. You may want to touch base with a few people and set up a time to have coffee to learn more about their goals and how you could be useful. Positioning yourself as a linchpin, connecting people to resources and each other, sets the stage for others to be receptive to you in

the future. Do not offer to help solely to have your favor reciprocated later, but the saying "what you put into the world comes back to you" is indeed true. A lifestyle built on mutuality and reciprocity is a win-win for all.

3. Guide the girls in your life to complete the social-capital exercise you completed in Power Boost #1. Relationships are so critical to a teen girl, and assessing her various communities and affiliations can prove useful for her in many ways: (1) She can see the map of her connections and how they are interrelated (or not), which may help her make changes or validate her feelings of connection. (2) She can create experiments that will expand her circles or become more invested in the ones she currently has. (3) She can think about how she could benefit others, e.g., bringing groups of circles together for a common cause, introducing people where it makes sense. Open up a dialogue about the diversity of her circles, asking her, "Are most of your circles filled with people who are similar types?" "What do you notice about the groups you participate in?" "What did you learn from doing this?" "If you could change one or two things about your map, what would it be?" She may discover she would like to venture out of her comfort zone and meet new people, and now is the time to experiment.

Afterword

O ur society is approaching a critical crossroads in gender reformation and revolution. One option is to accept that we are
as close to equality as we will ever be, moving on to address other
issues plaguing our society. The alternative is to admit that 51 percent of our country's population is barricaded by archaic stereotypes
and norms interwoven into the fabric of our culture, denying them
opportunities and advancement. We don a false veneer, pretending
the glass ceiling has been shattered; meanwhile, too many men and
women have denounced feminism, and as the United States ampli-
fies its disapproval of the egregious treatment of women and girls
across the globe, it suppresses its own females. Daunting quantitative evidence reveals that, in 2015, American women suffer from pay
disparities, limited leadership roles, budget cuts threatening health
and financial stability, child care issues, a dearth of mentors, and the
absence of a strong, supportive community. Sadly, these hard facts
are only the tip of the iceberg. Over the past twelve years, my work
with hundreds of women and girls, combined with the research I
conducted, has given me access to the inner life of today's female
(psychologically, emotionally, cognitively, and socially), the external

and internal barriers she confronts, personally and professionally. Regardless of whether she is twelve or thirty-five, the underlying issues are identical; context is the only difference. Girls develop into women; women were once girls.

By no means do I want to paint a bleak picture! At the heart of every social-change movement lies the truth; it is the platform propelling us to act. After years of interviewing powerful women, formulating a model of power based on the research, and writing a book proposal only to receive numerous rejections from the publishing industry, I tried to convince myself to set my findings aside and focus on my leadership consulting firm. Professionally, I had carved out a niche for myself, was partnering with thought leaders in the industry, and was reaping the benefits. It would have been easy for me to continue growing my own company. Yet, in the months after those rejection letters poured in, something was nagging me. One, I couldn't stop thinking about the finding that "early influences shape a woman's perception of her power." Additionally, I felt as though I was disappointing the women I had interviewed because their stories would go untold. My doctoral dissertation, "Adolescent Female Identity Development: The Second Stage of Separation Individuation," had examined the psychological and physiological processes girls undergo to solidify their cultural, social, and gender identities during this critical time. My conclusions centered on the need to establish a theoretical framework specific to girls' development rather than comparing it to the trajectory of boys'. Other than Carol Gilligan, few developmental psychologists made the distinction. When I decided to apply the research findings to design a program, adolescents seemed to be a natural target population.

The gender revolution is far from over. My vision is of a society willing to invest in the next generation of powerful female change-makers, unhinging itself from gender biases and stereotypes, digging deep beneath the surface, reevaluating itself, and committing to sustainable change. Men and women must join forces, engaging in gender bilingual dialogues that propel us forward. Implementing solutions will not be easy; we will need to address the root causes, become an emotionally intelligent community, narrow the existing divides, and identify and leverage common purpose. We cannot depend on IQ and test scores to change the world; the fundamental building blocks such as education, government, health care, and economic development must be revamped.

> *Never be afraid to innovate.*
> *Embrace your power; you were meant to do great things*
>   *in the world.*
> *Lead by example.*
> *Invest in building a strong sense of community.*
> *Follow your moral compass, never veering from your values.*
> *You have the capacity to be a hero.*
> *Respect and promote diversity.*
> *Encourage others to leverage their passion so they, too,*
>   *can create impact.*

These are powerful tenets to live by . . . ones Unleashed girls are privy to for twelve weeks, shaping their perspective, becoming embedded in their lives. Not only do our girls live by these principles; they model them for people of all ages to follow suit. Like the lyrics to the popular 2013 song "Brave" by Sara Bareilles, they learn to "say what [they] wanna say, and let the words fall out." Slowly but surely they change the world—one person, one dog, and one community at a time, becoming braver and braver.

Unleashed is fueled by my strong belief in the power of women, in the unique perspective and talent they offer that is so urgently needed by society. I want the world to be different for girls and women, so I am investing in our future female leaders and change-makers. Planting these seeds and skills early in girls' development will impact their later lives, subsequently influencing the decades and centuries that lie ahead. Now is the time to create revolutionary change; to think outside the box and engage women of all generations in a common cause; to rebuild a sense of sisterhood and create a transformational journey for girls and women.

What started out for me as a determination to dig deeper beneath the surface ended up to be one of the greatest journeys of my career. What I have observed over these past few years has been remarkable and has changed my life in so many ways. I have seen incredible transformations—shy girls finding their voices; socially alienated girls developing strong, intimate relationships; outspoken girls learning when to lead and when to give others the floor. Teachers and principals have reported a massive difference in their students, too. It is not always easy being an Unleashed girl; they are often challenged, "Why dogs?" or "Why don't you include boys?" They learn to state their opinions aloud and encourage others to support them, taking risks along the way. More important, they learn to trust themselves, following their instincts, minds, and hearts.

As of today, more than three hundred girls at twelve schools and three community centers have graduated from Unleashed, and 450 puppies have been rescued and adopted. But Unleashed is about so much more than animal rescue; it is about power, passion, leadership, and community. These girls have had such an enormous influence on me; I am attached to each and every one of them. As I write their stories, I distinctly remember their words and hear their voices.

They think they are changing the trajectory of dogs' lives, but in reality the welfare of dogs fuels these girls to venture into experiences that dramatically transform their own.

Unleashed was fueled by my passion to take a stand for a cause that I cared deeply about, advocating for the power of women and girls. It is, and was, a cause larger than myself, rooted deep within my soul. Thank you for taking this Unleashed journey, experiencing the development of power through the lens of the girls and women highlighted in these chapters. My hope is that they have inspired you the same way they have me; that this book has provoked you to think about power, civic engagement, gender, and community from a different perspective, providing you with insights and confidence so you are prepared to embark on your own transformational journey.

Acknowledgments

I need to acknowledge so many people for supporting me throughout my journey pre- and postbook. First and foremost is my family—my children, Justin and Jordyn, who are the reason I do what I
do every day of my life. My love for them always keeps me on track
and inspires me to reach beyond what seems possible. Thank you to
my husband, Brian, who has helped me in good times and bad and
is always the voice of reason when I can't see past the ideal. I owe a
lot to the furriest members of our family—Griffin, Shane, Kaylee,
and Rowan, our Unleashed rescue pup—who provide constant unconditional love, acceptance, and affection.

I am forever in debt to the influences in my life who are no longer here: my grandparents Marion and Sol Berman and my aunt Felice
Rubin. Most important, my father, who was my biggest fan and would
have been the first in line to buy this book. His unconditional love and
support gave me the strength to be who I am, challenge the status quo,
and stay true to my values.

I am extremely thankful for being surrounded by loving, supportive
friends and family members who have shaped me at critical moments
of my life. Thank you to my family: my mom, brother, and sister, and all

the Radins and Drimers who witnessed those defining moments when I practiced defying the status quo. Thank you to my friends: Suzanne Gerla, Beth Sussman, Ellen Simpao, Christina delBalso, Wendy Straker, Brandl Frey, Jacquie Tractenberg, Kaitlyn Falk Wong, Brittany Miaritis, Heather Cortes, Erin Riggins, Leanne Gluck, Marissa Miller, Mindy Schwarz, Ayelet Berger, Alison Dreizen, Cathy Beluch, Lisa Dell, Billy Shaw, Adam Zipkin, Beth Hooper, Donna Larosa, Tim Williams, Lori Myers, Jodi Garner, Karen Hayduk, and Anton Palushaj.

Thank you to my leadership colleagues who have stretched me and taught me so much: Dr. Stew Friedman; my circle of peers, Dr. Tom Ellett, Harriet Joynes, Alan Fried, Shari Cohen, and Josette Jean Francoise; and my own mentor, coach, and friend Meryl Moritz. Thank you to Leslie Grossman for hiring me as a consultant for Women's Leadership Exchange, allowing me to continue my journey. I am forever grateful to Leslie for joining the original Unleashed board and remaining with us since.

A huge thank you to Stephen Pollan, for his limitless generosity, coaching me to write my original book proposal. I would also not have written this book without Elizabeth Greenberg, who introduced me to a friend in the publishing industry, ultimately connecting me to my agent, Laura Nolan. I have to thank Laura for believing in me, taking me under her wing, and guiding me every step of the way. Thanks to Leslie Goldman for editing my work. And of course a special thank-you to Sarah Durand, my editor at Atria Books, who resonated with the vision and purpose of this book and brought it to life. This book would not have existed without the countless women who were part of my original research, who invited me into their corner offices and homes, sharing their experiences of being powerful, their challenges, their philosophies, values, and vision. There are too many to list, but I want to thank Deborah Roberts, Carolyn Everson, Kit Taylor, Marlene

Sanders, Prudence Bushnell, Eugenia Ulasewicz, Cyma Zarghami, Samantha Ettus, Bonnie Leff, Jaki Scarcello, Meredith Wagner, Marjorie Margolies Mezvinsky, Lisa Gersh, Nancy Richards, Lisa Sherman, Lauren Merkin, Nancy Richards, Ann Tisch, Alison Dreizen, Erikya Tisch, Kylie Sachs, Betsy Arons, Venetia Kontogouris, Karen Dykstra, Suzy Reingold, Geri Wang, Sheila Hollis, Sheila Marcelo, Barbara Stanny, Mary Suhm, Becky Gregory, Susan Jurevics, Divya Gugnani, Amy Dorn Kopelan, Alisa Levin, Catherine Sullivan, Christine Chang, Laura Washington, Lee Ann Daly, Julie Pukas, Laura Nissenbaum Slabin, Sarah Eder, and Christine Millen—to name just a few!

For the last four years, the animal-rescue/dog-training community across the country has provided me with so much information and resources that I share with our girls. Thank you to Liz Keller, Jerry Gaskins (my rescue partner and friend), Jim McGonigal, Deborah Farhi, April Gooch, Julie Sinaw, Denise Karamitsos, Jen Nall, Kristin Kucsma, Melissa Morgan, Michael Ripinsky, Mike O'Neill, Naresh Jessani, Ayelet Blumberg, Shelby Semel, Maggie O'Neill, Rachel Hirschfeld, the Mayor's Alliance, and all of my fosters, adopters, and puppy-rescue volunteers from Unleashed.

The women (and men) who have supported me daily as part of my board (past and present), advisory board, and committees cannot be thanked enough! A special thank-you to Shelly Wimpfheimer. I feel blessed and honored to have her in my corner. And surrounded by other powerful women (and men) such as Marnie Omanoff, Eileen Sullivan, Alexis Nixon, Melissa Porter, Vanessa Kuehn, Elizabeth Ross, Cheryl Benton, Kristine Bryan, Susan Toffler, Christina Alfonso, Lofton Holder, Zev Greenfield, Beth Lacey, Janet Salazar, Hannah Larkin, Constance Peak, Jennifer Moe, Kristin Barbato, Phillippe Danielides, Kate McCabe, and Elyse Staff. The committee members who volunteer endless hours: Julia Bray, Deirdre Curran, Corey

Levine, Robin Johnson, Julie Yeagley, Leigh Pasqual, Bari Toor, Lindsay Hair, Heather Hynes, Kyle Avery, Mary Jo Keeble, Corey Levine, and Kerri O'Toole. Thank you to Dr. Kate Gibson, Melissa Jhunja, Dr. Vanessa Lobue, and Marg Brown, who worked with me to create the coach certification program and evaluation protocol. Thank you to Rachael Ray, John Hall, and Judy Keane for investing in Unleashed and supporting "her." A huge thank-you to my support staff and interns over the years: Jamie Kilburn, Patricia Long, and Elizabeth Young.

Last but definitely not least are the school principals who were the first to believe in us, Noni Thomas from Nightingale-Bamford and Meg Adams from Lab School, and Dr. Karen Ezra, the school psychologist at Poly Prep. But the biggest thank-you goes to hundreds of Unleashed girls for changing my life in so many ways, inspiring me to continue my vision to change the world. Years from now, I am confident our society will reap the benefits of your activism; you will be at the helm, leading others in an effort to change the world for generations to come.

Notes

Introduction

1 Kerry Robinson and Cristyn Davies, "Tomboys and Sissy Girls: Exploring Girls' Power, Agency and Female Relationships in Childhood through the Memories of Women," *Australasian Journal of Early Childhood* 35 (2010), accessed June 29, 2013, http://www.earlychildhoodaustralia.org.au /australian_journal_of_early_childhood/ajec_index_abstracts/tomboys _and_sissy_girls.html.

2 Sheryl Sandberg, *Lean In: Women, Work, and the Will to Lead* (New York: Alfred A. Knopf, 2013).

Chapter 1: "Who Am I?": The Girl Problem

1 Erik Erikson, *Identity: Youth and Crisis* (New York: W. W. Norton, 1968).

2 Afterschool Alliance, "America After 3PM: The Most In-Depth Study of How America's Children Spend Their Afternoons," *Afterschool Alliance*, 2009, accessed July 2, 2013, http://www.afterschoolalliance.org/AA3_Full _Report.pdf.

3 Deloitte, "Survey: Teens Feel Intense Pressure to Succeed—Even If It Means Cutting Ethical Corners," *Corporate Social Responsibility Newswire*, 2006, accessed July 2, 2013, http://www.csrwire.com/press_releases/21907 -Survey-Teens-Feel-Intense-Pressure-to-Succeed-Even-if-It-Means-Cutting-Ethical-Corners.

4 Girls Incorporated, "The Supergirl Dilemma: Girls Grapple with the Mounting Pressure of Expectations," Girls Inc., 2006, accessed July 2, 2013, http://www.girlsinc.org/supergirldilemma/.

5 Michael Gurian, *The Wonder of Girls: Understanding the Hidden Nature of Our Daughters* (New York: Atria Books, 2002).

6 Judy Schoenberg et al., "The Ten Emerging Truths," *New Directions for Girls 11–17*, 2002: accessed July 2, 2013, http://www.girlscouts.org/research /pdf/ten_truths.pdf.

7 Martha Brady, "Safe Spaces for Adolescent Girls," *Safe Space for Girls*, accessed July 2, 2013, http://www.popcouncil.org/pdfs/AYSRH/7.pdf.

8   Nielsen BookScan, 2012, Adult Non-Fiction, Self-Help category; and Bowker Market Research, 2012.

9   Ariane Hegewisch et al., "The Gender Wage Gap by Occupation," Institute for Women's Policy Research, 2012, accessed July 2, 2013, http://www.iwpr .org/publications/pubs/the-gender-wage-gap-by-occupation-1.

Chapter 2: Strengths and Resilience

1   P. A. Linley et al., "Positive Psychology: Past, Present, and (Possible) Future," *Journal of Positive Psychology* 1 (2006): 3–16, accessed July 7, 2013, http://personalpages.manchester.ac.uk/staff/alex.wood/positive .pdf.

2   University of Pennsylvania, "Positive Psychology Center," 2013, accessed July 6, 2013, http://www.ppc.sas.upenn.edu/index.html.

3   American Academy of Pediatrics, "Strength Based Approach," 2013, accessed July 6, 2013, http://www.aap.org/en-us/advocacy-and-policy/aap -health-initiatives/HALF-Implementation-Guide/communicating -with-families/pages/Strength-Based-Approach.aspx.

4   National Technical Assistance and Evaluation Center for Systems of Care, "An Individualized, Strengths-Based Approach in Public Child Welfare Driven Systems of Care," *A Closer Look*, 2008, accessed July 6, 2013, https://www.childwelfare.gov/pubs/acloserlook/strengthsbased/.

5   Asset-Based Community Development Institute, "Welcome to ABCD," 2009, accessed July 6, 2013, http://www.abcdinstitute.org/.

6   Martin E. P. Seligman et al., "Positive Education: Positive Psychology and Classroom Interventions," *Oxford Review of Education* 35 (2009), accessed July 6, 2013, http://www.tandfonline.com/doi/abs/10.1080 /03054980902934563#.Udop4z7wKnY.

7   Ron Kral, *Strategies That Work: Techniques for Solutions in the Schools* (Milwaukee: Brieg Family Therapy Center, 1989).

8   Marcus Buckingham and Donald O. Clifton, *Now, Discover Your Strengths* (New York: Free Press, 2001).

9   Madeline Heilman and Tyler Okimoto, "Why Are Women Penalized for Success at Male Tasks?: The Implied Communality Deficit," *Journal of Applied Psychology* 92 (2007): 81–92, accessed July 6, 2013, http://www.ncbi .nlm.nih.gov/pubmed/17227153.

10 Thomas M. Buescher et al., "Influences on Strategies Adolescents Use to Cope with Their Own Recognized Talents" (paper presented at the Biennial Meeting of the Society for Research in Child Development, Baltimore, MD, April 23–26, 1987).

11 Betty A. Walker et al., "A Developmental Investigation of the Lives of Gifted Women," *Gifted Child Quarterly* 36 (1992): 201–6, accessed July 6, 2013, http://gcq.sagepub.com/content/36/4/201.abstract.

12 Daniel Pink, *A Whole New Mind: Why Right-Brainers Will Rule the Future* (New York: Penguin, 2005).

13 Ibid.

14 Andrew Delbanco, *The Real American Dream: A Meditation on Hope* (Cambridge, MA: Harvard University Press, 1999).

15 Hilary M. Lips, "The Gender Gap in Possible Selves: Divergence of Academic Self-Views among High School and University Students," *Sex Roles* 50 (2004), accessed July 6, 2013, http://geoff.rey.angelfire.com/res/papers /LipsHM.pdf.

16 Abraham Maslow, *Eupsychian Management: A Journal* (Homewood, IL: Dorsey Press, 1965).

17 Accenture, "Women Leaders and Resilience: Perspectives from the C-Suite," *International Women's Day 2010 Global Research Results*, 2010, accessed July 6, 2013, http://www.accenture.com/SiteCollection Documents/PDF/Accenture_Womens_Research_Women_Leaders_and _Resilience3.pdf.

18 Barbara A. Morrongiello and Tess Dawber, "Mothers' Responses to Sons and Daughters Engaging in Injury-Risk Behaviors on a Playground: Implications for Sex Differences in Injury Rates," *Journal of Experimental Child Psychology* 76 (2000), accessed July 6, 2013, http://www.science direct.com/science/article/pii/S0022096500925724.

19 Martin E. P. Seligman, *Learned Optimism: How to Change Your Mind and Your Life* (New York: Free Press, 1990).

20 Ibid.

21 Victor Frankl, *Man's Search for Meaning* (Boston: Beacon Press Books, 1959).

22 Princess Mathilde of Belgium, "Adult Responsibility: Listen to Adolescent Voices," *The State of the World's Children 2011: Adolescence: An Age of Opportunity*, 2011, accessed July 6, 2013, http://www.unicef.org/sowc2011 /princessmathilde.php.

Chapter 3: Social-Emotional Intelligence

1 Daniel Goleman, *Emotional Intelligence: Why It Can Matter More Than IQ* (New York: Bantam Books, 1995).

2 Karen F. Stone and Harold Q. Dillehunt, "Self Science: The Subject Is Me," 1978, accessed July 2, 2013, http://www.eric.ed.gov/ERICWebPortal /search/detailmini.jsp?_nfpb=true&_&ERICExtSearch_SearchValue_0 =ED165056&ERICExtSearch_SearchType_0=no&accno=ED165056.

3 R. P. Weissberg et al., "A New Conceptual Framework for Establishing School-Based Social Competence Promotion Programs," in *Primary Prevention and Promotion in the Schools* (Newbury Park, CA: Sage, 1989).

4 Maurice J. Elias et al., *Promoting Social and Emotional Learning: Guidelines for Educators* (Alexandria, VA: Association for Supervision and Curriculum Development, 1997).
5 National Commission on Children, *Beyond Rhetoric: A New American Agenda for Children and Families* (Washington, DC: National Commission on Children, 1991).
6 Ruth B. Ekstrom et al., "Who Drops out of High School and Why? Findings from a National Study," *Teachers College Record* 87 (1986), accessed August 19, 2013, http://eric.ed.gov/?id=EJ332413; Guy Mahan and Charles Johnson, "Dealing with Academic, Social, and Emotional Problems," *NASSP Bulletin* 67 (1983), accessed August 19, 2013, http://bul.sagepub.com/content/67/462/80.short; and Nadine M. Lambert, "Adolescent Outcomes for Hyperactive Children: Perspectives on General and Specific Patterns of Childhood Risk for Adolescent Educational, Social and Mental Health Problems," *American Psychologist* 43 (1988), accessed August 19, 2013, http://www.ncbi.nlm.nih.gov/pubmed/3195797.
7 James Heckman, "The Economics of Inequality: The Value of Early Childhood Education," *American Educator*, 2011, accessed August 19, 2013, http://www.aft.org/pdfs/americaneducator/spring2011/Heckman.pdf.
8 National Center for Education Statistics, "Dropout Rates in the United States: 2000," 2002, accessed August 19, 2013, http://nces.ed.gov/pubsearch/pubsinfo.asp?pubid=2002114.
9 Elias et al., *Promoting Social and Emotional Learning*.
10 Tierra M. Freeman et al., "Sense of Belonging in College Freshmen at the Classroom and Campus Levels," *Journal of Experimental Education* 75 (2006–7), accessed August 19, 2013, http://www.tandfonline.com/doi/abs/10.3200/JEXE.75.3.203-220#.UhJrh2TwKnY.
11 Peter Salovey and John D. Mayer, "Emotional Intelligence," *Imagination, Cognition, and Personality* 9 (1990), accessed August 2013, http://heblab.research.yale.edu/pub_pdf/pub106_Salovey,Mayer1990EmotionalIntelligence.pdf.
12 Ibid.
13 David Wechsler, *The Measurement and Appraisal of Adult Intelligence* (Baltimore, MD: Williams & Wilkins, 1958).
14 Joseph E. Zins, "Examining Opportunities and Challenges for School-Based Prevention and Promotion: Social and Emotional Learning as an Exemplar," *Journal of Primary Prevention* 21 (2001), accessed August 19, 2013, http://link.springer.com/article/10.1023%2FA%3A1007154727167#page-1.
15 David B. Wilson et al., "School-Based Prevention of Problem Behaviors: A Meta-analysis," *Journal of Quantitative Criminology* 17 (2001), accessed August 19, 2013, http://link.springer.com/article/10.1023%2FA%3A1011050217296#page-1.

16 Larry K. Brendtro et al., *Reclaiming Youth at Risk: Our Hope for the Future* (Bloomington, IN: Solution Tree Publishing, 1990); and Goleman, *Emotional Intelligence*.

17 Salovey and Mayer, "Emotional Intelligence."

18 Zins, "Examining Opportunities and Challenges."

19 Ellen F. Netting et al., "The Human-Animal Bond: Implications for Practice," *Social Work* 32 (1987), accessed August 19, 2013, http://eric .ed.gov/?id=EJ350452.

20 Alan M. Beck and Aaron H. Katcher, "Future Directions in Human-Animal Bond Research," *American Behavioral Scientist* 47 (2003), accessed August 19, 2013, http://abs.sagepub.com/content/47/1/79.short.

21 A. H. Katcher et al., "Interactions between People and Their Pets: Form and Function," in *Interrelations between People and Pets* (Springfield, IL: Charles C. Thomas Publisher, 1981).

22 ASPCA, "Pet Statistics," 2013, accessed July 2, 2013, http://www.aspca.org /about-us/faq/pet-statistics.aspx.

23 PETA, "Puppy Mills: Dogs Abused for the Pet Trade," 2013, accessed July 2, 2013, http://www.peta.org/issues/Companion-Animals/puppy-mills -dogs-abused-for-the-pet-trade.aspx?c=ptwit.

24 Daniel Goleman, *Working with Emotional Intelligence* (New York: Bantam Books, 2000).

25 Goleman, *Emotional Intelligence*.

26 J. Decety et al., "Who Caused the Pain? An fMRI Investigation of Empathy and Intentionality in Children," *Neuropsychologia* 46 (2008), accessed August 13, 2013, http://www.ncbi.nlm.nih.gov/pubmed/18573266.

27 John D. Mayer and Peter Salovey, "What Is Emotional Intelligence?," in *Emotional Development and Emotional Intelligence* (New York: Basic Books, 1997).

Chapter 4: Power

1 Maddy Dychtwald and Christine Larson, *Influence: How Women's Soaring Economic Power Will Transform Our World for the Better* (New York: HarperCollins, 2010).

2 United States Department of Labor, "General Facts on Women and Job-Based Health," accessed July 10, 2013, http://www.dol.gov/ebsa/news room/fshlth5.html.

3 Princeton Survey Research Associates, "Americans as Health Care Consumers: The Role of Quality Information," 1996, accessed July 7, 2013, http://www.ahrq.gov/legacy/qual/kffhigh.htm.

4 Catalyst, "Linking Performance and Gender Balance on the Board," *Bot-*

tom Line: Corporate Performance and Women's Representation on Boards, 2007, accessed July 7, 2013, http://www.catalyst.org/file/139/bottom%20 line%202.pdf.

5 Kellie A. McElhaney and Sanaz Mobasseri, "Women Create a Sustainable Future," 2012, accessed July 7, 2013, http://responsiblebusiness.haas .berkeley.edu/Women_Create_Sustainable_Value_FINAL_10_2012.pdf.

6 Jane Cunningham and Philippa Roberts, *Inside Her Pretty Little Head: A New Theory of Female Motivation and What It Means for Marketing* (London: Marshall Cavendish Business, 2006).

7 Girlpower Marketing, "Women—Not a Niche Market," 2013, accessed July 7, 2013, http://www.girlpowermarketing.com/niche_market.php.

8 Ibid.

9 *Richard Fry and D'Vera Cohn, "New Economics of Marriage: The Rise of Wives," Pew Research Center's Social & Demographic Trends Report, 2010, accessed June 7, 2013, http://www.pewsocialtrends.org/files/2010/11 /new-economics-of-marriage.pdf.*

10 Bureau of Labor Statistics, US Department of Labor, 2007.

11 Ariane Hegewisch et al., "The Gender Wage Gap by Occupation," Institute for Women's Policy Research, 2012, accessed July 2, 2013, http://www.iwpr .org/publications/pubs/the-gender-wage-gap-by-occupation-1.

12 Center for American Women and Politics, "Women in the U.S. Congress 2013," 2013, accessed July 7, 2013, http://www.cawp.rutgers.edu/fast_facts /levels_of_office/Congress-CurrentFacts.php.

13 Catalyst, "2011 Catalyst Census: Fortune 500 Women Executive Officers and Top Earners," *2011 Catalyst Census: Fortune 500,* 2011, accessed July 7, 2013, http://www.catalyst.org/knowledge/2011-catalyst-census-fortune-500 -women-executive-officers-and-top-earners.

14 McElhaney and Mobasseri, "Women Create a Sustainable Future."

15 Constance E. Helfat et al., "The Pipeline to the Top: Women and Men in the Top Executive Ranks of U.S. Corporations," *Academy of Management Perspectives* 20 (2006), accessed July 7, 2013, http://www.jstor.org/stable /4166270.

16 "Romney's LBO World Is Boys' Club with Few Women," *Bloomberg Businessweek,* 2012, accessed July 7, 2013, http://www.businessweek.com/news /2012-08-31/romney-s-lbo-world-is-boys-club-with-few-top-women.

17 Barack Obama, "A Message to Planned Parenthood Supporters from President Obama," 2012.

18 Gloria Feldt, "Own Your Power with New Ways of Activism," *Jewish Woman Magazine,* 2012, accessed July 7, 2013, http://www.jwi.org/page .aspx?pid=3406.

19 Ibid.

20 UNFPA, "Promoting Gender Equality: Frequently Asked Questions

about Gender," 2013, accessed July 7, 2013, http://www.unfpa.org/gender/resources_faq.htm.

Chapter 5: Leveraging Gender Differences

1   James Geary, "Doing It for Themselves," 2009, accessed July 8, 2013, http://rhodesproject.com/docs/articles/DoingItForThemselves.pdf.
2   Susannah Cahalan, "Inside the Male Brain and the Female Brain," *New York Post*, September 19, 2010, accessed July 8, 2013, http://www.nypost.com/p/news/opinion/opedcolumnists/inside_the_male_brain_female_brain_jvGvOr2EQM8J8SVWGdzYYI.
3   Geary, "Doing It for Themselves."
4   Ibid.
5   Susan Harter, *The Construction of Self: A Developmental Perspective* (New York: Guilford Press, 1999).
6   Kimberly Brennan-Parks et al., "Sex Differences in Smiling as Measured in a Picture Taking Task," *Sex Roles* 24 (1991), accessed July 8, 2013, http://link.springer.com/article/10.1007%2FBF00288310.
7   P. A. Katz et al., "Theories of Female Personality," in *Psychology of Women: A Handbook of Issues and Theories* (Westport, CT: Greenwood Press, 1993).
8   E. Ashby Plant et al., "The Influence of Gender and Social Role on the Interpretation of Facial Expressions," *Sex Roles* 51 (2004), accessed July 8, 2013, http://link.springer.com/article/10.1023%2FB%3ASERS.0000037762.10349.13#page-1.
9   Nancy J. Briton and Judith A. Hall, "Beliefs about Female and Male Nonverbal Communication," *Sex Roles* 32 (1995), accessed July 8, 2013, http://link.springer.com/article/10.1007%2FBF01544758.
10 Judith A. Hall, *Nonverbal Sex Differences: Accuracy of Communication and Expressive Style* (Baltimore, MD: Johns Hopkins University Press, 1984).
11 L. R. Brody, "Gender, Emotion, and Expression," in *Handbook of Emotions* (New York: Guilford Press, 2000).
12 Terri L. Bonebright et al., "Gender Stereotypes in the Expression and Perception of Vocal Affect," *Sex Roles* 34 (1996), accessed July 8, 2013, http://link.springer.com/article/10.1007%2FBF01547811#page-1.
13 Laura C. Lomelei, "Culture, Sex and Gender Role Attitudes in Relation to Transformational Leadership" (master's diss., California State University, 2007).
14 A. H. Eagly et al., "Gender and the Evaluation of Leaders: A Meta-analysis," *Psychological Bulletin* 111 (1992), accessed July 8, 2013, http://psycnet.apa.org/index.cfm?fa=buy.optionToBuy&uid=1992-16290-001.
15 Sylvia Ann Hewlett, *Off-Ramps and On-Ramps: Keeping Talented Women on the Road to Success* (Boston: Harvard Business School Press, 2007).

16   Alice H. Eagly and Selwyn W. Becker, "Comparing the Heroism of Women and Men," *American Psychologist* 60 (2005), accessed July 8, 2013, http://psycnet.apa.org/index.cfm?fa=buy.optionToBuy&id=2005-05480-014.
17   Health Resources and Services Administration, "Women's Health USA 2010: Organ Transplantation," 2010, accessed July 8, 2013, http://mchb.hrsa.gov/whusa10/hsu/pages/312ot.html.

Chapter 6: Fearless Communication

1   Jill McLean Taylor et al., *Between Voice and Silence: Women and Girls, Race and Relationship* (Cambridge, MA: Harvard University Press, 1996).
2   Michael Gurian, *The Wonder of Girls: Understanding the Hidden Nature of Our Daughters* (New York: Atria Books, 2002).
3   Nance Lucas and V. Scott Koerwer, "Featured Interview Sherron Watkins, Former Vice President for Corporate Development of Enron," *Journal of Leadership & Organizational Studies* 11 (2004), accessed July 9, 2013, http://jlo.sagepub.com/content/11/1/38.abstract.
4   Gary Toms, "The 'Bitch' Is Back," *Yahoo! Voices*, March 6, 2008, accessed July 9, 2013, http://voices.yahoo.com/the-bitch-back-1267831.html?cat=9.
5   Matthew Biedlingmaier, "CNN's, ABC's Beck on Clinton: '[She's] the Stereotypical Bitch,'" *Media Matters for America*, March 15, 2007, accessed July 9, 2013, http://mediamatters.org/research/2007/03/15/cnns-abcs-beck-on-clinton-shes-the-stereotypica/138303.
6   Judith Baxter, "Leadership Talk and Gender in Senior Management Business Meetings in the UK," *ESRC Impact Report*, 2012, accessed July 9, 2013, http://www.esrc.ac.uk/my-esrc/grants/RES-000-22-3409/outputs/read/6af616c9-2b3a-46c2-81fd-395635030f18.
7   Judith Baxter, *The Language of Female Leadership* (Basingstoke, UK: Palgrave Macmillan, 2010).

Chapter 7: Sisterhood

1   Kaiser Family Foundation and Nickelodeon, "Talking with Kids about Tough Issues: A National Survey of Parents and Kids," 2001, accessed July 16, 2013, http://www.talkwithkids.org/nickelodeon/charts.pdf.
2   Girl Scout Research Institute, "The Ten Emerging Truths," *New Directions for Girls 11–17*, 2002, accessed July 14, 2013, http://www.girlscouts.org/research/pdf/ten_truths.pdf.
3   Web MD, "10 Immune System Busters & Boosters," 2013, accessed July 14, 2013, http://www.webmd.com/cold-and-flu/10-immune-system-busters-boosters.

4   Luke McNally et al., "Cooperation and the Evolution of Intelligence," *Proceedings of the Royal Society* 279 (2012), accessed July 14, 2013, http://rspb .royalsocietypublishing.org/content/279/1740/3027.

5   Dan Buettner, *The Blue Zones: Lessons for Living Longer from the People Who've Lived the Longest* (Washington, DC: National Geographic Society, 2008).

6   Ibid.

7   Ibid.

8   Julianne Holt-Lunstad et al., "Social Relationships and Mortality Risk: A Meta-analytic Review," *PLOS Med* 7 (2010), accessed July 14, 2013, http:// www.plosmedicine.org/article/info%3Adoi%2F10.1371%2Fjournal .pmed.1000316.

9   Web MD, "10 Immune System Busters."

10 R. E. Adams et al., "The Presence of a Best Friend Buffers the Effects of Negative Experiences," *Developmental Psychology* 47 (2011), accessed July 14, 2013, http://www.ncbi.nlm.nih.gov/pubmed/21895364.

11 Lyn Mikel Brown and Carol Gilligan, *Meeting at the Crossroads: Women's Psychology and Girls' Development* (New York: Ballantine Books, 1992).

12 Rachel Simmons, *Odd Girl Out, Revised and Updated: The Hidden Culture of Aggression in Girls* (New York: Mariner Books, 2011).

13 Wendy M. Craig and Debra J. Pepler, "Observations of Bullying and Victimization in the School Yard," *Canadian Journal of School Psychology* 13 (1998), accessed July 14, 2013, http://cjs.sagepub.com/content/13/2/41 .abstract.

14 Bully Free Program, "Facts about Bullying," 2013, accessed July 14, 2013, http://bullyfree.com/free-resources/facts-about-bullying.

15 Simmons, *Odd Girl Out.*

16 Gary Namie, "2003 Report on Abusive Workplaces," *Workplace Bullying Institute Research Studies*, 2003, accessed July 14, 2013, http://www .workplacebullying.org/multi/pdf/N-N-2003C.pdf.

17 CBS News, "Poll: Women's Movement Worthwhile," 2005, accessed July 14, 2013, http://www.cbsnews.com/2100-500160_162-965224.html.

18 Ibid.

19 Pia Peltola et al., "The 'Feminist' Mystique: Feminist Identity in Three Generations of Women," *Gender and Society* 18 (2004), accessed July 14, 2013, http://www.jstor.org/discover/10.2307/4149377?uid=3739840&uid =2&uid=4&uid=3739256&sid=21102538942687.

20 Natasha Walter, "We Still Need Feminism," *Guardian*, July 2, 2003, accessed July 14, 2013, http://www.guardian.co.uk/world/2003/jul/03 /gender.comment.

21 Jack Mirkinson, "Rush Limbaugh: Sandra Fluke, Woman Denied Right to Speak at Contraception Hearing, a 'Slut,'" *Huffington Post*, February 29,

2012, accessed July 14, 2013, http://www.huffingtonpost.com/2012/02/29/rush-limbaugh-sandra-fluke-slut_n_1311640.html?ref=media.

22 Chloe, "Well, You Did Dare to Speak in Public, So I Guess You Deserve This," *Feministing*, October 18, 2012, accessed July 14, 2013, http://feministing.com/2012/10/18/well-you-did-dare-to-speak-in-public-so-i-guess-you-deserve-this/.

23 Sylvia J. Jaros, "A Comparative Analysis of Intergenerational Conflict between Women in the Workplace," *Scholarship at Seton Hall* (thesis, Seton Hall University, 2010).

24 Girlguiding UK, "Role Models," *Girls' Attitudes Explored*, 2012, accessed July 14, 2013, http://www.girlguiding.org.uk/pdf/GirlsAttitudesExplored RoleModels_FINAL.pdf.

25 GfK Custom Research North America, "To Get Her There: Girls' Insights on Leadership," *Girl Scouts Year of the Girl*, 2012, accessed July 19, 2013, http://marketing.gfkamerica.com/Roper_Report_Girls_Scouts_ToGetHer There.pdf.

Chapter 8: Change-Makers

1 United Nations Foundation, "Why Invest in Adolescent Girls: The Largest Girl Generation in History Desperately Needs Resources," accessed July 16, 2013, http://www.clintonglobalinitiative.org/ourmeetings/PDF/actionareas/Why_Invest_in_Adolescent_Girls.pdf.

2 UNICEF, "Adolescence: An Age of Opportunity," *The State of the World's Children 2011*, 2011, accessed July 17, 2013, http://www.unicef.org/adolescence/files/SOWC_2011_Main_Report_EN_02242011.pdf.

3 Ibid.

4 United Nations Foundation, "Why Invest in Adolescent Girls."

5 Murrey Jacobsen, "Venus Williams' Other Career: Pay Equality Activist," *Rundown*, July 2, 2013, accessed July 17, 2013, http://www.pbs.org/newshour/rundown/2013/07/venus-williams-other-career-pay-equity-activist.html.

6 NASA, "Remembering Sally Ride," 2008, accessed July 19, 2013, http://heasarc.gsfc.nasa.gov/docs/objects/heapow/archive/special/sally_ride.html.

7 "Women in Space: Female Astronauts before and after Sally Ride," *Huffington Post*, July 24, 2012, accessed July 17, 2013, http://www.huffington post.com/2012/07/24/astronaut-women-sally-ride-space_n_1698274.html.

8 Molly Peterson, "PG&E Makes $2.6 Million Settlement with Hinkley, Its Second in 20 Years," Southern California Public Radio, March 16, 2012, accessed July 17, 2013, http://www.scpr.org/news/2012/03/16/31664/pge-makes-36-million-settlement-hinkley-its-second/.

9   Leigh Richards, "Why Is Change Important in an Organization?," *Chron*, accessed July 17, 2013, http://smallbusiness.chron.com/change -important-organization-728.html.

10   UNICEF, "Adolescence."

11   Ibid.

12   Girl Scout Research Institute, "Change It Up! What Girls Say about Redefining Leadership," 2008, accessed July 17, 2013, http://www.girlscouts.org /research/pdf/change_it_up_executive_summary_english.pdf.

13   World Bank, "Gender Equality as Smart Economics: A World Bank Group Gender Action Plan," 2006, accessed July 17, 2013, http://siteresources .worldbank.org/INTGENDER/Resources/womens_economic _empowerment.pdf.

14   Foundation Center and Women's Funding Network, "Accelerating Change for Women and Girls: The Role of Women's Funds," 2009, accessed July 17, 2013, http://foundationcenter.org/gainknowledge/research/pdf /womensfunds2009_highlights.pdf.

15   Karen O'Connor, ed., *Gender and Women's Leadership: A Reference Handbook* (Thousand Oaks, CA: SAGE Publications, 2010).

16   United States Holocaust Memorial Museum, "Eichmann Trial," *Holocaust Encyclopedia*, 2013, accessed July 17, 2013, http://www.ushmm.org/wlc /en/article.php?ModuleId=10005179.

17   "Too Hard for Science? Philip Zimbardo—Creating Millions of Heroes," *Scientific American*, April 22, 2011, accessed July 28, 2013, http://blogs .scientificamerican.com/guest-blog/2011/04/22/too-hard-for-science -philip-zimbardo-creating-millions-of-heroes/.

18   Zeno Franco and Philip Zimbardo, "The Banality of Heroism," *Greater Good: The Science of a Meaningful Life* 3 (2006–7), accessed July 17, 2013, http://greatergood.berkeley.edu/article/item/the_banality_of_heroism.

19   J. P. Rushton et al., "Altruism and Aggression: The Heritability of Individual Differences," *Journal of Personality and Social Psychology* 50 (1986), accessed July 17, 2013, http://psycnet.apa.org/?&fa=main.doiLanding&doi =10.1037/0022-3514.50.6.1192.

20   Linda J. Skitka, "Moral Convictions and Moral Courage: Common Denominators of Good and Evil," in *Social Psychology of Morality: Exploring the Causes of Good and Evil* (Washington, DC: American Psychological Association, 2012).

Chapter 9: Building Her Entourage

1   Robert D. Putnam, *Bowling Alone: The Collapse and Revival of American Community* (New York: Simon & Schuster, 2000).

2   Wayne Baker, *Achieving Success through Social Capital: Tapping the Hid-

den Resources in Your Personal and Business Networks (San Francisco: Jossey-Bass, 2000).

3   Ibid.

4   S. Cohen et al., "Social Ties and Susceptibility to the Common Cold," *Journal of the American Medical Association* 277 (1997), accessed July 23, 2013, http://www.ncbi.nlm.nih.gov/pubmed/9200634.

5   Ithiel de Sola Pool and Manfred Kochen, "Contacts and Influence," *Social Networks* 1 (1978–79), accessed July 29, 2013, https://www.sfu.ca /cmns/courses/marontate/2009/801/ClassFolders/jmckinnon/(0)%20 Contacts%20and%20influence.pdf; and Wayne Baker, *Networking Smart: How to Build Relationships for Personal and Organizational Success* (New York: McGraw-Hill, 1994).

6   J. Richard Hackman, *Collaborative Intelligence: Using Teams to Solve Hard Problems* (San Francisco: Berret-Koehler Publishers, 2011).

7   Jonathan Tisch and Karl Weber, *Citizen You: Doing Your Part to Change the World* (New York: Crown Publishing Group, 2010).

8   Jonathan Tisch, "Introducing Citizen You: A New Kind of Citizenship," *Huffington Post*, April 8, 2010, accessed July 23, 2013, http://www .huffingtonpost.com/jonathan-tisch/introducing-citizen-you-a_b _530676.html.

9   Jonathan Tisch, "NYC's Most Active Citizens," *Huffington Post*, August 17, 2009, accessed July 23, 2013, http://www.huffingtonpost.com/jonathan -tisch/nycs-most-active-citizens_b_261290.html.

10 Barry Wellman and Keith Hampton, "Living Networked On and Off Line." *Contemporary Sociology* 28 (1999), accessed July 29, 2013, http:// www.mysocialnetwork.net/downloads/onandoff.pdf.

11 Andrei S. Markovits and Robin Queen, "Women and the World of Dog Rescue: A Case Study of the State of Michigan," *Society and Animals* 17 (2009), accessed July 23, 2013, http://www.andymarkovits.com/docs /TheNewDiscourseOfDogs.pdf.

Suggested Readings

Baker, Wayne. *Achieving Success through Social Capital: Tapping the Hidden Resources in Your Personal and Business Networks.* San Francisco: Jossey-Bass, 2000.

Baumgardner, Jennifer, and Amy Richards. *Manifesta: Young Women, Feminism and the Future.* New York: Farrar, Straus and Giroux, 2000.

Baxter, Judith. *The Language of Female Leadership.* Basingstoke, UK: Palgrave Macmillan, 2010.

Brendtro, Larry K., et al. *Reclaiming Youth at Risk: Our Hope for the Future.* Bloomington, IN: Solution Tree Publishing, 1990.

Brown, Lyn Mikel, and Carol Gilligan. *Meeting at the Crossroads: Women's Psychology and Girls' Development.* New York: Ballantine Books, 1992.

Buckingham, Marcus, and Donald O. Clifton. *Now, Discover Your Strengths.* New York: Free Press, 2001.

Buettner, Dan. *The Blue Zones: Lessons for Living Longer from the People Who've Lived the Longest.* Washington, DC: National Geographic Society, 2008.

Cunningham, Jane, and Philippa Roberts. *Inside Her Pretty Little Head: A New Theory of Female Motivation and What It Means for Marketing.* London: Marshall Cavendish Business, 2006.

Delbanco, Andrew. *The Real American Dream: A Meditation on Hope.* Cambridge, MA: Harvard University Press, 1999.

Dychtwald, Maddy, and Christine Larson. *Influence: How Women's Soaring Economic Power Will Transform Our World for the Better.* New York: HarperCollins, 2010.

Elias, Maurice J., et al. *Promoting Social and Emotional Learning: Guidelines for Educators.* Alexandria, VA: Association for Supervision and Curriculum Development, 1997.

Erikson, Erik. *Identity: Youth and Crisis.* New York: W. W. Norton, 1968.

Frankl, Victor. *Man's Search for Meaning.* Boston: Beacon Press Books, 1959.

Goleman, Daniel. *Emotional Intelligence: Why It Can Matter More Than IQ.* New York: Bantam Books, 1995.

Gurian, Michael. *The Wonder of Girls: Understanding the Hidden Nature of Our Daughters.* New York: Atria Books, 2002.

Harter, Susan. *The Construction of Self: A Developmental Perspective.* New York: Guilford Press, 1999.

Hewlett, Sylvia Ann. *Off-Ramps and On-Ramps: Keeping Talented Women on the Road to Success.* Boston: Harvard Business School Press, 2007.

Katcher, A. H., et al. "Interactions between People and Their Pets: Form and Function." In *Interrelations between People and Pets.* Springfield, IL: Charles C. Thomas, 1981.

Mayer, John D., and Peter Salovey. "What Is Emotional Intelligence?" In *Emotional Development and Emotional Intelligence.* New York: Basic Books, 1997.

O'Connor, Karen, ed. *Gender and Women's Leadership: A Reference Handbook.* Thousand Oaks, CA: SAGE Publications, 2010.

Pink, Daniel. *A Whole New Mind: Why Right-Brainers Will Rule the Future.* New York: Penguin, 2005.

Pipher, Mary. *Reviving Ophelia: Saving the Selves of Adolescent Girls.* New York: Putnam, 1994.

Putnam, Robert D. *Bowling Alone: The Collapse and Revival of American Community.* New York: Simon & Schuster, 2000.

Sandberg, Sheryl. *Lean In: Women, Work and the Will to Lead.* New York: Alfred A. Knopf, 2013.

Seligman, Martin E. P. *Learned Optimism: How to Change Your Mind and Your Life.* New York: Free Press, 1990.

Simmons, Rachel. *Odd Girl Out, Revised and Updated: The Hidden Culture of Aggression in Girls.* New York: Mariner Books, 2011.

Stoltz, Paul G. *Adversity Quotient: Turning Obstacles into Opportunities.* New York: John Wiley & Sons, 1997.

Taylor, Jill McLean, et al. *Between Voice and Silence: Women and Girls, Race and Relationship.* Cambridge, MA: Harvard University Press, 1996.

Tisch, Jonathan, and Karl Weber. *Citizen You: Doing Your Part to Change the World.* New York: Crown Publishing Group, 2010.

Wechsler, David. *The Measurement and Appraisal of Adult Intelligence.* Baltimore, MD: Williams & Wilkins, 1958.

Weissberg, R. P., et al. "A New Conceptual Framework for Establishing School-Based Social Competence Promotion Programs." In *Primary Prevention and Promotion in the Schools.* Newbury Park, CA: SAGE, 1989.

Wolf, Naomi. *The Beauty Myth: How Images of Beauty Are Used against Women.* New York: HarperCollins, 1991.

Index

bullying, 1, 2, 19–20, 140, 148, 162,
163, 168, 172–80, 195, 196–97,
205, 247
Blame Game in dismissal of, 175
cliques and, 162, 172, 175, 195
relational aggression and, 176–79,
195
technological innovation in,
172–73
see also cyberbullying
Burberry Americas, 6
burkas, 183
Bush, George H. W., 182
Bushnell, Prudence, 50, 129, 153–55
business:
community service and, 238
networking and, 224, 225, 228,
242–43
women and, 29–30, 35, 92–93,
95–96, 99–100, 242–43
Bystander Effect, 214–15, 217
Bystander Syndrome, 176

C
camps, 28
cancer, 27, 77, 81, 199, 200, 201, 210
CARE, 100
Carla (Unleashed coach), 193–94
catfights, 178
cell phones, 28
change-makers, 199–222, 224, 226
Charlotte (client), 141–42
charter schools, 129
Check Ins, 16–17, 27, 28, 68, 105
strengths identification and, 33
Chihuahuas, 69
child care, 4, 94, 126, 183, 251
children, 126
animal abusers and, 206
empathy in, 59
passive role assigned to, 205
pets and development of, 62–63

weakening cultural support
structures of, 82–83
see also adolescence; boys; girls
child welfare, positive psychology
and, 31
Chrissy (Unleashed participant),
23–24
cigarettes, 167
*Citizen You: Doing Your Part to
Change the World* (Tisch), 238
civil rights movement, 56, 99, 184
Claudia (Unleashed participant), 81
Clifton, Donald O., 33
Clinton, Hillary Rodham, 98, 121,
147, 247
Clique, The, 175
cliques, 16, 141, 161, 162, 169, 172,
175, 176, 191, 194, 195, 197,
214, 225, 227
CNN, 200
Coca-Cola, 199
cognition, 134, 135, 167, 204
collaboration, 56, 88, 89, 101, 103,
187, 190, 221, 227–28, 230,
236–37
collective identity, 228
Colleen (Unleashed participant),
217
Columbia University, 48
Columbine massacre, 57
communication, 34, 112, 176, 204,
228
elevator pitches and, 158
fearlessness in, 133–58
networking in, 231–33
community development, positive
psychology and, 31
community service, 3, 7, 15, 28, 51,
202–10, 238–39, 241
computers, 28
conflict resolution, 56, 103, 169,
171–80, 197, 235–36

Get email updates on

STACEY RADIN,

exclusive offers,

and other great book recommendations

from Simon & Schuster.

Visit **newsletters.simonandschuster.com**

or

scan below to sign up: